Contributions to Economics

The series *Contributions to Economics* provides an outlet for innovative research in all areas of economics. Books published in the series are primarily monographs and multiple author works that present new research results on a clearly defined topic, but contributed volumes and conference proceedings are also considered. All books are published in print and ebook and disseminated and promoted globally. The series and the volumes published in it are indexed by Scopus and ISI (selected volumes).

More information about this series at http://www.springer.com/series/1262

Robin Maialeh

Dynamic Models and Inequality

The Role of the Market Mechanism in Economic Distribution

Springer

Robin Maialeh
Department of Economics, Faculty of Economics
University of Economics
Prague, Czech Republic

Unicorn Research Centre
Prague, Czech Republic

ISSN 1431-1933 ISSN 2197-7178 (electronic)
Contributions to Economics
ISBN 978-3-030-46312-0 ISBN 978-3-030-46313-7 (eBook)
https://doi.org/10.1007/978-3-030-46313-7

This Springer imprint is published by the registered company Springer Nature Switzerland AG.
The registered company address is: Gewerbestrasse 11, 6330 Cham, Switzerland

Contents

Chapter 1
Introduction

It has been decades since Douglass North (1977) pointed out on the peculiarity that despite market is the central institution, economic literature discusses its role so rarely. Similarly, George Stigler (1967) pondered the question why too little attention has been paid to the theory of markets notwithstanding economic theory is based on markets. Our current situation is not, in this particular sense, much better. Ongoing specialization diverts attention from general economic questions. It is almost believed, or at least such impression is usually spread out through the current economic discourse, that "big questions" are already solved; that the thing we need the most is more detailed research on particular aspects of market economies which could fix minor deficiencies occurring in the economic system. Abstract theorizing of market principles belongs to the past. But the difficulty we then face is that specialized insights are hardly aggregable without understanding fundamental motion of a system driven by market mechanism.

In the light of recent development, economic distribution is the issue that is worth to contextualize with general market principles. Not only in economics, but also in other branches of social sciences, the issue of inequality is gaining ground and it is slowly becoming the leading theme for contemporary social research. Reasons behind this trend are sensible since current tendencies in economic distribution affect (if not determine) various fields of our lives and society's reproduction as a whole. The common consent on these tendencies generally refer to relatively high and rather rising economic inequality in advanced Western economies, with the United States as the typical example of deepening gaps between the richest and the rest of the population.

The book therefore utilizes two main strands of literature. Firstly, we will inspect the main findings on contemporary economic inequality, and, secondly, we scrutinize fundamental market forces. The goal is to achieve a theoretical explanation which connects observable phenomena in economic distribution and underlying theoretical principles of market mechanism. As a result, we should be able to formulate a theoretical model which explains market inequalities as the intrinsic feature of the market mechanism. Our aim is therefore to provide a different

R. Maialeh, *Dynamic Models and Inequality*, Contributions to Economics,
https://doi.org/10.1007/978-3-030-46313-7_1

perspective on established economic doctrine that effective markets tend to produce convergence.

The second chapter will introduce readers to basic concepts of inequality, its measuring and methods. These opening parts help to distinguish between various types of inequalities and present all mainstream methods which are used to investigate economic inequality including their specifics and limitations. Here we will also review empirical findings on inequality and their broader context. It will particularly focus on how inequality has been evolving over the last decades of economic progress in advanced economies where the connection between market and inequality is more dynamic and transparent. A literature review will be then dedicated to global inequality and its ambivalences as well as to contextualizing the question of inequality with economic growth. The purpose of this chapter is to contribute to revealing main trends and stylized facts of today's inequality.

Although we bear in mind inconsiderable difficulties with the role of empirical findings, one of the central arguments for this book is an obvious and markable discrepancy between what is observed on data and conclusions of the general theoretical background. The third chapter will therefore present established theories that laid the foundations of converging tendencies in modern economics. Before starting with formal explanation of the relevant models, the chapter will argue for the importance of theory in understanding any scientific subject matter. This is particularly important in our times of enormously increasing data availability and processability that naturally incline toward highly empiricalized inequality research. Economic models representing the theoretical background for economic convergence will be then examined in detail with an emphasize on their converging tendencies.

As the reaction to the Ramsey-Cass-Koopmans model in the third chapter, the aim of the fourth chapter will be to clarify methodological aspects of economic agents. Firstly, we will cope with behavioural allegations against rationality of economic agents. After proving that behavioural critique is of low importance when following a general-theoretical approach, we will discuss central questions of agent-based modelling. Lucas (1988) posited that application of economic theory require assumptions about both the individual behaviour and the mode of interaction among agents. In line with this statement, the existence of economic agents will be put into two conflicting domains—internal agent's motivations and her external market environment. This conflict, which consists of self-preserving behaviour leading to competitive struggle for scarce resources, establishes the driving force of any action of the agent on the market.

The fifth and sixth chapters will deal with these two domains separately. Firstly, we will concern internal self-preserving stimuli which are already present in models of subsistence consumption. It will be shown how incorporation of subsistence constraints into agents' optimization causes structural changes in their behaviour. Moreover, we will prove that attained results principally do not rely on the level of subsistence which support its further theoretical potential and generalizability. The last model which contains subsistence consumption will then use simulations with the objective to get the answer to the question of how subsistence constraints affect economic inequality.

The second theme will contend with market environment. Under these circumstances, resource allocation is, from the agent's perspective, dominated by competitive principles. The aim of this chapter is to interlink competition as the fundamental feature of the market mechanism with inequality in economic distribution. For this purpose, we will present three models with different viewpoints on competition. Each of these models accentuates different aspects of competition: innovations and monopolistic rent, disproportionate holdings of corporate assets and rising market power, and immanent 'trickle-up principles' in resource competition. These models will also demonstrate ambivalent effects of competition on inequality, underlying a combination of converging and diverging tendencies.

The general model of market inequality will be formulated in the last chapter. The aim of the model is to grasp market interaction of rationally behaving agents. Hence, we combine approaches of models from previous chapters in order to operationalize fundamental market principles based on competition with inherent self-preserving stimuli mirroring themselves in subsistence constraints. As a means to isolate the effect of market mechanism on inequality we will use homogeneous agent model so that resulting inequality will not be caused by differences among agents, but by the market principles that govern agents' interaction. The final model therefore aims to comprehend not only empirical surface with its stylized facts, but also abstract nature of the market mechanism and its connection to economic distribution.

The models presented in this book are formulated and interpreted with the intention of accentuating decisive tendencies for economic distribution. Despite slight modifications of these models, I tried to keep notations—when it does not harm clarity—as in original papers, so that readers can easily skip back to the former context of the model. Also, at places where it does not disrupt a logic of the model, selected technical problems are not explained in detail as is usual in textbooks. So as to fully enjoy richness of all presented models, it is advised to have (upper) intermediate knowledge of quantitative tools including differential calculus or dynamic programming. Nevertheless, for the convenience of readers from different fields of expertise, each problem has a non-reduced verbal interpretation. Furthermore, the final model of market inequality is technically simplified as much as possible. The solution to the model is also reached through simulations and not via mathematical derivation so that both problem definitions and conclusions should be accessible to all social scientists.

Although economic inequality closely relates to various normative (value-based), economic-political and even moral questions, it is beyond the scope of this book to provide insights into these spheres. We are fully aware of the importance of this broader context that is desperately needed for a comprehensive assessment of the researched relationship. The aim of the book is to contribute to mere quantitatively capturable aspects of general laws in economic distribution. This "mechanistic" approach is thus unable to decide how a just and fair distribution should look like, what state of matters is desired and which ways should we follow in order to reach our established goals. On the other hand, adopted approach is supposed to be sufficiently reliable in demystifying ideological proclamations regarding economic inequality, which helps to clarify the role of market mechanism in economic distribution.

References

Lucas RE (1988) Adaptive behaviour and economic theory. J Bus 59:401–426

North D (1977) Markets and other allocation systems in history: the challenge of Karl Polanyi. J Eur Econ Hist 6:703–716

Stigler G (1967) Imperfections in the capital market. J Polit Econ 75:287–292

Chapter 2
Contemporary Economics and Inequality

2.1 Introduction to Inequality: Concepts, Methods and Data

Despite that classical economists and their contemporaries in other social sciences were significantly focused on inequality in economic distribution and the question of inequality indeed played the central role, social scientists in the last century and economists paradoxically the most, partly overlook the question of how wealth (in its broadest sense) is distributed. Fortunately, this trend is dramatically changing. A proponent of these classical economists and their contemporaries was Adam Smith who had been convincing us that the demand of those who live by wages increases with the increase of aggregate wealth. By this he has inspired many thinkers of political economy. Empirical findings however do not correspond to such trickle-down idea. This fact causes that research on inequality comes to the forefront of social sciences' interest. Recent development in economics indicate that inequality is slowly becoming the most burning issue throughout the whole spectre of economic disciplines.

The first thought is dedicated to the notion of 'inequality'. The term intuitively stands in contraposition to equality which, however, entails numerous points of view. Such standards of equality (Rein and Miller 1974) may be based on income shares so that equality demands to maximise the share of disadvantaged lowest social strata, which corresponds to a typical Rawlsian maximin principle. This focus on the bottom of economic distribution may lead to equalizing policies that no one falls below a given minimum standard of well-being. Or, equality may refer to the opposite, i.e. lowering the ceiling for a relatively advantaged social stratum. The idea is that the top of the economic distribution is from a certain level restricted in accumulation of additional resources. Equality could also refer to eliminating the influence of political power, education and many other social phenomena that may cause disproportionate advantages (or disadvantages) in economic distribution. The benchmark of equality can be also set up as the endeavour to keep inequality at the

R. Maialeh, *Dynamic Models and Inequality*, Contributions to Economics,
https://doi.org/10.1007/978-3-030-46313-7_2

level of (or below) inequality of another comparable economic unit (e.g. national state). A more theoretical approach could define equality as the complete horizontal equity, where equal agents are treated equally. Conversely, equal treatment of unequal agents may lead to reproducing inequality which is particularly the motive for discussing today's inequality. Equality can be also based on lifetime income profiles. This means that rather than the actual position of the agent in the economic pyramid, the important aspect of equality is connected to future income prospects. It also relates to possibilities of economic mobility which eliminate the difference between initial barriers on the one side, and initial advantages of occupational groups on the other side. Finally, equality can be explained in more abstract terms of social exclusion. In this regard, the aim is to eradicate possible social exclusion caused by differences in economic power.

Either way, the list is undoubtedly not exhaustive. The present chapter meets standards of the current inequality research in economics and focuses mainly on empirical description of inequality. This means that inequality is understood mechanistically in terms of general economic differences among economic agents, may they be individuals, households or national states. It follows that inequality thus has various interpretations which vary according to used method.

It is a hard task to rigorously capture all necessary factors of inequality. Europe was a highly unequal rentier society with intergenerational spillovers of inherited wealth in the early twentieth century. At the same time, the United States were already a society with high inequality, but the distribution of wealth was predominantly self-made. Today's inequality is in addition affected by the role of supermanagers who triturate traditional analysis based on two main social classes. Each of these examples has different driving forces and researching inequality means using different variables and methods according to the source of inequality.

Following the classics, Malthus (1998 [1798]) predicted a misery of the masses based on the 'iron law of wages' in combination with population growth. In a similar fashion, Ricardo (2001 [1817]) puts fixed land supply into play, because as the land becomes more and more scarce, the landowners are supposed to capture an ever-growing fraction of national income. Marx (2015 [1867]) sees the process of accumulation on competitive markets as the main diverging factor. Rousseau as one of the first problematized the relationship between private property and inequality, distinguishing inequality in its full richness as natural and moral (2013 [1755]).

It is evident today that none of these giants was fully successful in his predictions and all of them underestimated partly equalizing power of economic growth. A slight 'renaissance' of the issue appeared around the middle of the twentieth century. The one who seemingly overestimated the equalizing power of economic growth was Kuznets (1953 and 1955). His famous curve hypothesis depicts inequality following an inverted U-shaped development over economic progress. More recent studies, e.g. Cornia and Kiiski (2001), however present that the assumed shape is empirically untenable. We are witnessing that the question of economic distribution has arisen again during the recent decades. Economic research in the field is mainly empirical as the data availability and their quality is incomparably higher than classical economists had, and also much higher than Kuznets had at his disposal more than half a century ago.

Notwithstanding, methods and data, both in terms of availability and quality, remain to be one of the most complicated and simultaneously the most important aspects in researching economic inequalities. Despite enormous advances, contemporary economics still faces difficulties with interpretation of inequality, ambivalent tendencies on different societal levels, comparability or at the end with the technical side of measuring of inequality itself. With wide-range databases and growing data availability the proper classification has an increasing importance. Survey data are often used as the source for interpersonal inequality measurements, famously e.g. by Milanovic (2005, 2002 etc.). These datasets are provided for example by Luxembourg Income Study Database or Luxembourg Wealth Study Database, World Bank Living Standard Measurement Studies and so on. Practical problems related to data surveys are mainly response rate, under-reporting at the top income level and omission of the very poor population as noted by Anand and Segal (2008) and researched by Korinek et al. (2006).

Another source of data for measuring inequality are tax data which were firstly used by Kuznets (1953). These data were also extended and systematized in the World Wealth and Income Database (WID). Still, tax data are connected to few problems. One of the greatest problems is tax evasion. Not surprisingly, research on evasion rate by wealth group clearly shows that tax evasion is connected almost exclusively to the top 1%, while the richer the household is, the bigger the fraction of household taxes evades. Similarly, the share of offshore wealth on total wealth is increasing with the position in the wealth distribution. To give an illustration, one third of the wealth of the top 0.1% in Norway is in offshores and the 0.01% richest households evade about 25% of their taxes (Alstadsaeter et al. 2019). In other words, the richer you are, the greater is your tax evasion rate and the greater is the share of your wealth in offshores. Among other difficulties with tax data we can name tax-exempt incomes. For example, tax data in the United States capture only 60% of the national income and such data obviously does not reflect the bottom income strata. Most of capital income is, for obvious reasons, not reflected as well. Tax data could therefore contribute to both overestimating and underestimating inequality.

Distributional national accounts (DINAs) are another frequently used source of data. These accounts are supposed to resolve discrepancies between micro and macro level and also to derive measures of the distribution across households' groups. Analyses based on national income, on the contrary to those based on gross domestic product, reflect capital depreciation and net foreign income. This is crucial when considering countries with substantial GDP and GNI gap. On a typical example of Ireland, it can be clearly seen that e.g. extensive capital outflows significantly decrease income which is available to be distributed among residents of the country. In the global context, it is evident that developing countries face this problem. The second important feature of DINAs is that they allow to capture the evolution of the distribution of national income and wealth by different percentiles of the distribution. On the contrast to GDP-based measures, which focus solely on aggregates and averages, by using DINAs we can be informed about the extent to which various social groups—e.g. rich and poor—benefit from total economic growth. World Bank's PovcalNet is usually the source for general distributional data with global coverage.

2.2 Measuring Inequality

Before we start with basic introduction of inequality measures, it is useful to remind readers specifics of discrete and continuous distributions since both can be easily incorporable into most of inequality measures. Discrete distributions assume arithmetic mean:

$$\bar{y} = \frac{1}{n} \sum_{i=1}^{n} y_i, \tag{2.1}$$

where y_i represents income of the i-th agent, $\bar{y}$ is the mean income and n is the number of observations (agents). Arithmetic mean can be smoothly used to define the agent's share on total income:

$$share_i = y_i / (n\bar{y}). \tag{2.2}$$

Geometric mean then takes the form:

$$y^* = \exp\left(\frac{1}{n} \sum_{i=1}^{n} \log y_i\right). \tag{2.3}$$

Continuous distributions operate with arithmetic mean as follows:

$$\bar{y} = \int y \, dF, \tag{2.4}$$

where $F(y)$ represents the proportion of n with income $\leq y$, for $y \geq 0$. Geometric mean is then defined as:

$$y^* = \exp\left(\int \log y \, dF\right), \tag{2.5}$$

and with the well-defined density function $f(\cdot)$ we get the following arithmetic and geometric means:

$$\bar{y} = \int yf(y)dy, \tag{2.6}$$

$$y^* = \exp\left(\int \log y\, f(y)\, dy\right). \tag{2.7}$$

The proportion of total income that satisfies $\leq y$ thus follows:

$$\Phi(y) = \frac{1}{\bar{y}} \int_0^y z dF(z), \tag{2.8}$$

which is greatly important since it establishes the Lorenz curve defined on (F, Φ).

As regards inequality measures, the aim is to recapitulate basic measurement methods and point out at their specifics. But even more importantly, presented measures remind the reader that final empirical findings on economic inequality, however exact they seem to be, are results of compromises in computational methodology. As we will see, that is exactly why the theoretical approach, adopted in upcoming chapters, is a viable complement to any empirical analysis of inequality.

The simplest approach in measuring inequality is based on ranges. It measures differences for instance between the maximum and minimum values of income. Here we can claim the good old truth that the simplest approach can likely be appropriate when applied on simple phenomena. Hence, ranges would not suit to large and heterogeneous samples. And above that, such a simple approach as ranges do not refer properly to what is happening between these two extreme values.

The second possible measure is the relative mean deviation. This measure improves the range-based inequality by considering not only extreme values on the top and the bottom, but it includes information about the distribution of the whole sample. It is defined as the average absolute distance of agent's income from the mean expressed as a proportion of the mean. For discrete distribution we have:

$$RMD = \frac{1}{n\bar{y}} \sum_{i=1}^{n} (y_i - \bar{y}), \tag{2.9}$$

and for continuous distributions it reads:

$$\int \left|\frac{y}{\bar{y}} - 1\right| dF. \tag{2.10}$$

Naturally, perfectly equal distribution of income yields $RMD = 0$. The main problem with this measure is insensitiveness when resources among households on a given side of the mean income are transferred. Simply put, if we transfer resources only among poorer or only among richer than the mean is, the inequality measured by relative mean deviation stays the same. It might be useful to note that, in the context of social welfare analysis, this may be contradictory to Pigou-Dalton principle which generally ends up with more equitable allocations.

Further, they can be used measures that capture dispersion of any frequency distribution. For this purpose, we may use the variance of income:

$$V = \frac{1}{n}\sum_{i=1}^{n}(y_i - \bar{y})^2. \tag{2.11}$$

But, variance has also its own limitations in capturing inequality. Assume that if we double incomes of all agents, i.e. that income distribution remains unchanged and the mean income gets doubled as well, the variance will quadruple. Since the variance increases with the mean, our difficulty can be solved through logarithmic transformation:

$$\nu_1 = \frac{1}{n}\sum_{i=1}^{n}\left[\log\left(\frac{y_i}{\bar{y}}\right)\right]^2, \tag{2.12}$$

which is merely logarithmized variance; or we may formulate the variance of logarithmized incomes, which states:

$$\nu_2 = \frac{1}{n}\sum_{i=1}^{n}\left[\log\left(\frac{y_i}{y^*}\right)\right]^2, \tag{2.13}$$

and where y^* represents the mean of the logarithm of income. However, the simplest way to sort out this problem with variance is to employ the coefficient of variation, defined as:

$$c = \frac{\sqrt{V}}{\bar{y}}. \tag{2.14}$$

Starting with c, it can be read that a transfer of a given amount of resources (say 1 USD) will not change the value of c, regardless 1 USD goes from an agent with 20 USD to an agent with 15 USD, or from an agent with 1000 USD to an agent with 995 USD. This feature favorizes using c to measure high incomes but at the expense of information about the rest of the distribution. Regarding ν_1 and ν_2, we observe that 1 USD transferred from the agent with 1000 USD to the agent with 995 USD reduces values ν_1 and ν_2 more than 1 USD transferred from the agent with 20 USD to the agent with 15 USD. If we calculated these changes with all necessary values, we would also see that this effect is so strong that it distorts the final evaluation of inequality. It is easy to imagine a situation of high incomes where a transfer from richer agents to those slightly underneath may even lead to an increase in inequality; for more details see e.g. Foster and Ok (1999).

The most common quantifier of inequality is undoubtedly Gini coefficient. This non-entropic measure of statistical dispersion says what fraction of aggregate population owns what fraction of aggregate income, usually on national or global level. The index is based on Lorenz curve which represents the cumulative proportion of certain variable (income, wealth…) linked to individuals who are ordered from lowest to highest in terms of the cumulative proportion of their sizes. The easiest way of defining Gini coefficient for discrete distributions is:

$$g = \frac{1}{2n^2\bar{y}} \sum_{i=1}^{n} \sum_{j=1}^{n} |y_i - y_j|, \tag{2.15}$$

and in the case of continuous distributions we get:

$$g = 1 - 2 \int \Phi dF. \tag{2.16}$$

It might be helpful, exclusively in the case of the Gini coefficient, to outline a more sophisticated approach (Chatterjee et al. 2015). The Lorenz curve traditionally represents the relationship between the cumulative distribution and the cumulative first moment of $P(m)$; hence:

$$X(r) = \int_{m_0}^{r} P(m)dm,$$

$$Y(r) = \frac{\int_{m_0}^{r} mP(m)dm}{\int_{m_0}^{\infty} mP(m)dm}; P(m) \in [m_0, \infty). \tag{2.17}$$

The Lorenz curve is given by the set ($X(r)$, $Y(r)$), where X represents cumulative proportion of ordered (low → high) individuals who hold the cumulative proportion of Y (e.g. wealth). Perfect equality occurs when all individuals hold the same amount of wealth m^e and then $P(m) = \delta(m - m^e)$, where $m_0 < m^e < \infty$. Then we get:

$$X(r) = \int_{m_0}^{r} \delta(m - m^e)dm = \theta(r - m^e), \tag{2.18}$$

and

$$Y(r) = \frac{\int_{m_0}^{r} m\delta(m - m^e)dm}{\int_{m_0}^{\infty} m\delta(r - m^e)dm} = \frac{m^e\theta(r - m^e)}{m^e} = X(r), \tag{2.19}$$

where $\theta(x)$ is a step function:

$$\theta(x) = \begin{cases} 1, & x \geq 1, \\ 0 & x < 1. \end{cases} \tag{2.20}$$

This situation denotes perfect equality since the fraction of total wealth corresponds to the same fraction of individuals, e.g. 70% of individuals own 70% of wealth. Perfect inequality, on the other hand, would occur in the society of N individuals if $P(m) = (1 - \varepsilon)\delta_{m,\ 0} + \varepsilon\delta_{m,\ 1}$, with total wealth normalized to 1 and $\varepsilon \sim O\left(\frac{1}{N}\right)$. Then, we obtain:

$$X(r) = 1 - \varepsilon + \varepsilon\delta_{r,1} \quad \text{and} \quad Y(r) = \delta_{r,1} \tag{2.21}$$

from which we derive $Y = 1 \Leftrightarrow X = r = 1$ and hence perfect inequality line is $Y = \delta_{X,\ 1}$, while $\delta_{x,\ \nu}$ is Kronecker's delta.

Finally, the Gini coefficient is computed as twice the area between the Lorenz curve $(X(r), Y(r))$ and perfect equality line $X = Y$; thus:

$$g = 2\int_{0}^{1} (X - Y)dX = 2\int_{r_0}^{\infty} (X(r) - Y(r))\frac{dX}{dr}dr, \tag{2.22}$$

where $X^{-1}(0) = r_0$ and $X^{-1}(1) = \infty$ hold. Then, $g = 1$ applies for perfect inequality and $g = 0$ for perfect equality. Naturally, there is a number of computation methods of Gini coefficient which depend on adopted functions, e.g. discrete or continuous probability function, probability density function; income distribution is above that frequently represented by Pareto, log-normal or exponential distribution functions. The main drawback of using Gini coefficient in its pure form is its selective sensitivity. In concrete, transfers between agents around the middle of the distribution have a greater effect on g than if we transfer the same amount at either end of the distribution (top or bottom).

Another index that is widely used to measure economic inequality is the Theil index. The index belongs to the entropy class of inequality indexes and it can be interpreted as income-share weighted average of the logarithmic difference between each economic unit's income and mean income. The theory behind this index (Theil 1967) is based on entropy, representing a measure of disorder in various scientific disciplines. For the purpose of capturing economic inequality, it can be used as a deviation from perfect equality. In technical terms, a class of such inequality indexes can be defined as:

$$E(\alpha) = \frac{1}{n(\alpha^2 - \alpha)}\left[\sum_{i=1}^{n}\left(\frac{y_i}{\bar{y}}\right)^{\alpha} - 1\right], \tag{2.23}$$

where $\alpha \neq 0, 1$. As can be seen, the value of α is the crucial as regards the sensitivity to a specific part of the income distribution. High values of α denote higher sensitivity to the upper tail of the income distribution, while lower values of α pushes the index to be more sensitive to what is happening at the bottom of the income distribution. Since we had to adopt the restriction $\alpha \neq 0$, 1, we need to apply the l'Hôpital's rule. Then we get:

$$\frac{d\left(\frac{y}{\bar{y}}\right)^{\alpha}}{d\alpha} = \left(\frac{y_i}{\bar{y}}\right)^{\alpha} \log\left(\frac{y_i}{\bar{y}}\right), \tag{2.24}$$

and since $d[n(\alpha^2 - \alpha)]/d\alpha = n(2\alpha - 1)$ we can continue to evaluate limits $\alpha \rightarrow 0$ and $\alpha \rightarrow 1$ for the term:

$$\frac{\sum_{i=1}^{n}\left(\frac{y_i}{\bar{y}}\right)^{\alpha} \log\left(\frac{y_i}{\bar{y}}\right)}{n(2\alpha - 1)}. \tag{2.25}$$

Applying the rule then allows to formulate the Theil index for discrete distributions:

$$E(1) = \frac{1}{n}\sum_{i=1}^{n}\left(\frac{y_i}{\bar{y}}\right) \log\left(\frac{y_i}{\bar{y}}\right) = T, \tag{2.26}$$

and for continuous distributions:

$$E(1) = \int \frac{y}{\bar{y}} \log\left(\frac{y}{\bar{y}}\right) dF = T. \tag{2.27}$$

In addition, if we put $\alpha = 0$, we get the mean logarithmic deviation for discrete distributions:

$$E(0) = -\frac{1}{n}\sum_{i=1}^{n} \log\left(\frac{y_i}{\bar{y}}\right) = MLD, \tag{2.28}$$

and, similarly for continuous distributions it reads:

$$E(0) = \int \log\left(\frac{y}{\bar{y}}\right) dF = MLD. \tag{2.29}$$

A rather technical limit in using Theil index and mean logarithmic deviation lies in the fact that they are not defined when zero incomes are present. Obviously, it suggests itself that this can be overcome by replacing zero incomes with "insignificantly" small numbers. However, the maximum value of the mean logarithmic deviation will necessary be sensitive on how small these numbers are, which, at the end, potentially distorts inequality interpretation.

To conclude, among other important tools for capturing inequality we also find top shares and Pareto coefficients. Just briefly and starting with the latter, Pareto coefficient is of great help due to its (Pareto) distribution[1] properties when focusing on dynamics of top incomes. Pareto distribution has a probability density function

$$f(y) = \frac{ac^a}{y^{1+a}}, \tag{2.30}$$

and a cumulative distribution function $1 - F(y) = (c/y)^a$, where $c =$ const. and a is the Pareto coefficient. Countries with a narrow dispersion of top incomes (e.g. Cyprus or Ireland) therefore report lower coefficients. A fruitful discussion on the relationship and possible corrections between Gini and Pareto coefficients was held by Hlasny and Verme (2018). As regards income and wealth shares, the main advantage is concreteness even when data are not available for all percentiles; additionally, inequality interpreted by top and bottom shares is simple to understand, without getting into abstract computations, e.g. in comparison to Gini coefficient. An interesting study on the relationship between Gini coefficients and top shares was elaborated by Alvaredo (2011). For more details on measuring inequality see especially Cowel (2011) and Atkinson (1970 and 1983:53–58).

To use the most common indexes Gini and Theil in international extent, it requires a method which converts national currencies into a common numeraire. Two main options are market exchange rates and purchasing parity power. Whereas the latter takes into account price differences across countries and therefore generates lower, most likely even underestimated values of inequality (due to possibly overestimated relative incomes of developing countries), market exchange rates suffer with 'traded sector bias', which omits domestic prices of internationally non-traded goods and services, which most likely leads to the opposite—an overestimation of inequality. Additionally, purchasing parity power—the application of the law of one price to a basket of goods—is usually calculated by three different methods: Geary-Khamis method used by Penn World Tables (PWT); Elteto-Koves-Szulc (EKS) used by the World Bank (WB); and less used Afriat index.[2] A combination of market exchange rates and purchasing parity power is Exchange Rate Deviation Index (ERDI), however it has limited applicability in the issue of inequality.

Further, we can distinguish three concepts of world income inequality. The first one refers to inequality among countries based on their average per capita income, with each country as a unit. This measure does not reflect population weighting and

---

[1]Since we seek general laws of contemporary inequality and their market connectedness, we omit vast of problems related to types of distributions (not only to widely used Lognormal distributions and the whole family of Pareto distributions), whose success in use is heavily fixed on particular circumstances. For more details on functional forms in modelling economic distributions see e.g. Kleiber and Kotz (2003).

[2]Differences in results can be significant according to used method. For instance, GDP of India in 1990 was estimated about 15% higher by PWT (GK) than in case of WB (EKS).

hence small and big countries have the same importance for global inequality. Calculated Gini index was then rising from 1950s to the end of millennium and then slightly decreasing up to 2010. Second concept refers to inequality among individuals in the world, with each individual assigned the average per capita income of individual's country of residence. This measure therefore takes population sizes into account. Conversely to the first concept, the second one had a tendency to decrease over time. A considerable downfall of Gini coefficient was captured since 1990s. Third concept focuses on inequality among individuals in the world with each individual assigned his income. It is evident that the last concept is individual-based and emphasizes economic differences between individuals, not national states as in the previous two concepts. Naturally, the greatest challenge is the calculation since we need access to household surveys with individual incomes or consumption, which must have, on top of that, comparable methodology. It is no surprise that not all countries of the world meet such requirements. In any case, the trend of the third concept is about to follow slightly rising inequality in terms of Gini coefficient (Milanovic, 2005).

And lastly, we can differentiate between relative income inequality and absolute income inequality. The relative inequality stays constant when incomes change proportionately, absolute inequality stays constant when incomes change by the same amount. It must be also noted that income is still the most common reference point representing economic inequality, nevertheless other variables like consumption and especially wealth help to capture real economic differences with higher interpretative preciseness.

An attentive reader might notice that several problems have been, from various reasons, omitted. There are countless measuring methods, methods of data processing or even perspectives on economic inequality, all of which would suffice for a separate book. The opening subchapter however adequately introduces into (more or less) technical aspects of measuring economic inequality. The reason is simple—the aim is to facilitate the reader with knowledge which is necessary to understand *general trends* in economic distribution. Furthermore, presenting these basic concepts helps to explain, albeit indirectly, various controversies connected with economic inequality. For instance, the subchapter should clarify how does it possible that incomes at the very top can be rising, as well as the income share of the very top, and simultaneously we observe decreasing Gini coefficient? This example on the United Kingdom from the early 1990s pointedly illustrates the complexity of the inequality measurement and the need to properly understand various techniques used for capturing inequality.

2.3 Production Process: Attributes and Decomposition of the Output

The following subchapter offers an overview of how the output in modern economies is distributed and what makes the composition of the output. For this purpose, we consider the role of capital, labour and wealth.

Table 2.1 World growth since industrial revolution

Average annual growth rate	World output (%)	World population (%)	Per capita output (%)
0–1700	0.1	0.1	0.0
1700–2012	1.6	0.8	0.8
1700–1820	0.5	0.4	0.1
1820–1913	1.5	0.6	0.9
1913–2012	3.0	1.4	1.6

Source: Piketty (2014)

Firstly, it is shown what actually is the result of production process and its development. The discussion on population growth and its role on economic output was famously held by Malthus (1998 [1798]) who believed that population growth leads to falling wages and inevitable poverty. Conversely, e.g. Kremer (1993) believed that population growth produces more ideas/innovations (supply of innovators) and thus the population growth (increasing the potential size of the market) has a positive effect on economic growth. This idea can be in several combinations found in various innovation-based theories (for instance, the product-variety model with horizontal innovations or the Schumpeterian model with vertical innovations). The Table 2.1 depicts the development of growth and population.

It is seen that during the recent century global society experienced the highest growth rate per capita. By the sum of demographic and productivity growth we get income growth. Income is the first variable when evaluating economic inequality. At the national level, income is the sum of net domestic output and net foreign income. Net domestic output is generally described as a function of labour and capital, more concretely as GDP minus capital depreciation. Depreciation can vary with asset mix (e.g. tangible fixed assets and financial assets) or geography (Hsiang and Jina 2015). Net foreign income is the sum of net foreign labour income and net foreign capital income. Net foreign asset position is then the difference between foreign assets and foreign liabilities. In order to calculate income, it is also viable to sum up capital income and labour income which allows to capture shares of capital and labour on national income. Capital income is composed of rents, corporate profits, interest and capital component of mixed income; labour income is the sum of wages, supplements to wages and labour component of mixed income. Such division of income is known as factor income.

Piketty and Zucman (2014) demonstrates on the sample of advanced economies (USA, France, Australia, Japan, UK, Italy, Germany and Canada) that capital share on national wealth is growing since late 1970s; an increase in capital share at global level was captured by Karabarbounis and Neiman (2014). When considering government, the situation gets complicated a bit more. If we abstract from government, individual's income is given by incomes from capital and particularly from labour. If the government is in play, which usually means through tax and pension systems, disposable incomes vary from the ones which are based on production factors ownership; for more detailed decomposition of pre-tax income and disposable income on the example of the United States see Piketty et al. (2018). Then, income inequality must be also distinguished between market inequality and net (final) inequality since governments usually strive to moderate pure market distribution. It is easy to prove that governments are principally successful in this goal since reduction in Gini coefficients before and after taxes and transfers is, at least among OECD countries, considerable. In countries like Sweden, Belgium, Denmark, Czech Republic or even Luxembourg, we observe that the percentage reduction in Gini coefficient is between 43% and 46%, which means that the market inequality is reduced almost by half. On the other end we find United States, where market Gini coefficient is reduced after government interventions only by 16.6% (OECD 2008). These facts are the main reason why we repeatedly refer to the United States when aiming at market inequality.

The question of how the benefits of economic growth are shared among economic agents is the crucial one. Let us have a look on the Great Britain and the United States as typical examples of Anglo-Saxon countries with U-shaped evolution of inequality. Based on microdata from the Luxembourg Income Study Database, it can be clearly demonstrated that the highest growth of real disposable household income during 1979–2013 (up to 2010 in the case of Great Britain) was experienced by the top decile (followed by the subsequent upper deciles), while the lowest decile (again, followed by the subsequent lower deciles) is connected with the lowest growth of real disposable income.[3] On the contrary, many continental Europe countries, for instance Denmark or Sweden, have exactly the opposite evolution of real disposable income by income deciles, so that the lower deciles grow faster than the top deciles. The income growth with a very low variance across income deciles in developed countries is observed e.g. in Norway. This is then mirrored in the median (disposable) income growth since 1980, where Norway experienced the most significant growth, in contrast to the United States which demonstrates the lowest dynamics of the median income growth. It is then no surprise that the difference between median and mean disposable income was during the period 1979–2013 on the rise in the United States (Thewissen et al. 2019).

A global perspective is captured by the famous "elephant graph" (Lakner and Milanovic 2013) which is based on panel database of national household surveys between 1988 and 2008. It shows that most significant increases in per-capita income can be found among the "emerging global middle class" and especially among the very top of the global income distribution. The real income of the top 1% has risen by more than 60% between 1988–2008. The largest increases were however monitored between 50th and 60th percentiles of global income distribution, whose incomes have risen by more than 70%. These include mainly people in fast growing and populated countries like China, India, Brazil, Egypt or Indonesia. Despite the income increases among the bottom third, the real income increases of

[3]The relationship between growth of real disposable income and respective income decile in the United States is perfectly clean—the higher the income decile, the higher the growth of disposable household income and vice-versa. To mention a continental European country, the same development can be observed e.g. in Belgium and a bit surprisingly also in relatively egalitarian countries like Finland or the Czech Republic.

the poorest 5% of the global population were insignificant. Even lower dynamics of real incomes than experienced by the poorest 5% belong to those between 75th and 90th percentiles of global distribution, whose real incomes have not experienced any change. These include global upper middle class, mainly people in post-communist countries and countries of Latin America.

Highly important is a reference to differences in distribution of labour and capital incomes worldwide. As is widely recognized, capital income is more concentrated than labour income: top 10% owns 20–30% of total labour income and 50–90% of total capital income. The bottom 50% owns 20–30% of total labour income and 0–10% of capital income. Gini coefficients are then calculated between 0.2 and 0.4 for labour income distribution and between 0.6 and 0.8 for capital income distribution (Piketty 2014).

Despite the distribution of labour income is more equal than is the case of capital income, the situation on the labour market cannot be overlooked. Probably the most common feature is skill premium which relates to both ‘textbook’ points on labour income inequality derived from marginal productivity: the nature of work that the worker is able to perform and relative scarcity. The rise in the skill premium vastly affects wage inequality—according to Goldin and Katz (2010) the rise in the skill premium explains 60–70% of the rise of the wage inequality in the United States between 1980–2005. On the other hand, Card (2009) did not find any significant evidence that immigrants, classified by education (college/high school), would have an impact on native wage inequality. Labour market institutions also play a key role: strong correlation between the decline in union density and rising top 10% income share (Jaumotte and Buitron 2015) in combination with minimum wage policy, examined in details e.g. by the Center on Wage and Employment Dynamics (UC Berkeley) and top tax rates (Piketty et al. 2014; Bertrand and Mullainathan 2001) heavily contributes to deepen labour market inequality.

When referring to income shares, it is inevitable to mention the question of the top 1%. Data for income shares are usually reconstructed from income tax records. The great advantage of these data is that, in some cases, it allows to monitor the evolution of inequality over more than 100 years. The increase in the top 1% income is too relevant to be omitted, especially in the context of the United States. Decomposition of labour income of the top 1% over the past century in the United States shows that the labour component of mixed income as a share on national income is stagnating, while other compensations has grown significantly since 1970s. In case of capital income of the top 1% we observe an increase as a share on national income since 1980s (Piketty et al. 2018). Altogether, the top 1% income share received almost 11% of total US income in 1980, while the bottom 50% income share received almost 21% of total income. Monitoring the situation 36 years later, the top 1% received more than 20% of national income, while the bottom 50% dropped down to 13% of national income. In contrast, according to statistics of the Internal Revenue Service (2018), the top 1% of income earners in the United States, whose share on total income equalled 20%, paid 37% of all income taxes. On the other hand, the bottom 50% of income earners, who earned 12% of total income, paid only 3% of all income taxes in 2016.[4]

Wealth is another variable which is crucial to understand when researching inequality. Private wealth equals the subtraction of liabilities of households from households' assets (financial and non-financial). Public wealth equals the similar subtraction but instead of households the government is taken into account. National wealth is then the sum of private and public wealth, while it can be further decomposed as the sum of domestic capital and net foreign assets. Piketty (2014:113–139) shows how the nature of wealth is changing over time, for instance the declining share of agricultural land and increasing share of housing on national wealth. The significance of private wealth is increasing during the last four decades, while government wealth in most advanced economies is on the decrease. Private wealth is given by the sum of non-financial and financial assets minus financial liabilities (household and non-profit sectors). On the other hand, average return on private wealth has a downward trend. National wealth is then given by the sum of domestic capital (land, housing and other domestic capital) and net foreign assets. An important indicator for further analysis is the capital/income ratio (β), which was pioneered by Harrod-Domar-Solow and is given by the relation of saving and growth rate. The formula plays a central role also in Piketty and Zucman (2014). Transitional dynamics is then as follows:

$$W_{t+1} = W_t + s_t Y_t, \tag{2.31}$$

where W is wealth, s denotes saving rate and Y represents income. Since future income is given by the present income and growth rate:

$$Y_{t+1} = Y_t(1 + g_t), \tag{2.32}$$

we get:

$$\beta_{t+1} = \frac{W_t + s_t Y_t}{Y_t(1 + g_t)} = \frac{\beta_t + s_t}{1 + g_t}. \tag{2.33}$$

There are no variances over time in the steady state, hence:

$$\beta = \frac{\beta + s}{1 + g} \Rightarrow \beta = \frac{s}{g}. \tag{2.34}$$

As was indicated, current trends refer to increasing private wealth on national income in advanced economies. In addition, more than half of the gross private

[4]To complete the mosaic, individual income taxes make up less than half of the US federal revenues.

Table 2.2 Thresholds and average wealth in top wealth groups (USA, 2012)

Wealth group	Number of families	Wealth threshold (USD)	Average wealth (USD)	Wealth share (%)
A. Top wealth groups				
Full population	160,700,000			100
Top 10%	16,070,000	660,000	2,560,000	77.2
Top 1%	1,607,000	3,960,000	13,840,000	41.8
Top 0.1%	160,700	20,600,000	72,800,000	22.0
Top 0.01%	16,070	111,000,000	371,000,000	11.2
B. Intermediate wealth groups				
Bottom 90%	144,600,000		84,000	22.8
Top 10–1%	14,463,000	660,000	1,310,000	35.4
Top 1–0.1%	1,446,300	3,960,000	7,290,000	19.8
Top 0.1–0.01%	144,600	20,600,000	39,700,000	10.8
Top 0.01%	16,070	111,000,000	371,000,000	11.2

Source: Saez and Zucman (2016)

savings in advanced economies is spend on capital depreciation (Piketty and Zucman 2014).

In order to capture wealth inequality, researchers have to overcome many methodological difficulties related to estate tax multiplier method, capitalization of investment income or survey data with top-end correction. Uncertainty also arises when considering offshore wealth (Zucman 2015). One of the most insightful studies on the topic was written by Saez and Zucman (2016). In the case of the United States, authors come up with the following numbers:

The Table 2.2 depicts the share of total household wealth held by the given income percentile as estimated by capitalizing income tax returns. Authors refer to a rapid increase of wealth of the top 0.1% since late 1970s. Even more dramatic is the situation among the very top richest individuals—the wealth share of the top 0.01% jumped from around 2% in late 1970s to more than 11% in 2008. Conversely, the magnitude of wealth held by the bottom 90% is declining during the same time period. This dynamic is further supported by average returns on foundation wealth. Saez and Zucman (2016) shows that returns (including realized and unrealized gains) increases with foundation wealth.

A similar development between top and bottom wealth holders is also observable in income. All in all, we see that the share of income and wealth of the bottom 90% wealth holders have been declining since 1980s and, conversely, the share of income and wealth of the top 1% wealth holders have been rising during the same time period (Saez and Zucman 2016). Identical trend is confirmed by many others, e.g. Duménil and Lévy (2003). The same also applies on income shares by quintiles available in the Poverty and Equity database of the World Bank—the only quintile which got in the United States better-off is the top 20%; all the rest, i.e. the bottom

80%, got worse-off during 1979–2013. Average growth rate of GDP per person for the top 0.1% was 0.72%; and 2.3% for the bottom 99.9% between 1950 and 1980. Between 1980–2010 average growth rate of GDP per person for the top 0.1% was 6.86% and 1.83% for the bottom 99.9% (Jones 2015).

Authors often attribute these changes to saving rate. The rationale consists in a generalization of Harrod-Domar-Solow formula $\beta = s/g$; concretely for i-th agent we have wealth accumulation equation:

$$W_{t+1}^{i} = \left(1 + r_{t}^{i}\right)\left(W_{t}^{i} + s_{t}^{i} Y_{t}^{i}\right), \tag{2.35}$$

where W is wealth, $1 + r$ is rate of capital gains, Y is income and s is saving rate. Then, if we have a population fractile p and share of wealth (W_{share}) and income (Y_{share}) a long-run steady state (without price effect linked to the rate of capital gains) determines:

$$W_{share}^{p} = Y_{share}^{p} \frac{s^{p}}{s}, \tag{2.36}$$

where s^p/s is relative saving of a given fractile. The data show the following: while the average saving rate in the United States has been 9.8% over 1913–2013, the saving rate at the top was fold higher and at the bottom was slightly above zero. The saving rate of the top 1% oscillated around 40% in recent decades (culminating in 1980s with almost 50%), while the saving rate of the bottom 90% is decreasing since 1980s to zero level (Saez and Zucman 2016).

The fact that wealth is much more concentrated than labour income determines types of model which can be used for studying wealth inequality. A typical precautionary saving model assumes uncertainty of income and hence individuals save a part of their income to cover job loss risks. Within this framework, the richer the individual is, the lower is the motivation to save which causes decreasing saving rate with increasing income. Wealth is then less unequally distributed than income. Another historically influential framework stems from Modigliani's "Life cycle theory". The theory says that savings are solely driven by the need of savings in retirement. Individuals therefore save a part of their income during their working period and accumulated savings melt away during retirement. Individuals then die with zero wealth. Intuitively, such kind of models do not properly fit to data in Western countries where developed pension systems reduce the need of savings in retirement. Secondly, the theory based on assumptions of the model, life-cycle theory generates proportional inequality between wealth and income. However, as data demonstrates, none of these two approaches satisfactorily explains greater wealth inequality than income inequality. The following chapters therefore work with dynamic approaches which allow to model saving rate more accurately.

On the other side, development of consumption relates to general consumption-smoothing theories quite well. The empirical evidence comes from the Survey of Consumer Finances and the Consumer Expenditure Survey for the distribution of consumption, income and corporate equity across US households between 1989 and

2016. It shows that bottom 20% of income distribution spent 9% of all expenditures in 1989, while the top 20% accounted for 38%. In 2016, the share of consumption of the bottom 20% remained the same and the highest-income group's share had risen only by 1 percentage point. During 1989–2016, the lowest-income 20% increased their corporate equity from 1.1% to 2%. But, during the same period the second-bottom quintile share dropped from 3.5% to 1.6%, so the total share of corporate equity of the bottom 40% felt. On the contrary, the top 20% held 77% of corporate equity in 1989, and 89% in 2016. To conclude with income—the lowest-income group's share equalled to 3% of pre-tax income at the start and the end of the observed period. Conversely, the top 20% increased their share of income by 7 percentage points—from 57% in 1989 to 64% in 2016 (Gans et al. 2019).

The data clearly displays that consumption shares remain *de-facto* constant, whereas income and holdings of corporate equity demonstrate widening gaps among the top and bottom income shares. The dynamics of the real average annual growth of income is depicted in the Graph 2.1:

We observe that market (pre-tax) real average annual growth of income between 1980 and 2014 was faintly increasing with income percentile, until reaching the 99th percentile. The situation within the top 1% however differs enormously. Data shows that the top 0.1 witnessed more than 3% real average annual growth of income; 0.01 experienced almost 4.5% growth and the top 0.001 enjoyed 6% growth of their income.

The view of the top 1% was partially confronted by Acemoglu and Robinson (2014) who oppose general Piketty's conclusions, summarized in (Piketty 2014). Beside the role of the top 1% also formula $r > g$, which purportedly does not explain historical patterns of inequality, authors point out at imperfect elasticity between labour and capital. Acemoglu and Robinson argue with the example of South Africa and Sweden for which they run statistical regression. According to their analysis, the development of the top 1% went through the same pattern in both countries, however their national inequalities were substantially different.[5] However, this could be explainable through the inequality measure computations presented in the previous part. The question is also whether a particular empirical counterexample could disqualify the whole theory.

In spite of partial uncertainties, the dynamics of production process allows basal conclusions. Firstly, aggregate wealth has increased enormously during the last century. It is also apparent that changes affecting inequality the most are placed in late 1970s and early 1980s; wealth and income shares of the bottom social strata is declining while wealth and income shares of the top strata are rising. Wealth share of the top 0.01% in the United States is six times larger than in late 1970s; saving rate at the top wealth shares is significantly higher than for the bottom 90%. At least on the examples of the United States and Great Britain, it can be concluded that the richer the economic unit (household) is, the more rapidly its income was growing. It is also

[5]Empirical challenge of Piketty's work (2014) was also held by Magness and Murphy (2015), however their corrections are rather formal with no change in general trends.

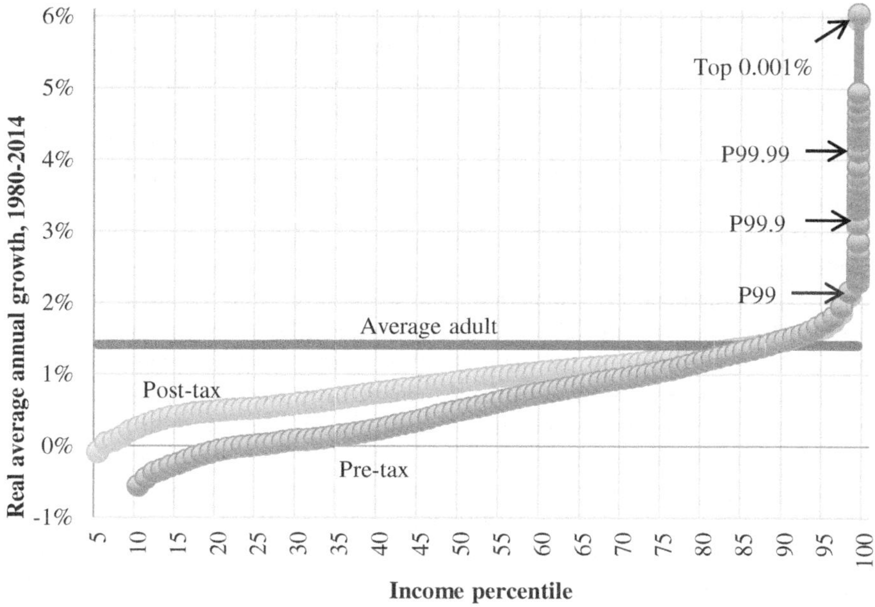

Graph 2.1 Average annual growth by percentile, US 1980–2014. Source: Piketty et al. (2018)

evident that richer households had much greater corporate equity holdings than poorer households, and that capital incomes, the crucial parameter of economic distribution, are growing in favour of the richest.

2.4 Quantification of Global Inequality

Most researchers throughout the world would agree that global income inequality is high. Estimates and calculations nevertheless exhibit ambiguous results, or at least, there is no simple answer as to whether global inequality is increasing or decreasing. Despite the fact that the vast majority of papers incline toward increasing inequality, it would require tremendous effort to conjure highly confident research on global inequality. When considering recent and widely discussed books, let us name e.g. Milanovic (2016), Piketty (2014), Atkinson (2015) or Stiglitz (2012), we also focus on the most respected academic papers which have remarkably contributed to the issue of measuring global income inequality in the recent past. The aim is to provide an influential sample of what the development of worldwide inequality is; it is not meant to be a complete review of the subject.

Inequality in the global context varies widely across regions. Generally, Europe has the lowest inequality while the highest inequality is measured in the Middle East. Recent two decades were characterized by rising inequality in all countries of former Soviet Union and its satellites. China has experienced an immense economic growth, which was, however, accompanied by an immense increase of inequality. Traditionally unequal societies in modern history like countries of sub-Saharan Africa or Latin America remain relatively stable at extremely high levels. The important breaking point, which this book refers to with the highest importance, occurred in 1980s since when inequality has risen sharply, most notably in Anglo-Saxon countries.

Global inequality itself is the product of converging and diverging factors of global production processes. From the first group, we might name catch-up growth in developing countries, migration from poor to rich countries or diffusion of technologies through trade. On the other hand, the rise in top-end inequality within countries, international tax competition and evasion or rising inherited wealth are supposed to cause greater divergence on global scale. The following research results are structured according to the method—Gini results based on purchasing parity power and Gini results based on market exchange rates. Researches are then sum up according to interpretation of inequality: a) increasing, b) constant or ambiguously interpreted and c) decreasing.

Dorwick and Akmal (2005) deal with the question whether inequality values based on purchasing parity power (PPP) and market exchange rates converge since globalization makes national states trade a bigger fraction of their GDP. By using Deininger and Squire's (1996) data for within-country inequality and GDP PPPs from Penn World Table (PWT 5.6). Authors present that global Gini coefficient decreased from 0.659 in 1980 to 0.636 in 1993 when using standard PPP conversion factors (Geary-Khamis method) for measuring relative incomes. On the contrary, by using their own 'Afriat' conversion factors the inequality slightly rose from 0.698 to 0.711.

Milanovic (2005) used his own dataset of household surveys for within-country inequality and PWT and World Bank data for PPP. He informs about increasing Gini coefficient from 0.622 to 0.641 between 1988 and 1998. Milanovic comes out with other calculations—as if he used GDP per capita instead of household surveys, Gini coefficient would increase almost by 2 percentage points. In his previous work (2002) Milanovic observed an increase from 0.628 to 0.660 between 1988 and 1993 as the result based on household surveys for 91 countries. Between-country inequality explains between 75% and 88% of overall inequality, depending on whether the author uses Gini or Theil index. Real incomes of the bottom 5% of the world population decreased by one-fourth, while the richest quintile went up. The world top 1% receive as much as the bottom 57%, which means that 50 million of the richest receive as much as 2.7 billion poor. Milanovic continues that the ratio between average income of the world top 5% and world bottom 5% increased from 78:1 in 1988, to 114:1 in 1993. UNDP (1999) adds that the ratio of GDP per capita in the richest and the poorest country rose from 35:1 in 1950 to 44:1 in 1973 and finally 72:1 in 1992.

Milanovic (2013) also uses Theil's mean log deviation. Such analysis is easily decomposable and at the same time the importance of each component does not depend on the rest of the decomposition. This attitude is also shared by Anand and Segal (2008). It allows measuring global inequality by the index value and decomposing the aggregate value into two main factors—location and social class.

The results show that the importance of location prevails class affiliation over time, which subsequently confirms that between-country inequality has become decisive in explaining global inequality.

Sala-i-Martín (2006) used Deininger and Squire's (1996) and United Nations University—World Institute for Development Economics Research data (UNU–WIDER) for within-country inequality; GDP PPPs from PWT 6.0. Based on these datasets the author found a decrease of the Gini coefficient from 0.660 to 0.637 between 1980 and 2000. Sala-i-Martín therefore presents that countries were converging. However, he reminds that if China were excluded from the sample, we would get results that sign economic divergence on the interpersonal level. In this particular case, Gini coefficient would increase from 0.620 to 0.648, which represents an increase of global interpersonal inequality by 4.4%. (2006, 388) When computing logarithm of income, the method also used e.g. by Schultz (1998), inequality in 2000 is higher than in 1970.

Bhalla (2002) used his own data for within-country inequality; as a source of GDP PPPs he used World Development Indicators and PWT 5.6. Bhalla recorded a reduction from 0.686 in 1980 to 0.651 in 2000. This means that median person in the developing world is slightly catching up world richer counterparts.

Bourguignon and Morrison (2002) found no change in the Gini coefficient between 1980 and 1992 which remained at 0.657. Authors also used their own data for within-country inequality and Maddison's data (1995) for GDP PPPs. Bourguignon and Morrison found in their sample of 33 countries that between 1820–1920 inequality grew according to every method. Income share of the top quintile grew from 1970 to 1992. From 1820 to 1992 the Gini coefficient grew by 30% and Theil index grew by 60%. Their results also show that higher social mobility decreases inequality. Authors further claim that inequality in the early nineteenth century was mainly due to within-country disparities, while later on the driver was between-country inequality.

Dikhanov and Ward (2001) came up with an increase in Gini from 0.683 to 0.668 during 1970–1999. They used Milanovic's (2002) data for within-country inequality and World Bank data for PPPs.

The previous researches above were calculated by using PPPs. The second option is to compare national incomes through market exchange rates. Dorwick and Akmal (2005) argue with increasing Gini from 0.779 to 0.824 between 1980 and 1993. Milanovic (2002) had recorded an increase as well, concretely from 0.782 to 0.805 between 1988 and 1993. Three years later (Milanovic 2005) he presented an increase from 0.778 to 0.794 between 1988 and 1998. Finally, Korzeniewicz and Moran (1997) identified an increase of Gini from 0.749 to 0.796 between 1965 and 1992. Authors also use the Theil index to prove that between-country inequality is the most important in capturing global interpersonal income inequality, while between-country inequality explains roughly 90% of interpersonal global inequality (Table 2.3).

Among other influential empirical researches, which are from various (more or less methodical) reasons non-comparable with the researches above, we might find Cornia and Kiiski (2001). Their dataset covers 80% of the world population and 91%

Table 2.3 Research's results on global inequality

Author(s)	Inequality trend	Method	Data sources
Dorwick and Akmal (2005)	Decreasing	PPPs (Geary-Khamis)	Deininger and Squire (1996); PWT 5.6
Dorwick and Akmal (2005)	Increasing	PPPs (Afriat index)	Deininger and Squire (1996); own calculations of Afriat index
Dorwick and Akmal (2005)	Increasing	Market exchange rates	Deininger and Squire (1996)
Milanovic (2005)	Increasing	PPPs (consumption)	Household surveys; PWT; WB
Milanovic (2005)	Increasing	Market exchange rates	Household surveys
Milanovic (2002)	Increasing	Market exchange rates	Household surveys
Milanovic (2002)	Increasing	PPPs (consumption)	Household surveys; PWT; WB
Sala-i-Martín (2006)	Decreasing	PPPs	Deininger and Squire (1996); UNU-WIDER; PWT 6.0
Bhala (2002)	Decreasing	PPPs	Own dataset; WDI; PWT 5.6
Bourguignon and Morrisson (2002)	Constant	PPPs	Own dataset; Maddison (1995)
Dikhanov and Ward (2001)	Increasing	PPPs (consumption)	Milanovic (2002); WB
Korzeniewicz and Moran (1997)	Increasing	Market exchange rates	WB

Source: Maialeh (2017)

of the world GDP. Authors claim that 59% of the world population lived in countries where inequality is increasing, meanwhile only 5% of the world population lived in countries where inequality is decreasing. The research shows that since the 1980s there has been a significant increase in inequality in both developing and developed countries. To provide an economic policy outlook, their analysis shows that liberalization of domestic financial and job markets led to the increase in inequality, as well as did privatization.

Schultz's (1998) research covers 93% of the world population. The variance in the logarithms of per capita GDP PPPs increased worldwide between 1960 and 1968; and decreased since the mid 1970s. Schultz also argues that subsequent convergence in intercountry incomes offset any increase in within-country inequality. In contrast to Korzeniewicz and Moran (1997) and Milanovic (2002), Schultz assigns two-thirds of world inequality to inter-country differences. Further, three-tenths to inter-household within-country inequality, and one-twentieth to between-gender differences in education. If China is excluded from the world sample, the decline in world inequality after 1975 is not evident. Schultz's research also underlines the intuitive fact that the bigger the sample is, the higher the chance of estimate errors is.

Minoiu (2007) analyses poverty based on kernel density estimates for 94 countries. Minoiu's outcomes show that global poverty rates are highly sensitive to the choice of smoothing parameter. As the result, the estimated proportion of people who live for 1 USD/day in 2000 varies by a factor of 1.8, while the estimated number of people who live for 2 USD/day in 2000 varies by 287 million people. According to Minoiu's research, 23–27% of the world population lived for 2 USD/day in 1990, whereas Sala-i-Martín (2006) identifies only 16% of the world population on this economic level. The outlined difference can be explained by using income clusters in case of Minoiu's research, and the difference might also reveal why Sala-i-Martín identified decreasing global inequality. As the author admits, there exists serious concerns about the validity and robustness of poverty analysis based on kernel density estimation on grouped data.

With an eye to one of the newest contributions, we read no surprise. It concludes that global interpersonal income inequality measured by income per capita on the sample of 145 countries has been declining over the period 1988–2015, especially due to the most recent dynamics. Again, excluding China and India, i.e. reducing the sample on 143 countries, would cause rising interpersonal income inequality (Darvas 2019).

In summary, on the basis of this sample of papers it can be concluded that increasing inequality in recent decades was detected by Milanovic (2002 and 2005), Dikhanov and Ward (2001), Korzeniewicz and Moran (1997), Cornia and Kiiski (2001). Constant or ambiguously interpreted inequality was detected by Dorwick and Akmal (2005), Schultz (1998) and Bourguignon and Morrisson (2002). Decreasing inequality was detected by Sala-i-Martín (2006) and Bhala (2002). Still, most researchers outside this sample agree with increasing global inequality since the 1980s. An eloquent in this regard may be Milanovic (2003) whose sample includes 144 countries and each country/year represents one observation. The study clearly demonstrates sharp rise of inequality since the 1980s which contrasts with generally declining tendencies since the 2WW. It must be also noted that both Sala-i-Martín and Bhalla use quintile shares which most likely explains their results; whereas Milanovic (2002 and 2005) and Dikhanov and Ward (2001) calculate PPPs for consumption.[6]

[6]For more details on variances in income and consumption inequality see well known Krueger and Perri (2005), Deaton and Grosh (2000) or the study of Aguiar and Bils (2015). The conclusion is intuitive since the consumption is, for obvious reasons, smoother than income. Hence, we can again conclude that inequality in consumption tends to be lower than inequality in income.

2.5 Inequality, Growth and Other Social Phenomena

The following subchapter reveals interrelatedness between inequality and economic growth and put the issue of inequality to a broader socioeconomic context. This subchapter thus contributes to the core idea of growth and inequality as the results of the production process itself. Elaborated literature also suggests that theory dealing with these issues transfers from theories of capital accumulation to theories of human capital.

The first one is Galbraith et al. (1999) who argue that the Gini coefficient tends to undervalue high incomes, for which they research inequality through Theil index. According to authors' calculations, Theil index is more appropriate for measuring changes in income within countries. Their results show, exactly as was the case of Cornia and Kiiski (2001), that liberalization contributes to generally rising inequality. Authors also claim that economic growth equalizes economic disparities and hence increasing inequality since the 1980s was caused by lower growth rates.

One of the most prominent authors who refers to the relationship between inequality and growth is Philippe Aghion. The complexity of the issue has however caused that Aghion et al. (1999) do not find any substitution effect between inequality and effectivity in cases of imperfect capital markets. This implies that convergence depends vastly upon the existence of perfect capital markets. When considering imperfect capital market, authors conclude that the level of wealth does not converge. Further, faster growth is rather a matter of more egalitarian countries. On the other hand, economic growth might increase wage inequality within and between educational groups. The research also shows that technologies are not neutral and especially general-purpose technologies (GPT) significantly drive wage inequality.

The underlying source of growth frequently consists in vertical innovations, a fruit of competitive research sector. The optimum is derived from differential equations which reflects intertemporality of current and past costs on research and development. It is then sensible to incorporate the notion of 'creative destruction' which is based on the idea that new research destroys rents of the previous one.[7] Growth is then mainly a function of the magnitude of resources allocated to innovation process. We can also assume that e.g. innovations are divided into 'drastic' and 'non-drastic', while the latter allow that the other subjects realize profit despite an innovation was introduced. Such type of model then concludes that laissez-faire environment shrinks the magnitude of innovations due to 'business-stealing effect' (Aghion and Howitt 1992).[8] Single-sector growth model was also elaborated by Romer (1990), who, however, assumes the product as non-rival. The

[7]This idea is frequently assigned to J. A. Schumpeter, however the first who elaborated the issue was Marx and Engels—we read in Communist Manifesto that old industries are destroyed and replaced by new industries as a result of the very motive to survive (2008 [1848]), which basically represents the antagonistic character of society on macro-level.

[8]This model is presented in more details in the Chap. 6.

similarity with the previous model derives from the fact that Romer, too, incorporates the magnitude of capital (human) in research and development as the foremost driving force of growth. Innovation process, consuming today's resources with an intention to benefit from them in the future, is then considerably sensitive on interest rate.

Emphasizing the role of the research sector naturally increases the interest in the Schumpeterian growth theory. Upon growing inequality in the United States and the Great Britain since the 1980s, a simple model deals with wage inequality (skill premium) in the context of technologies. The model presents two main effects (supply and demand-oriented) that explain rising skill-premium and therefore wage differences. 'Market size effect' says that increasing supply of skilled labour generates increasing monopolistic rent deriving from innovations. Based on that, the whole sector is growing as well as skill-premium.[9] The second effect concerns GPT. Since diffusion of technology requires greater amount of skilled labour, the demand for skilled labour is growing and skill-premium as well. It is also important to decipher the ambivalence of a new technology implementation. From the intertemporal perspective, the long run enhancement in productivity is preceded by costly restructuralization of the production process and temporary reduction in productivity. The aggregate effect on the economy could be captured by introducing coefficient of proportionality which measures inter-sectoral spillovers (Aghion 2002). This redirects back to Aghion and Howitt's article (1992) because their 'business stealing effect' might be also seen in this perspective. The higher the coefficient of proportionality is, the easier the diffusion of innovation among sectors is and hence the higher the growth it generates. Yet this would have to call for considering the crucial fact that the higher the coefficient of proportionality, the lower the initiative to innovate and the lower the growth it generates. The issue of technological changes and their negative impacts on wage inequality are summarized in Aghion and Howitt (2009). An interesting viewpoint on skill-biased technological changes in the context of inequality provides Acemoglu (2002).

Alesina and Perotti (1996) tested a hypothesis whether higher inequality leads to socio-political instability and through higher uncertainty whether it decreases investments and growth. Socio-economic instability is not measured by changing governments as in many other studies, but by social instability index that is composed of numerous social phenomena. Their results suggest that lower inequality causes rapid growth (e.g. in South-East Asia). The question of capital taxation is also briefly discussed—taxation reduces propensity to invest with negative effect on growth, but on the other hand reduces social tensions with positive effect on growth. The net effect of capital taxation thus remains unclear.

The question of capital taxation was discussed also earlier in Alesina and Rodrik (1994). The authors define two social groups, workers and capitalists, and for each group formulate utility function with regards to capital taxation. The role of

[9]Upon closer inspection it must be admitted that the effect is not corresponding with early twentieth century data.

government is to maximize weighted average of welfare for both groups. In democratic society results show that the more unequal the distribution of wealth the lower the rate of growth. Economic policies maximizing growth are then optimal only for governments representing the 'capitalist' group. To conclude, the model posits that democracies with lower inequality grow faster and that redistribution of wealth from the top quintile to middle class supports economic growth.

Another research reports that characteristics of industrial countries like skill-intensive technologies, low barriers to knowledge spillovers and high redistribution have a positive growth-inequality correlation. The opposite characteristics, assigned to non-industrial countries, have a negative correlation between growth and inequality (Bandyopadhyay and Parantap 2005).

Similar division was earlier elaborated by Barro (2000) who identified that higher inequality slows down economic growth in poorer countries, meanwhile accelerates economic growth in advanced countries—economic growth slows down with higher inequality in countries where GDP per capita is lower than 2000 USD/person/year and accelerates with higher inequality in countries where GDP per capita is higher than 2000 USD/person/year. Redistribution of wealth then might cause a decrease in growth rate in advanced countries and increasing growth in developing countries. Barro also discusses the fact that poor cannot afford investments in human capital. This implies that redistribution in favour of poor, who would consequently afford investments in human capital with high rate of return, might lead to the increase in average aggregate productivity. Barro also mentions that income share of the top quintile rises with rising GDP per capita; however, it decreases when GDP reaches 3500 USD/capita/year which intuitively may correspond to the idea embedded in Kuznets curve. The question is whether these results would be obtained if Barro used e.g. decile or even top 1% computation whose income shares may be dragged down by the rest of the quintile.

There are few examples in the literature that observed an inverse relationship between growth and inequality. One of them are Berg and Sachs (1988) who focus on debt crises and restructuralization of national debts. They claim that extending the maturity of the debt is closely related to higher inequality. This account presumes that higher inequality decreases economic performance of the country and leads to rescheduling of the debt etc. Authors conclude that internationally oriented countries (in terms of trade) have lower probability of restructuralization. On the other hand, such orientation usually requires lower real wages and devaluation of currency and therefore initial inequality should be relatively small. Empirical evidence on the effect of trade on economic growth, despite the uneasiness to establish a causality between the two, was also provided by Frankel and Romer (1999) who conclude that trade has a large and positive effect on income.

de la Croix and Döpke (2003) emphasize the status of fertility and education. By using data for 68 countries, authors posit that fertility-differential derives from the fact that poor parents with many children cannot afford investments in human capital of their children and the next generation is even poorer with no significant contributions to growth. According to authors, it does not matter how many children are born, but to whom, as they apply trade-off between 'quality' and 'quantity' of children. Their 'social engineering approach' then suggest rather to liberalize an access to education instead of redistributive tax policies.

Another article elaborated on the topic was written by Deininger and Squire (1996). Authors compiled a new dataset for 108 countries with 682 observations, but they did not identify a systematic relationship between growth of aggregate income and inequality measured by Gini coefficient. During 88 periods of growth, in 45 cases was recorded a decline of inequality, in the rest of the 43 cases there was an increase of inequality. During these periods, the lowest quintile experienced growth of its income in 77 cases and decline in the remaining 11 cases. Statistically significant relationship, based on the income of the lowest quintile, was detected between aggregate growth and poverty reduction which leads them to conclusion that positive growth makes poor better-off, negative growth makes them worse-off. Additionally, Kuznets curve pattern corresponded only to five countries, four countries had the opposite pattern and for the rest of countries the pattern was statistically insignificant.

Consequently, it is worthwhile noting that different stages of economic development require different types of stimuli. To give an illustration, during industrialization, where physical capital accumulation is a prime source of economic growth, inequality enhances the process of economic development by channelling resources to those whose marginal propensity to save is higher. Later stages require (due to capital-skill complementarity) more human capital and human capital becomes the prime source of growth. Such a classification necessarily has an impact on credit constraints: more equal distribution of income, when considering credit constraints, stimulates investments in human capital and economic growth at the end. As economies become wealthier, credit constraints might become less binding and the aggregate effect of income distribution on economic growth becomes less significant (Galor 2009).

An article summarizing studies on growth and inequality was elaborated by Bénabou (1996). The paper compares 13 respected studies which used all major measures of inequality (Gini coefficient, Theil index, and income shares). It concludes that ten of them found a consistent and statistically significant negative relationship between growth and inequality; two studies demonstrated the same negative relationship but with low statistical significance and magnitude; and one paper found no relationship between these two variables.

Conversely, concentrating on several statistical and econometric aspects of the relationship between inequality and growth may lead to quite opposite conclusions. As an example, Forbes (2000) demonstrates that income inequality has a positive relationship with subsequent economic growth in the short and medium term. Increasing inequality therefore goes hand in hand with economic growth and these statistical results are supposed to be highly robust across samples, variable definitions and further model specifications.

Gomez and Foot (2003) research age structures and their impact on income distribution. Authors claim that credit constraints serve as an intensificator of income inequality. Such inequality is detrimental to economic growth since it leads to redistributive policies. These policies consequently harm private ownership because private profit, which stems from investments, cannot be fully appropriated. They also incline to suggest that more egalitarian countries grow faster than unequal countries, similarly as Aghion et al. (1999).

Perhaps the most famous article on the relationship between growth and inequality was written by already mentioned Kuznets (1955). The general idea is as follows: countries start with low economic performance and low inequality. Inequality is rising simultaneously with economic performance over the period of their economic development. In later stages, economic growth generates, through inter-sectoral migration, converging forces that result in economic growth with decreasing inequality. Kuznets also states four factors impeding concentration of savings: (1) government intervention; (2) demographic changes; (3) dynamic free market; and (4) structure of top incomes with lower growth potential. Nevertheless, those parts referring to insufficient data and Kuznets' own conclusion became often forgotten, especially that the article "is perhaps 5 per cent empirical information and 95 per cent speculation, some of it possibly tainted by wishful thinking." (1955:26) A theoretical model that supports Kuznets' curve was developed by Aghion and Bolton (1997)[10] who attribute widening inequality to earlier stages of capital accumulation, which, however, reduce inequality in later stages. The model works with capital market imperfections, the phenomenon that plays its role e.g. in Gomez and Foot (2003), Aghion et al. (1999) or Mookherjee and Ray (2003).

Korzeniewicz and Moran (1997) confront Kuznets' 'modernization paradigm' (1955) with Schumpeterian 'creative destruction'. By following contemporary research on inequality, authors focus on between-country inequality in contrast to Kuznets' within-country inequality (which under current globalizing conditions has significantly lower explanatory power). Authors argue that between 1970 and 1990 lower income countries had decreasing inequality, middle income countries had stagnating inequality and high-income countries had increasing inequality. In sum, their results stand in opposition of what Kuznets assumed. On the examples of South Korea and Taiwan authors argue that these countries experienced enormous increase of income per capita without rising inequality.[11] The authors also point out at rapidly rising inequality since the 1980s. Korzeniewicz and Moran concludes that if we substitute Kuznets' 'modernization paradigm' with 'creative destruction', and hence stationarity with continual processes of development, a "drive toward inequality" prevails.

Lundberg and Squire (2003) firstly follow Kuznets' 'mechanistic' heritage, but the most interesting part of their paper lies in separate causal analysis of growth and inequality. They use Deininger and Squire (1996) data and extended their dataset for 125 countries with 757 observations. For calculating GDP per capita authors use PWT. After composing vectors of variables for growth, equality and common vector of variables for growth and equality (inequality), they got the following results:

[10]This paper is one of the very few which endeavours to theorize the 'trickle-down' idea.

[11]To challenge authors' partial conclusion, Korzeniewicz and Moran completely neglect political aspects of the economic success in South Korea and Taiwan.

firstly, growth and inequality should be analysed together since several variables are statistically significant only when both equations for growth and inequality were employed. Secondly, expansion of education leads to lower inequality but at the expense of slower growth. This substitution effect however might be solvable by policymakers, e.g. by improving Sachs-Warner index or equalizing distribution of land without losing growth rate. The estimates of the common equation for growth and inequality show that equality negatively affects growth at 10% significance level. Growth has high statistically significant negative impact on equality, however relatively small quantitatively. Authors conclude that civil liberties generate conflict between growth and equality; conversely education, redistribution of land and lower inflation supports both growth and equality.

The article written by Persson and Tabellini (1994) researches the relationship between growth and inequality in two periods: from 1830 to the 2WW and from 2WW onward. Authors accentuate, as was also the case of Gomez and Foot (2003), that inequality harms growth since it leads to taxation of growth promoting activities. The model however suffers with estimate errors. The measure of inequality in the model is income share of the top 20% and inequality purportedly explains roughly one-fifth of growth variances. Persson and Tabellini's model is rather applicable on democracies. The same is valid for their findings inasmuch as equality has a positive effect on growth in democracies. The conclusion therefore does not support Barro (2000) or Bandyopadhyay and Parantap (2005) since the 'democracy' classification rather corresponds to higher income countries, where the relationship between growth and inequality is supposed to be positive. Nevertheless, according to authors' computations, growth is mainly driven by capital accumulation, human capital and knowledge usable in production processes.

A pioneering question whether inequality is bad for poor or rich was the subject matter for van der Weide and Milanovic (2018). They criticize other researches for considering growth and inequality homogeneously; i.e. how overall inequality affects average growth. Authors calculate impacts of overall inequality on different income groups in the United States between 1960 and 2010. Authors conclude that high overall inequality hurts only income growth of the poor, while the positive effect on growth is exclusively reserved for the top end of the income distribution. This also offers an alternative explanation for why the relationship between average income growth and inequality is so fragile, since those two effects from the different ends of the income distribution may offset each other. Incomes of poor (the lowest 40%) were growing faster in the 1960s and 1970s, while incomes of rich (top 40%) have been growing faster since the 1980s. Based on authors' computations, total inequality seems to be negatively associated with growth of the poorest and positively with growth of the top decile, while there is no statistically significant effect on growth of the middle of income distribution. The article tends to conclude that rich have been getting richer at the expense of the poor.

Many of today's questions regarding the relationship between growth and inequality in OECD countries over the past 30 years were researched recently by Cingano (2014). His econometric analysis suggests that income inequality has a considerable and statistically significant negative impact on growth; and that redistributive policies achieving greater equality in disposable income do not cause adverse growth consequences. Another recent study elaborated by Berg and Ostry (2013) claims that in the cross-section of developing countries, more equal countries tend to grow more. On the other hand, there is no such correlation for rich countries and the study says nothing about the direction or even existence of any causal relationship.

A possible link can be seen, even intuitively, between inequality and social mobility. Corak (2013) shows that the higher the inequality is, the less mobility across generations the country experiences. The study measures inequality as the Gini coefficient for disposable income and intergenerational mobility is measured as the elasticity between paternal and son's adult earnings. Corak's results clearly show that the lower the social mobility the country has, the higher the inequality is detected.

The discussion on whether wealth is predominantly inherited or self-made has been held by Modigliani (1986 and 1988) and Kotlikoff and Summers (1981) and Kotlikoff (1988). The first claims that 80% of the wealth in the United States is self-made while the latter claims the complete opposite. This is based on whether wealth comes from the past (inherited) or the present (self-made). The Kotlikoff-Summers-Modigliani controversy was re-examined by Piketty (2011) and corrected by Piketty et al. (2013), in more details in Piketty and Zucman (2015). The apparent motivation for further examination of this controversy arises from Modigliani's zero-capitalization and Kotlikoff's and Summers' full capitalization (of past inheritance flows using economy's average rate of return). Obviously, both of these two assumptions are theoretically weak and gave unreasonable outcomes. The role of inherited wealth is then captured in Piketty and Zucman (2015) who computed that in developed countries like France, United Kingdom or Germany, about 50–60% of total wealth comes from inheritance; in Sweden between 40 and 50%. Benchmark estimates for Europe and the United States were then elaborated by Alvaredo et al. (2017).

Nevertheless, differences are observable also among developed countries themselves. Inequality was significantly rising Anglo-Saxon countries while continental Europe and Japan more or less persisted on the values right after the 2WW. It suggests itself, especially in the case of Anglo-Saxon countries, that inequality can be linked to tax rates. Experience from Anglo-Saxon countries shows that top income tax rates and income inequality were changing inversely. The data also show that top inheritance tax rates play the crucial role in differences in overall inequality in developed countries (Piketty 2014).

2.6 Chapter Summary

The second chapter presents how inequality in economic distribution is reflected in contemporary economic research. To summarize empirical findings of inequality in economic distribution, we might claim the following: there are expectable methodological difficulties in both measuring inequality and making connections to other socioeconomic variables. Most of the authors inspected rising long-term global inequality, supported by all major quantitative methods used in economics. Also, wealth and income shares of the top are rapidly rising, especially in Anglo-Saxon countries since the 1980s, which also corresponds to differences in saving rates between the top and the bottom shares. In the context of this book it is also important to note that the period of widely recognized rising inequality corresponds to the period of political releasing market mechanism.

When concerning production process, it is inevitable to research relationship between growth and inequality. None of the models however includes all relevant variables; every author works on different assumptions about included variables and estimate error or multicollinearity play their roles. To conclude, the majority of authors incline toward negative relationship between growth and inequality, despite few respected studies showing right the opposite. Therefore, this prevailing statement, that more egalitarian societies stimulate growth, should be taken into account with relatively low explanatory power. Firstly, it is still not clear if the relationship between growth and inequality is statistically relevant. Secondly, if the relationship is present, it is not clear if the relationship is causal. And lastly, if the relationship is causal the question is what causes what—growth causes inequality or inequality causes growth? Equal society drives growth or rapid growth equalizes society? Further, the relationship between inequality and growth is affected by measures that might cause rising between-country inequality and declining within-country inequality or *vice versa* (e.g. in the case of China). Overall global inequality then depends on what effect prevails. These questions require research on their own since it is very complex theoretical interplay with highly diversified national histories and politico-economic conditions. The chapter, despite all outlined ambivalences, equips the following parts with observed data and stylized facts showing that the 'trickle-down' idea, which formed the discourse without any theoretical insight (see e.g. Sowell 2012), is not backed by empirical evidence.

References

Acemoglu D (2002) Technical change, inequality, and the labor market. J Econ Lit 40(1):7–72

Acemoglu D, Robinson JA (2014) The rise and fall of general laws of capitalism. J Econ Perspect 29(1):3–28

Aghion P, Bolton P (1997) A theory of trickle-down growth and development. Rev Econ Stud 64 (2):151–172

Aghion P, Howitt PW (1992) A model of growth through creative destruction. Econometrica 60 (2):323–351

Aghion F (2002) Schumpeterian growth theory and the dynamics of income inequality. Econometrica 70(3):855–882

Aghion P, Howitt PW (2009) The economics of growth. MIT Press, Cambridge, MA

Aghion P, Caroli E, García Penalosa C (1999) Inequality and economic growth: the perspective of the new growth theories. J Econ Lit 37(4):1615–1660

Aguiar MA, Bils M (2015) Has consumption inequality mirrored income inequality? Am Econ Rev 105(9):2725–2756

Alesina A, Perotti R (1996) Income distribution, political instability, and investment. Eur Econ Rev 40(6):1203–1228

Alesina A, Rodrik D (1994) Distributive politics and economic growth. Q J Econ 109(2):465–490
Alstadsæter A, Johannesen N, Zucman G (2019) Tax evasion and inequality. Am Econ Rev 109 (6):2073–2103
Alvaredo F (2011) A note on the relationship between top income shares and the Gini coefficient. Econ Lett 110:274–277
Alvaredo F, Garbinti B, Piketty T (2017) On the share of inheritance in aggregate wealth Europe and the United States, 1900–2010. Economica 84:239–260
Anand S, Segal P (2008) What do we know about global income inequality? J Econ Lit 46(1):57–94
Atkinson AB (1970) On the measurement of inequality. J Econ Theory 2:244–263
Atkinson AB (1983) The economics of inequality, 2nd edn. Clarendon Press, Oxford
Atkinson AB (2015) Inequality: what can be done? Harvard University Press, Cambridge, MA
Bandyopadhyay D, Parantap B (2005) What drives the cross-country growth and inequality correlation? Can J Econ 38(4):1272–1297
Barro RJ (2000) Inequality, growth and investment. J Econ Growth 5(1):5–32
Bénabou R (1996) Inequality and growth. NBER Macroecon Annu 11(1450):11–92
Berg A, Ostry J (2013) Inequality and unsustainable growth: two sides of the same coin? Int Organ Res J 8(4):77–99
Berg A, Sachs J (1988) The debt crisis: structural explanations of country performance. NBER. Working Paper No. 2607, Cambridge (MA)
Bertrand M, Mullainathan S (2001) Are CEOs rewarded for luck? The ones without principals are. Q J Econ 116(3):901–932
Bhala SS (2002) Imagine there's no country: poverty, inequality and growth in the era of globalization. Peterson Institute for International Economics, Washington, DC
Bourguignon F, Morrisson C (2002) Inequality among World citizens: 1820–1992. Am Econ Rev 92(4):727–744
Card D (2009) Immigration and inequality. Am Econ Rev 99(2):1–21
Chatterjee A, Ghosh A, Jun-Ichi-Inoue, Chakrabarti BK (2015) Social inequality: from data to statistical physics modelling. J Phys Conf Ser 638(1):012014
Cingano F (2014) Trends in income inequality and its impact on economic growth. OECD social, employment and migration Working Papers. No. 163, OECD Publishing
Corak M (2013) Income inequality, equality of opportunity and intergenerational mobility. J Econ Perspect 27(3):79–102
Cornia GA, Kiiski S (2001) Trends in income distribution in the post-World War II period: evidence and interpretation. United Nations University, World Institute for Development Economics Research. Discussion Paper No. 2001/89
Cowel F (2011) Measuring inequality, 3rd edn. Oxford University Press, New York
Darvas Z (2019) Global interpersonal income inequality decline: The role of China and India. World Dev 121:16–32
de la Croix D, Döpke M (2003) Inequality and growth: why differential fertility matters. Am Econ Rev 93(4):1091–1113
Deaton A, Grosh M (2000) Consumption. In: Grosh M, Glewwe P (eds) Designing household survey questionnaires for developing countries: lessons from 15 years of the living standards measurement study. The World Bank, Washington DC
Deininger K, Squire L (1996) A new dataset measuring income inequality. World Bank Economic Revue 10:565–591
Dikhanov Y, Ward M (2001) Evolution of the global distribution of income in 1970–99. Fourth Meeting of the Expert Group on Poverty Statistics, Rio de Janeiro, Brazil
Dorwick S, Akmal M (2005) Contradictory trends in global income inequality: a tale of two biases. Rev Income Wealth 51(2):201–229
Duménil G, Lévy D (2003) Économie marxiste du capitalisme. La Découverte, Paris
Forbes KJ (2000) A reassessment of the relationship between inequality and growth. Am Econ Rev 90(4):869–887
Foster JE, Ok EA (1999) Lorenz dominance and the variance of logarithms. Econometrica 67:901–907
Frankel J, Romer D (1999) Does trade cause growth? Am Econ Rev 89(3):379–399

Galbraith JK, Lu J and Darity WA Jr. (1999) Measuring the evolution of inequality in the global economy. UTIP Working Paper No. 7
Galor O (2009) Inequality and economic development: the modern perspective. Edward Elgar, Cheltenham
Gans JS, Leigh A, Schmalz MC, Triggs A (2019) Inequality and market concentration, when shareholding is more skewed than consumption. Oxf Rev Econ Policy 35(3):550–563
Goldin C, Katz L (2010) The race between education and technology. Harvard University Press, Cambridge, MA
Gomez R, Foot DK (2003) Age structure, income distribution and economic growth. Can Public Policy 29:141–161
Hlasny V, Verme P (2018) Top incomes and inequality measurement: a comparative analysis of correction methods using the EU SILC data. Econometrics 6(2):1–21
Hsiang SM, Jina AS (2015) Geography, depreciation, and growth. Am Econ Rev 105(5):252–256
Jaumotte F, Buitron CO (2015) Inequality and labor market institutions. IMF Working Paper
Jones CI (2015) Pareto and Piketty: the macroeconomics of top income and wealth inequality. J Econ Perspect 29(1):29–46
Karabarbounis L, Neiman B (2014) The global decline of the labor share. Q J Econ 29(1):61–103
Kleiber C, Kotz S (2003) Statistical size distributions in economics and actuarial sciences. Wiley, Hoboken NJ
Korinek A, Mistiaen A, Ravallion M (2006) Survey nonresponse and the distribution of income. J Econ Inequal 4(1):33–55
Korzeniewicz RP, Moran TP (1997) World-economic trends in the distribution of income, 1965–1992. Am J Sociol 102(4):1000–1039
Kotlikoff L (1988) Intergenerational transfers and savings. J Econ Perspect 2(2):41–58
Kotlikoff L, Summers L (1981) The role of intergenerational transfers in aggregate capital accumulation. J Polit Econ 89(4):706–732
Kremer M (1993) Population growth and technological change: one million B.C. to 1990. Q J Econ 108(3):681–716
Krueger D, Perri F (2005) Does inequality lead to consumption inequality? Evidence and theory. CFS Working Paper Series 2005/15, Center for Financial Studies (CFS)
Kuznets S (1953) Shares of upper income groups in income and savings. National Bureau of Economic Research, New York, pp 171–218
Kuznets S (1955) Economic growth and income inequality. Am Econ Rev 45(1):1–28
Lakner C, Milanovic B (2013) Global income distribution: from the fall of the Berlin Wall to the great recession. Policy Research Working Paper; No. WPS 6719. World Bank Group, Washington, DC
Lundberg M, Squire L (2003) The simultaneous evolution of growth and inequality. Econ J 113 (487):326–344
Maddison A (1995) Monitoring the world economy: 1820–1992. Paris: OECD Development Centre. http://www.ggdc.net/MADDISON/Monitoring.shtml. Accessed 24 Dec 2019
Magness WP, Murphy PR (2015) Challenging the empirical contribution of Thomas Piketty's capital in the 21st century. Journal of Private Enterprise 30(1):1–34
Maialeh R (2017) Persisting inequality: a case of probabilistic drive towards divergence. Acta Oeconomica 67(2):215–234
Malthus T (1998 [1798]) An essay on the principle of population. Electronic Scholarly Publishing, London
Marx K (2015 [1867]) The capital: a critique of political economy, vol I. Progress Publishers, Moscow
Milanovic B (2002) True world income distribution, 1988 and 1993: first calculation based on household surveys alone. Econ J 112(476):51–92
Milanovic B (2005) Worlds apart: measuring international and global inequality. Princeton University Press, Princeton, NJ
Milanovic B (2003) The two faces of globalization: against globalization as we know it. World Dev 31(4):667–683

Milanovic B (2013) Global income inequality in numbers: in history and now. Global Pol 4 (2):198–208

Milanovic B (2016) Global inequality: a new approach for the age of globalization. Harvard University Press, Cambridge, MA

Minoiu C (2007) Poverty analysis based on kernel density estimates from grouped data. Columbia University Institute for Social and Economic Research and Policy. Working Paper, No. 07-07

Modigliani F (1986) Life cycle, individual thrift, and the wealth of nations. Am Econ Rev 76 (3):297–313

Modigliani F (1988) The role of intergenerational transfers and life cycle saving in the accumulation of wealth. J Econ Perspect 2(2):15–40

Mookherjee D, Ray D (2003) Persistent inequality. Rev Econ Stud 70(2):369–393

OECD (2008) Growing unequal? Income distribution and poverty in OECD countries. OECD, Paris

Persson T, Tabellini G (1994) Is inequality harmful for growth? Am Econ Rev 84(3):600–621

Piketty T (2011) On the long-run evolution of inheritance: France 1820–2050. Q J Econ 126 (3):1071–1131

Piketty T (2014) Capital in the twenty-first century. Harvard University Press, Cambridge

Piketty T, Zucman G (2014) Capital is back: wealth-income ratios in rich countries 1700–2010. Q J Econ 129(3):1255–1310

Piketty T, Zucman G (2015) Wealth and inheritance in the long run. In: Atkinson AB, Bourguignon F (eds) Handbook of income distribution, vol 2. Elsevier, Amsterdam

Piketty T, Postel-Vinay G, Rosenthal J-L (2013) Inherited vs self-made wealth: theory and evidence from a Rentier society (Paris 1872–1927). Explor Econ Hist 51:21–40

Piketty T, Saez E, Stancheva S (2014) Optimal taxation of top labor incomes: a tale of three elasticities. American Economic Journal 6(1):230–271

Piketty T, Saez E, Zucman G (2018) Distributional national accounts: methods and estimates for the United States. Q J Econ 133(2):553–609

Rein M, Miller SM (1974) Standards of income redistribution. Challenge 17(3):20–26

Ricardo D (2001 [1817]) On the principles of political economy and taxation. Batoche Books, Kitchener

Romer P (1990) Endogenous technological change. J Polit Econ 98(5):71–102

Rousseau J-J (2013 [1755]) A discourse on inequality. Aziloth Books, London

Saez E, Zucman G (2016) Wealth inequality in the United States since 1913: evidence from capitalized income tax data. Q J Econ 131(2):519–578

Sala-i-Martín X (2006) The world distribution of income: falling poverty and...convergence, period. Q J Econ 121(2):351–397

Schultz TP (1998) Inequality in the distribution of personal income in the world: how it is changing and why. J Popul Econ 11(3):307–344

Sowell T (2012) Trickle-down theory and tax-cuts for the rich. Hoover Institution Press, Stanford University, Stanford

Stiglitz JE (2012) The price of inequality: how today's divided society endangers our future, 1st edn. WW Norton & Company, New York

Theil H (1967) Economics and information theory. North-Holland Publishing Company, Amsterdam

Thewissen S, Nolan B and Roser M (2019) Incomes across the distribution. https://ourworldindata.org/incomes-across-the-distribution. Accessed 24 Dec 2019

UNDP (1999) Human development report. Oxford University Press, New York

U.S. Department of the Treasury. Internal Revenue Service (2018) Statistics of income, individual income rates and tax shares. U.S. Dept. of the Treasury, Internal Revenue Service, Washington, DC

van der Weide R, Milanovic B (2018) Inequality is bad for growth of the poor (but not for that of the rich). World Bank Econ Rev 32(3):507–530

Zucman G (2015) The hidden wealth of nations. Chicago University Press, Chicago

Chapter 3
Growth Theories and Convergence Hypothesis

3.1 The Importance of Theory: Why Empirical Results Do Not Speak for Themselves?

In ancient Greek, the word *theorein* and its connected noun *theoría* link to observation, consideration and looking more closely at the subject matter; they simply lead to scientific contemplation and seeking truth. Today, in the context of highly specialized fields of science, seeking the eternal truth is not at stake. But still, each field of scientific exploration aims to increase understanding of its subject matter through formulating theories. Above that, theoretical insights do not contribute to interpretation and understanding of a system for its own sake. It is hard to imagine that a system can be modified without understanding its fundamental laws, when only disordered empirical facts are on the table. The everlasting struggle to master conditions that determine human lives therefore lies in theoretical comprehension, which gives possibilities to actively shape researched systems including socioeconomic order. Empirical findings thus refer to the surface, how a phenomenon demonstrate itself to human senses, while theoretical insights, based on logical explanation of the empirical dimension, reveals the underlying 'nature' of a phenomenon. In terms of time, purely empiricist approach may refer only to what has already happened, while theoretical insights, which forms the underlying model, furnish our understanding with a certain extrapolating power. In response to empirical findings on inequality, the present chapter focuses on distributional dynamics of mainstream economic theories.

A theory comprises of hypotheses, assumptions and facts which in coherent and consistent way capture the researched phenomena. It strives to formulate general principles and laws to which empirical appearance, i.e. the available to the senses, is subordinated. Put it in other words, theory is about to explain observable facts. Building a theory therefore requires an interplay of two different but necessarily connected domains—abstract world of concepts and ideas and concrete world of empirical appearances. Observable and calculable facts then, intuitively, should

R. Maialeh, *Dynamic Models and Inequality*, Contributions to Economics,
https://doi.org/10.1007/978-3-030-46313-7_3

correspond to theoretical insights. Complementarity of these two domains suggests itself when thinking of these domains separately: the world of abstract concepts and ideas which is not backed by empirical reality risks to be a mere fiction, and, conversely, lacking the abstract theoretical background causes that empirical findings devalues into a mass of data with no interpretation, meaning and purpose.

Here we come to the difference between natural and social sciences. Obviously, natural sciences can hardly accept a theory which contradicts observed facts. This derives from the fact that several fields in natural sciences are able to isolate various effects. For instance, an interaction between two materials can be put into specific conditions, e.g. into vacuum. Then, it is easy to prove that the interaction of the two materials or substances under identical conditions will lead to identical results, no matter how many times such experiment is repeated. Empirical verification is therefore the essential aspect of theories in many fields of natural sciences.

The situation in social sciences is complicated a bit more since social scientists face a frequent problem of non-isolability of the researched phenomena. This causes that general (economic) theories are hardly verifiable or falsifiable through experimental procedures. The aim of social science theories, however, remains the same—to explain the logic of a given system through understanding the fundamental relationships among elements of the system. The cardinal challenge stems from the fact that a valid theory may capture the decisive forces of the researched system despite particular elements empirically deviate from the central theoretical concept. The reason is that lawfulness of phenomena in social sciences is of a lower level than is the case of phenomena in natural sciences. An example for all is provided in Maialeh (2019): If a central bank pushes-down interest rates, it will always generate universal positive incentives for consumption and investments. Under *ceteris paribus* condition we can claim that both consumption and investments will go up. The final empirical moment—whether falling interest rates truly caused increasing consumption and investments—simply cannot validate or falsify general economic theory as far as it is backed by another consistent theory. What is important for economic theory at this point is the general law that lower interest rates make the present consumption and investments cheaper and therefore stimulate economic agents with scarce resources to a certain behaviour (this might be an equivalent to gravity in physics). Whether it happens what economic theory assumes or not is a case of narrowly defined empirical research which could hardly confront the general tendency caused by falling interest rates. The lawfulness therefore concerns underlying forces operating within economic system, not the final empirical result. As we want to explain the final empirical moment, we come to the conclusion that the same empirical fact could have different theoretical explanations. It would be a fallacy of economics to seek for empirical demonstration of its results with accuracy and generalizability as seen in natural sciences.

On the other hand, it does not mean that economic theory is detachable from our empirical reality. The simplified representation of complex reality, which aims to capture the essential, is rarely disconnected from the observable. In other words, the essential is mirroring in the empirical world and the goal of a researcher is to decipher the substance in a mass of empirical complexity. The more it applies to economics where the abstract representation usually takes the form of a model which naturally inclines to be connected with the empirical representation. As the second chapter suggests, economic inequality is generally on the rise. On the other hand, all main theories that concern economic divergence are burdened with their particular point of view. We could have a (short) list of theories that assign economic divergence, for instance, to various positive externalities, foreign trade, increasing returns to scale or—to provide even more practical example—due to transport costs. In a greater historical perspective, economic inequality could have source in colonial and post-colonial policies of the Western countries. But, does it mean that disappearance of positive externalities or increasing returns to scale would lead to parallel development or even economic convergence? Could we imagine that eliminating transaction costs (which are anyway on the decline) would cause more equitable economic growth? Complexity of the issue, outlined in the second chapter, signs that the answer is most likely "No".

Unlike converging tendencies, which are usually based on neoclassical growth theories or some other 'diminishing marginal value' theory, divergence is due to its disequilibria possibility much less theorized. Another fact is that available concepts of divergence rely on too narrow explanations. The narrowness causes that already developed concepts of economic divergence lack of universal applicability and hence theoretical robustness. In sum, there is no *general* theory of diverging tendencies in economics.

Upon knowledge from the second chapter, diverging tendencies are present on both individual/household level as well as on macro level, it means among national states. Going back to the neoclassical framework, the convergence hypothesis asserts that poor economies (*ceteris paribus*) should grow faster than rich economies and this idea was later on sophisticated within the new (endogenous) growth theory (especially Barro and Sala-i-Martín 1992). Based on this we formulate the so called β-convergence which implies a negative relationship between the growth rate per capita and the initial level of income. The comparative dynamics (see e.g. Gandolfo 2010) then says that we evaluate the dynamics of two economies which are identical except for the one variable under consideration. The element of difference in convergence hypothesis is the distance from the steady state, which is, in neoclassical sense, changing over time and over considered economies. The often-asserted misinterpretation (and confusion with the absolute convergence) is then that poor economies should grow faster than rich economies. The correct understanding of the outlined dynamics of conditional convergence is that the growth rate is the function of the distance of a particular economy from *its own* steady state. A poor economy will therefore catch-up the rich one only if both economies have the same steady state. In other words, we assume identical economies except for the distance from the same steady state, and only then the poor economy will grow faster than the rich economy. As could be proved in the deterministic environment, β-convergence implies the so called σ-convergence, which relates to diminishing dispersion of income per capita over time. On the other hand, the dispersion of per capita income, measured for instance as the variance of per capita income, tends to increase in the presence of random shocks in a stochastic environment. If we concern microeconomic foundations of the agent-based modelling within this neoclassical framework, which is particularly important for the upcoming chapters of this book, we cannot miss Ramsey-Cass-Koopmans model.

In sum, if we consider identical agents, naturally with the same steady state, competitive markets should lead them through different growth rates (when different initial levels of income are considered) to that predetermined steady state. If we transmit the idea to micro-level agents, the empirical findings speak differently. As has been showed, the richer the agent (or group of agents, e.g. decile) is, the greater growth rate is experienced by the agent and *vice versa*. A possible explanation of empirical results then would be that rich agents have incomparably higher steady state than poor agents. But what if we insist on the assumption that agents are homogeneous?

As was argued, especially social scientists must accept that no matter how detailed their theorizing is, in a sense of empirical correspondence it remains inherently reductive. Infinitely complex reality remains elusive but reductive abstractions still may contribute to our understanding of that complex reality. This fact underlines the importance of theory. Theory can be detached from empirical appearances as far as it still explains general laws of motion of a given system. But does the neoclassical theory capture the essence of contemporary economic distribution? To find the answer, we should have a look on the fundamental converging ideas in economics in more details.

3.2 The Solow-Swan Model

The most profound theory of growth was stimulated by Solow (1956) and Swan (1956). This model belongs to exogeneous theories of growth and the final idea of the model is present in most of macroeconomics courses for decades. The model inspired numerous authors to pursue uncountable modifications and extensions, especially after a revival of growth theories at the turn of the 1980s and 1990s.

The model is composed of three main parts. The first concerns production function:

$$Y(t) = AF(K(t), L(t)), \tag{3.1}$$

where Y is total production, K is the capital stock, L quantifies employed labour, and A is a technological parameter (sometimes interpreted as TFP), all of them at time t. The production function follows $F : \mathbb{R}^3_+ \to \mathbb{R}_+$, i.e. considers non-negative arguments ($K, L \in \mathbb{R}_+$) and non-negative output ($Y \in \mathbb{R}_+$). The function is increasing in both arguments, so that marginal products are positive:

$$F_K(A, K, L) \equiv \frac{\partial F(A, K, L)}{\partial K} > 0, \tag{3.2}$$

$$F_L(A, K, L) \equiv \frac{\partial F(A, K, L)}{\partial L} > 0, \tag{3.3}$$

while the second partial derivation of the production function with respect to each argument is negative:

$$F_{KK}(A, K, L) \equiv \frac{\partial^2 F(A, K, L)}{\partial K^2} < 0, \tag{3.4}$$

$$F_{LL}(A, K, L) \equiv \frac{\partial^2 F(A, K, L)}{\partial L^2} < 0, \tag{3.5}$$

and hence we assume decreasing marginal returns to each factor. Moreover, F exhibits constant returns to scale in both factors, as long as it is linearly homogeneous in both of these factors. For that:

$$AF(K\lambda, L\lambda) = \lambda AF(K, L), \forall \lambda, K, L \geq 0, \tag{3.6}$$

where λ is a non-negative constant. The production function also satisfies well-known Inada conditions[1]:

$$\lim_{K \to 0} F_K(A, K, L) = \infty \text{ and } \lim_{K \to \infty} F_K(A, K, L) = 0 \ \forall L > 0 \& \forall A,$$

$$\lim_{L \to 0} F_L(A, K, L) = \infty \text{ and } \lim_{L \to \infty} F_L(A, K, L) = 0 \ \forall K > 0 \& \forall A.$$

For the sake of readers' familiarity, one of the functions which satisfies all outlined conditions is Cobb-Douglas production function:

$$Y = AK(t)^{\alpha} L(t)^{1-\alpha}, 0 < \alpha < 1. \tag{3.7}$$

The second part concerns the law of motion for the stock of capital. In other words, we seek dynamics of capital; in continuous time[2] we have

[1] A bit less known is that these conditions were firstly introduced by Uzawa (1963).

[2] Continuous time is considered in order to be in line with upcoming Ramsey-Cass-Koopmans model.

$$\dot{K}(t) = I(t) - \delta K(t), \tag{3.8}$$

where a dot over a variable denotes a time derivative; i.e. $\dot{X}(t) \equiv \partial X(t)/\partial t$. As usual, δ is the depreciation rate and I represents net investments. To complete the model, we assume that a constant fraction s of income Y is saved. Keynesian nature of the model relies on the fact that investment and savings are computed identically as a fraction of income. The new capital thus accumulates in line with the aggregate flow of savings sY and decumulates with δK. Net investments are given by

$$I(t) = sY(t) = S(t), \tag{3.9}$$

where S represents savings and the fundamental differential equation of neoclassical growth theory states:

$$\dot{K}(t) = sY(t) - \delta K(t). \tag{3.10}$$

By assuming population growth at rate n, we get:

$$L(t) = L_0 e^{nt}, \tag{3.11}$$

since

$$\ln L(t) = \ln L_0 + nt$$

and taking the derivative with respect to time gives:

$$\frac{L(t)}{L(t)} = n.$$

The intensive form (per unit of effective labour) of the production function follows[3]:

$$y(t) = \frac{Y(t)}{L(t)} = \frac{AK(t)^{\alpha} L(t)^{1-\alpha}}{L(t)} = A\left(\frac{K(t)}{L(t)}\right)^{\alpha} = Ak(t)^{\alpha}. \tag{3.12}$$

The law of motion of capital states:

$$\frac{\dot{K}(t)}{L(t)} = \frac{I(t)}{L(t)} - \frac{\delta K(t)}{L(t)} \Rightarrow i(t) - \delta k(t) = \dot{k}(t), \tag{3.13}$$

where the last term is:

[3]Variables in the intensive form use small letters.

$$\dot{k}(t) = \frac{\partial k(t)}{\partial t} = \frac{\partial\left(\frac{K(t)}{L(t)}\right)}{\partial t} = \frac{\dot{K}(t)L(t) - \dot{L}(t)K(t)}{L(t)^2} = \frac{K(t)}{L(t)} - \frac{\dot{L}(t)}{L(t)}\frac{K(t)}{L(t)}, \tag{3.14}$$

and thus,

$$\dot{k}(t) = \frac{\dot{K}(t)}{L(t)} - nk(t) \Rightarrow \frac{\dot{K}(t)}{L(t)} = \dot{k}(t) + nk(t). \tag{3.15}$$

Substituting this equation into Eq. (3.13) then yields:

$$\dot{k}(t) = i(t) - (\delta + n)k(t). \tag{3.16}$$

The intensive form of investment function (Eq. 3.9) is:

$$i(t) = sy(t) = sAk(t)^{\alpha}, \tag{3.17}$$

and putting into Eq. (3.16) yields a nonlinear first order differential equation that describes capital accumulation:

$$\dot{k}(t) = sAk(t)^{\alpha} - (\delta + n)k(t). \tag{3.18}$$

This growth equation says that capital accumulation is the decisive driver of economic growth, while the capital grows over time with savings and declines with population growth and depreciation of capital. Naturally, equilibrium ($k(t) = k^*$) is reached when $\dot{k}(t) = 0$, i.e. for:

$$sAk(t)^{\alpha} = (\delta + n)k(t). \tag{3.19}$$

The equilibrium for capital is reached when:

$$sAk^* = (\delta + n)k^* \Rightarrow k^* = \left(\frac{sA}{\delta + n}\right)^{\frac{1}{1-\alpha}} \tag{3.20}$$

and substituting into production yields:

$$y^* = (k^*)^{\alpha} = (\frac{sA}{\delta + n})^{\frac{\alpha}{1-\alpha}}. \tag{3.21}$$

Since steady-state consumption is the difference between income and investments (savings) in equilibrium, we also get:

$$c^* = (1-s)y^* = (1-s)\left(\frac{sA}{\delta+n}\right)^{\frac{\alpha}{1-\alpha}}. \tag{3.22}$$

The economy therefore tends to grow the faster the smaller is the initial level of capital. This can be seen if (3.16) is divided by $k(t)$:

$$g_k(t) = \frac{sA}{k(t)^{1-\alpha}} - (\delta+n), \tag{3.23}$$

from which we also see that in equilibrium growth $g_k(t) = 0$.

3.2.1 Golden Rule of Capital Accumulation

As trained readers already know, the golden rule of capital accumulation refers to the level of capital which maximizes consumption in equilibrium. The equilibrium is defined as:

$$sf(k^*) = (\delta+n)k^* \Rightarrow c^* = f(k^*) - (\delta+n)k^*, \tag{3.24}$$

and solving the equation as a function of k^* yields:

$$\max_{k^*} c^*(k^*) = \left\{\max_{k^*} f(k^*) - (\delta+n)k^*\right\}, \tag{3.25}$$

where the solution is:

$$f_k(k^* = \delta+n), \tag{3.26}$$

and for the Cobb-Douglas form the 'golden-rule' states:

$$\alpha A (k_g)^{\alpha-1} = \delta+n \Rightarrow k_g = \left(\frac{\alpha A}{\delta+n}\right)^{\frac{1}{1-\alpha}}. \tag{3.27}$$

For our purpose it is important to understand optimal savings. The situation $\alpha < s$ means that the economy tends to over-save and as a consequence $k_g < k^*$. In such cases we detect dynamical inefficiency since reduction of savings in favour of consumption should lead to higher welfare. In other words, aggregate utility from consumption is higher than potential increments of income stemming from high level of capital. On the contrary, $\alpha > s$ signifies under-saving and hence $k_g > k^*$.

Sustain growth per unit of effective labour is then possible only when the technological parameter A is allowed to grow exogenously over time. Let us denote that:

$$A(t) = A_0 e^{\gamma t} \Leftrightarrow \frac{\dot{A}(t)}{A(t)} = \gamma, \tag{3.28}$$

while $A(t)$ is Harrod-neutral (i.e. labour augmenting), so that

$$Y(t) = K(t)^{\alpha} (A(t)L(t))^{1-\alpha}, \tag{3.29}$$

and the intensive form follows:

$$Y(t) = K(t)^{\alpha} (A(t)L(t))^{1-\alpha}. \tag{3.30}$$

Differentiating with respect to time yields:

$$\frac{\dot{y}(t)}{y(t)} = (1-\alpha)\frac{\dot{A}(t)}{A(t)} + \alpha\frac{\dot{k}(t)}{k(t)} = (1-\alpha)\gamma + \alpha\frac{\dot{k}(t)}{k(t)}. \tag{3.31}$$

The growth rate of capital is obtained by following Eq. (3.18), hence:

$$\frac{\dot{k}(t)}{k(t)} = sA(t)^{1-\alpha}k(t)^{\alpha-1} - \delta - n = \frac{sA(t)^{1-\alpha}k(t)^{\alpha}}{k(t)} - \delta - n = \frac{sy(t)}{k(t)} - \delta - n. \tag{3.32}$$

It reads that growth rate of capital is constant if capital and income per unit of effective labour grow at the same rate. The balanced growth path, i.e. the situation when all variables grow at the same constant rate q, is derived from Eq. (3.31). Then, we get:

$$\frac{\dot{y}(t)}{y(t)} = (1-\alpha)\gamma + \alpha\frac{\dot{k}(t)}{k(t)} \Rightarrow (1-\alpha)g = (1-\alpha)\gamma \Rightarrow g = \gamma. \tag{3.33}$$

Now, Eq. (3.18) is divided by $A(t)$:

$$\frac{\dot{k}(t)}{A(t)} = s\left(\frac{k(t)}{A(t)}\right)^{\alpha} - (\delta + n)\frac{k(t)}{A(t)}, \tag{3.34}$$

where the capital-technology ratio is for further analysis defined as $\widetilde{k}(t) \equiv k(t)/A(t)$. To explain the left-side of the equation, we have:

$$\frac{d\left(\frac{k(t)}{A(t)}\right)}{dt} = \frac{\dot{k}(t)A(t) - \dot{A}(t)k(t)}{A(t)^2} = \gamma_{\tilde{k}} \approx -(\alpha - 1)(\delta + n + \gamma)(\frac{\tilde{k} - \tilde{k}^*}{\tilde{k}^*}), \quad (3.35)$$

which transforms the fundamental equation in the intensive form (Eq. 3.18) into:

$$\dot{\tilde{k}}(t) = s\tilde{k}(t)^\alpha - (\delta + n + \gamma)\tilde{k}(t), \quad (3.36)$$

so that the system includes technological progress in terms of capital-technology ratio. The steady state is then:

$$\widetilde{k}^* = \left(\frac{s}{\delta + n + \gamma}\right)^{\frac{1}{1-\alpha}} \quad (3.37)$$

The dynamics of the model denotes that the steady-state $\widetilde{k}^*$ corresponds to a balanced-growth path where all relevant variables grow at the same constant rate γ, since

$$\widetilde{k}^* = \frac{k^*(t)}{A(t)} \Rightarrow k^*(t) = \left(\frac{s}{\delta + n + \gamma}\right)^{\frac{1}{1-\alpha}} A(t). \quad (3.38)$$

The economy is thus able to generate long-run growth which is of exogeneous nature. That is to say that if we assume an economy on its balanced growth path which suddenly increase its saving, the balanced growth path shifts upward, and the economy will be no longer in optimum. Hence, it will grow faster than γ in order to converge to the new balanced growth path.

3.2.2 Speed of Convergence

To compute the speed of convergence, we follow Eq. (3.36) in a sense that $\widetilde{k}^*$ is redefined as:

$$\gamma_{\widetilde{k}} \equiv \frac{\dot{\tilde{k}}}{\tilde{k}} = s\widetilde{k}^{\alpha-1} - (\delta + n + \gamma) = G\left(\widetilde{k}\right), \quad (3.39)$$

while in the steady-state we have $\gamma_{\widetilde{k}}^* = G\left(\widetilde{k}^*\right) = 0$. Further, the first-order Taylor approximation of $G\left(\widetilde{k}\right)$ around k^* states:

$$G\left(\widetilde{k}\right) \approx G\left(\widetilde{k}^*\right) + G'\left(\widetilde{k}^*\right)\left(\widetilde{k} - \widetilde{k}^*\right) \tag{3.40}$$

and substituting the derivative $G'\left(\widetilde{k}^*\right)$ from Eq. (3.39) yields:

$$G\left(\widetilde{k}\right) \approx (\alpha - 1)s\widetilde{k}^{\alpha-1}\left(\frac{\widetilde{k} - \widetilde{k}^*}{\widetilde{k}^*}\right). \tag{3.41}$$

In order to capture the speed of convergence, we should eliminate $A(t)$. Hence,

$$\widetilde{k}^* = \left(\frac{s}{\delta + n + \gamma}\right)^{\frac{1}{1-\alpha}} \tag{3.42}$$

and substituting the term gives:

$$\gamma_{\widetilde{k}} \approx -(\alpha - 1)(\delta + n + \gamma)\left(\frac{\widetilde{k} - \widetilde{k}^*}{\widetilde{k}^*}\right). \tag{3.43}$$

Typically, $\beta \equiv (\alpha - 1)(\delta + n + \gamma)$ is considered as the speed of convergence which measures how much $\widetilde{k}$ changes when $\widetilde{k}^* > \widetilde{k}$.

The same applies for income. Taking the first-order Taylor approximation of $\ln \widetilde{k}$ around $\widetilde{k}^*$ posits:

$$\ln \widetilde{k} \approx \ln \widetilde{k}^* + \frac{1}{\widetilde{k}^*}\left(\widetilde{k} - \widetilde{k}^*\right) \Leftrightarrow \left(\ln \widetilde{k} - \ln \widetilde{k}^*\right) \approx \frac{\widetilde{k} - \widetilde{k}^*}{\widetilde{k}^*}. \tag{3.44}$$

Substituting the term into Eq. (3.43) yields:

$$\gamma_{\widetilde{k}} \approx -(\alpha - 1)(\delta + n + \gamma)\left(\ln \widetilde{k} - \ln \widetilde{k}^*\right), \tag{3.45}$$

and respecting Cobb-Douglas form of production implies $\ln \widetilde{y} = \alpha \ln \widetilde{k}$. Then we can write:

$$\gamma_{\widetilde{y}} \approx -(1 - \alpha)(\delta + n + \gamma)(\ln \widetilde{y} - \ln \widetilde{y}^*) \tag{3.46}$$

where $\beta \equiv (1 - \alpha)(\delta + n + \gamma)$ again represents the speed of convergence which measures how much $\widetilde{y}$ changes when $\widetilde{y}^* > \widetilde{y}$.

Finally, let us summarize the main findings of the model. The steady-state capital k^* is (in the first instance) decreasing with depreciation rate δ and population growth n. On the contrary, the steady-state capital is increasing with the technological parameter A and with the saving rate s, while the saving rate determines the amount of investment. It also increases with the share of capital on income α, since the closer is α to 1, the smaller is the effect of diminishing returns and the more the economy can grow without contributions of exogenously given technological progress. Simply put, the income per unit of effective labour can grow as long as capital per unit of effective labour grows.

As can be seen, the income increases with the capital stock. But exactly due to the effect of diminishing marginal productivity the capital will grow faster than income, which means that depreciation will also grow faster than savings. The Solow model therefore presumes that potentially increasing saving rate and consequent raise of capital accumulation will have just temporary effect on the growth rate. But there is also long-run effect of increasing saving rate. The increase in saving rate and the subsequent temporary increase in capital shift the long-run levels of income and capital upward. As regards growth effects (as opposed to absolute level effects), these come only from technological progress.

To conclude, the so called 'conditional convergence', as the result of the model settings, postulates that if poor economies have the same steady-state as the rich economies, poor economies will converge due to higher rates of growth than experienced by their richer counterparts, which is caused by the greater distance to this steady-state and lower level of capital stock. The main driver of convergence is thus diminishing marginal productivity. Finally, we can also read that income is driven by capital accumulation and that the capital stock is determined by the already existing amount of capital, despite the capital accumulation does not account for long-run welfare implications.

3.3 The Ramsey-Cass-Koopmans Model

The following model reacts on Solow's model in a way that the fraction of output devoted to investment (i.e. saving in closed economy) ceases to be constant. In other words, households are allowed to optimize between consumption and savings. The capital stock is therefore the results between utility-maximizing households which supply savings and profit-maximizing firms which demand investments. This setup of the model is important for our subsequent approach since Ramsey-Cass-Koopmans (RCK) model is among pioneers in representative-agent modelling.

3.3.1 Firms

As outlined, the solution in RCK model is derived from the setting of two main actors—firms and households. Let us start with firms. We assume a large number of identical firms with the same production function (and its properties) as seen in

Solow's model.[4] The price of capital is r and firms also hire labour at real wage W, while both production factors are available on perfectly competitive markets. The profit is assumed to be transferred to firms' owners. Finally, we work with non-negative initial values K, L, A.

The goal of a representative firm is to maximise its present value of a future expected stream of profits $V(t)$:

$$V(t) = E(t)\sum_{s=1}^{\infty}\left[\frac{\pi(t+s)}{(1+r)^{s}}\right], \tag{3.47}$$

where π is profit and r is interest rate. Based on this, we can formulate the simplest version of profit equation:

$$\pi(t) = p(t)F(K(t), A(t)L(t)) - W(t)L(t) - r(t)K(t), \tag{3.48}$$

where $p(t)F(K(t), A(t)L(t))$ is total revenue and L and K represent quantity of labour and capital, respectively. Due to omitting depreciation and having perfectly competitive markets, the return to capital equals the marginal product of capital:

$$r(t) = \frac{\partial F(K, AL)}{\partial K}. \tag{3.49}$$

We also know that $\partial F(K, AL)/\partial K = f'(k)$, where $f(k) \equiv F(k, 1)$ and $k = K/AL$, which means that firms find themselves cost-effective when

$$f'(k(t)) = r'(t). \tag{3.50}$$

The same logic applies for labour—firms will hire workers up to the point where the marginal product of labour equals real wage:

$$W(t) = \frac{\partial F(K, AL)}{\partial L}, \tag{3.51}$$

where

$$\frac{\partial F(K, AL)}{\partial L} = Af(k) - ALf'(k)\left(\frac{K}{AL}\right) = A(f(k) - kf'(k)). \tag{3.52}$$

The wage per effective unit of labour $w(t) \equiv W(t)/A(t)$ then must satisfy:

[4]For the sake of simplicity, it is abstracted from depreciation.

$$w(t) = f(k) - kf'(k),$$

where

$$f(k) = kf'(k) + \frac{F_L(K, AL)}{A} = kf'(k) + w.$$

3.3.2 Households

In order to be coherent with subsequent parts of this book, we will examine the household's position in more details. The number of households is H, the whole population is $L(t)$ and the size of each household must be $L(t)/H$. The size of each household and population grow at rate n. Wages and interest rates are exogenously given and workers (all people within the economy, $L(t)$) supplies 1 unit of labour inelastically. Each household initially holds $K(0)/H$ units of capital and receives income from selling their labour, renting out capital and from the firms' profits.

The main difference compare to Solow's model is that households optimize between consumption and capital accumulation (savings). Each household is thus endowed with lifetime utility:

$$U = \int_{t=0}^{\infty} e^{-\rho t} u(C(t)) \frac{L(t)}{H} dt, \tag{3.53}$$

where ρ denotes discount rate and $C(t)$ is the consumption per worker, the aggregate consumption then must be $C(t)L(t)$. By this we adjust the representative agent instantaneous utility formulated by Blanchard and Fischer (1989), as opposed to objective functions asserted by Acemoglu (2009) or Barro and Sala-i-Martín (2004). To formulate a concrete form of the utility function, we have a standard constant relative risk aversion (CRRA) preferences:

$$u(C(t)) = \frac{C(t)^{1-\theta}}{1-\theta},$$

with

$$\theta > 0; \rho - n - (1 - \theta), q > 0, \tag{3.54}$$

where the right-hand condition secures that life-time utility is well-defined.[5] The relative risk aversion is typically defined as $\theta = -Cu''(C)/u'(C)$. This coefficient is also helpful, especially in our deterministic model where risk considerations are irrelevant, for intended intertemporal approach since it refers to willingness of the household to transfer consumption in time. The intertemporal elasticity of substitution (IES) is defined as:

$$\sigma_{t,s} = -\frac{d \ln \frac{C_s}{C_t}}{d \ln \frac{u(C_s)}{u(C_t)}}, \tag{3.55}$$

and taking the limit for $s \to t$ yields:

$$\sigma = -\frac{u'(C)}{Cu''(C)} = \frac{1}{\theta}. \tag{3.56}$$

High θ therefore generates low IES which signifies high impatience of the agent in consumption, and *vice versa*. If we simplify the settings by noting $H = 1$, the household faces the following problem with dynamic budget constraints:

$$\max_{\{C(t)\}} U = \int_{t=0}^{\infty} e^{-\rho t} u(C(t)) L(t) dt$$

s.t.

$$\dot{B}(t) = r(t)B(t) + W(t)L(t) - C(t)L(t). \tag{3.57}$$

Here, $B(t)$ is defined as the household's stock of saving in t, in other words household's wealth; r denotes return to capital; and W represents wages. In line with the assumption of closed economy, the equilibrium requires $B(t) = K(t)$, so that households' savings are equal to the stock of physical capital. Alternatively, we might also define $B(t)$ as the result of households' saving optimization and $K(t)$ as the firms' capital optimization. From the households' perspective, the path of wages {W

[5]The reason is that along the balanced growth path, where the consumption per capita grows at rate g, the integrand term in U grows at rate $-\rho + n + (1 - \theta)g$. As we want the integral to converge, the term must be negative.

$(t)\}$ and the path of rental rates $\{r(t)\}$, as well as the condition $K(0) = B(0) > 0$ are all given. In order to avoid an 'infinite-borrow strategy', but on the other to allow temporary indebtedness, we impose No-Ponzi Condition (NPC) so that household's debt cannot grow asymptotically faster than the real interest rate (e.g. Blanchard and Fischer 1989):

$$\lim_{t\to\infty} e^{-\int_0^t r(u)du} B(t) \geq 0, \tag{3.58}$$

where $\int_0^t r(u)du$ is the continuously compounded interest rate[6] between 0 and t.

An intertemporal budget constraint can be derived from the dynamic budget constraint through multiplying Eq. (3.57) by $e^{-\int_0^t r(u)du}$ and integrating between t and $T > t$. For the sake of clarity, we make the substitution $-\int_0^t r(u)du = R(t)$:

$$\int_t^T e^{-R(s)} \cdot B(s)ds = \int_t^T e^{-R(s)} r(s)B(s)ds + \int_t^T e^{-R(s)}(W(s) - C(s))L(s)ds. \tag{3.59}$$

Using *per partes* method and considering the fact that $dR(s)/ds = d\left(\int_0^s r(u)du\right)/ds = r(s)$ yields:

$$\int_t^T e^{-R(s)} \cdot B(s)ds = B(T)e^{-R(T)} - B(t)e^{-R(t)} + \int_t^T e^{-R(s)} r(s)B(s)ds, \tag{3.60}$$

and substituting into the budget constraint generates after basic arrangement:

$$B(T)e^{-R(T)} - B(t)e^{-R(t)} = \int_t^T e^{-R(s)}(W(s) - C(s))L(s)ds. \tag{3.61}$$

After taking the limit for $T \to \infty$ we obtain:

$$\lim_{T\to\infty} B(T)e^{-R(T)} = B(t)e^{-R(t)} = \int_t^\infty e^{-R(s)}(W(s) - C(s))L(s)ds. \tag{3.62}$$

[6]For Albert Einstein the most powerful force in the universe.

Considering the NPC ensures that the left-hand-side term is positive; hence:

$$B(t) + \int_{t}^{\infty} e^{-R(t,s)} (W(s) - C(s))L(s)\, ds \geq 0. \tag{3.63}$$

The term $R(t, s) = R(s) - R(t)$ also enables to define $\int_t^s r(u)du = R(t, s)$ as the continuously compounded return between t and $s > t$. Equation (3.63) then represents the intertemporal budget constraint which says that total wealth, defined as the sum of current assets and future labour income, has to be greater than the present value of consumption.

To continue, we transform the problem into the intensive form, i.e. per unit of effective labour. As was the case of the Solow model, we denote all variables in intensive form with lower case. From now, we optimize $\{c(t)\}$, where $c(t) = C(t)/A(t)$, and hence:

$$u(C(t)) = \frac{(A(t)c(t))^{1-\theta}}{1-\theta} = A(0)^{(1-\theta)} e^{(1-\theta)gt} u(c(t)), \tag{3.64}$$

where $A(t) = A(0)e^{gt}$ The lifetime utility (Eq. 3.53) now takes the form:

$$U = A(0)^{(1-\theta)} L(0) \int_{t=0}^{\infty} e^{-(\rho-n-(1-\theta)g)t} u(c(t))dt. \tag{3.65}$$

By substituting $\rho - n - (1 - \theta)g = \beta$, the maximization problem follows:

$$\max_{\{c(t)\}} U = \int_{t=0}^{\infty} e^{-\beta t} u(c(t))dt \tag{3.66}$$

and the dynamic budget constraint is thus redefined as:

$$\dot{b}(t) = (r(t) - g - n)b(t) + w(t) - c(t), \tag{3.67}$$

with the initial condition $b(0) = k(0) > 0$. NPC also transforms into:

$$\lim_{t\to\infty} e^{-R(t)+(n+g)t} b(t) \geq 0. \tag{3.68}$$

The final form of the household's problem is therefore defined as:

$$\max_{\{c(t)\}} U = \int_{t=0}^{\infty} e^{-\beta t} u(c(t))\, dt \tag{3.69}$$

s.t.

$$\dot{b}(t) = (r(t) - g - n)b(t) + w(t) - c(t)$$
$$c(t) \geq 0$$
$$b(0) > 0, \{r(t), w(t)\} \text{ given}$$
$$\lim_{t\to\infty} e^{-R(t)+(n+g)t} b(t) \geq 0,$$

with $c(t)$ and $b(t)$ as the control and the state variables, respectively.

3.3.3 The Maximum Principle

Now, we are going to examine the maximum principle for our problem. It is useful since it provides a set of necessary conditions for any thinkable solution while transforming a complex dynamic problem into a static one. Let the consumption sequence $c^*(t)$ be the solution to the problem and $\lambda(t) \geq 0$ is a co-state variable such that the following Hamiltonian

$$\mathcal{H}(c(t), b(t), \lambda(t)) = u(c(t)) + \lambda(t)[(r(t) - g - n)b(t) + w(t) - c(t)] \tag{3.70}$$

is maximized at $c^*(t)$ with respect to $b(t)$ and $\lambda(t)$:

$$\frac{\partial \mathcal{H}}{\partial c}(c^*(t), b(t), \lambda(t)) = 0. \tag{3.71}$$

The co-state variable satisfies:

$$\dot{\lambda}(t) = \beta\lambda(t) - \frac{\partial \mathcal{H}}{\partial b}(c^*(t), b(t), \lambda(t)), \tag{3.72}$$

which can be, for interpretation purposes, simply rewritten as:

$$\beta = \frac{\dot{\lambda}(t) + \frac{\partial \mathcal{H}}{\partial b}(c^*(t), b(t), \lambda(t))}{\lambda(t)}. \tag{3.73}$$

The Hamiltonian provides an important insight—it associates gains from additional current consumption $u(c(t))$ with the loss in capital accumulation $\dot{b}(t)$. Such a loss is weighted by $\lambda(t)$, which is, in a sense, a shadow value of wealth $b(t)$. This allows to optimize e.g. a lower current utility with a higher wealth in the future (in terms of utility), so that in equilibrium these two effects must offset each other.

Additionally, the shadow price of wealth can be further reinterpreted as a price of an asset. In this sense, the right side of Eq. (3.73) is composed of a yield based on changes in the value of the Hamiltonian $\partial \mathcal{H}/\partial b$; and, it also reflects a kind of 'capital gain' based on changes of the co-state variable itself. These two components on the right-hand side of Eq. (3.73) altogether form a return on the asset which must be equal to household's discount rate β. Asset prices in the economy therefore must evolve in line with the shadow value of wealth, which is secured by the dynamic evolution of the co-state variable.

The co-state variable also satisfies the transversality condition of the form:

$$\lim_{t \to \infty} e^{-\beta t} b(t)\lambda(t) \leq 0, \tag{3.74}$$

where $b(t)$ can be interpreted as the quantity of wealth and $\lambda(t)$ as the price of this wealth; $b(t)\lambda(t)$ is then the shadow value of total wealth. The explanation of the transversality condition is simple: a strictly positive limit would mean that the discount rate is lower than the growth rate of wealth, which would necessarily lead households to increase current consumption at the expense of wealth holdings in the future. The term $e^{-\beta t}$ then secures that the household is not motivated to accumulate a great amount of wealth in the long run.

By following Eq. (3.71), the necessary FOC for our problem is:

$$u'(c(t)) = c(t)^{-\theta} = \lambda(t), \tag{3.75}$$

which demonstrates that the co-state variable $\lambda(t)$, and hence the shadow value of wealth, simply equals the marginal utility of consumption. Substituting $\lambda(t)$ in Eq. (3.72) and combining it with Eq. (3.70) produces:

$$\dot{\lambda}(t) = \beta\lambda(t) - \lambda(t)(r(t) - g - n), \tag{3.76}$$

from which we can write:

$$\frac{\dot{\lambda}(t)}{\lambda(t)} = -\theta\frac{\dot{c}(t)}{c(t)} = \beta - (r(t) - g - n), \tag{3.77}$$

and rearranging the terms and substituting for β yields:

$$\frac{\dot{c}(t)}{c(t)} = \frac{r(t) - g - n - \beta}{\theta} = \frac{r(t) - g\theta - \rho}{\theta}. \tag{3.78}$$

From this we easily obtain the Euler equation that captures the growth rate of consumption per unit of effective labour:

$$\frac{\dot{C}(t)}{C(t)} = \frac{\dot{c}(t)}{c(t)} + g = \frac{r(t) - \rho}{\theta}. \tag{3.79}$$

It can be seen that the household is not motivated to deviate in situations when the interest rate $r(t)$ equals the discount factor ρ. The relationship between these two variables therefore establishes the ground for consumption/saving optimization. For instance, the situation $r(t) > \rho$ pushes the household to save more and hence consumption will be on the rise over time. The role of θ is obvious as well—higher IES is mirrored in smaller θ, which means that the change in consumption has lower sensitivity to the interest rate. It is also important to note that Eq. (3.79) defines the slope (dynamics) of consumption, while the level of consumption is determined by the intertemporal budget constraint (Eq. 3.63).

In addition, if we express $\lambda(t)$ from the differential Eq. (3.72) and then integrate it between 0 and t, we get:

$$\lambda(t) = \lambda(0)\exp[-R(t) + (n + g)t], \tag{3.80}$$

and substituting into the transversality condition yields:

$$\lim_{t\to\infty} e^{-\beta t} b(t)\lambda(t) = \lim_{t\to\infty} b(t) \exp[-R(t) + (n + g)t] \leq 0. \tag{3.81}$$

As in the previous case, neither this limit motivates the household to accumulate wealth massively. The reason is simple: a strictly positive limit would lead to a situation when aggregate wealth holdings $B(t)$ would grow faster than the compound interest rate $R(t)$, which corresponds to a disequilibrium where households would have to save more than is the interest income earned on their wealth.

By combining NPC (Eq. 3.58) and transversatility condition (Eq. 3.81) we receive optimal consumption path that satisfies:

$$\lim_{t\to\infty} b(t) \exp[-R(t) + (n + g)t] = 0, \tag{3.82}$$

and the intertemporal budget constraint (Eq. 3.63) will transform into:

$$B(t) + \int_t^{\infty} e^{-R(t,s)}(W(s) - C(s))L(s)\,ds = 0. \tag{3.83}$$

The maximum principle applied on households implies the optimal trade-off between consumption and saving which satisfies:

$$\frac{\dot{c}(t)}{c(t)} = \frac{r(t) - g\theta - \rho}{\theta}, \tag{3.84}$$

$$\dot{b}(t) = (r(t) - g - n)b(t) + w(t) - c(t). \tag{3.85}$$

Considering that $b(t) = k(t)$, we obtain a dynamical system $(c(t), k(t))$ of the form:

$$\frac{\dot{c}(t)}{c(t)} = \frac{f'(k(t)) - g\theta - \rho}{\theta}, \tag{3.86}$$

$$\dot{k}(t) = f(k(t)) - (g + n)k(t) - c(t), \tag{3.87}$$

with the initial condition $k(0) > 0$ and terminal condition:

$$\lim_{t\to\infty} \exp\left[-\int_0^t f'(k(s))ds + (n + g)t\right]k(t) = 0. \tag{3.88}$$

As can be seen, $\dot{k}(t) = 0$ when the difference between the actual output $f(k(t))$ and break-even investments $(g + n)k(t)$ equals consumption $c(t)$. Consumption $c(t)$ is therefore increasing in $k(t)$ until $f'(k) = g + n$, i.e. until reaching the level corresponding to the golden-rule of k, and then is decreasing.

3.3.4 Speed of Convergence

The important question is where the convergence comes from? Widely recognized converging tendencies in Ramsey-Cass-Koopmans model will be detected through linear approximations of the non-linear Eqs. (3.86) and (3.87) around the balanced growth path ($k^* = k, c^* = c$). For the purpose of clarity, equations in the upcoming part do not contain time factor t. In order to find out the answer on convergence in the RCK model, we can simply follow e.g. Romer (2006). Hence, first-order Taylor approximations state:

$$\dot{c} \cong \frac{\partial \dot{c}}{\partial k}(k - k^*) + \frac{\partial \dot{c}}{\partial c}(c - c^*) \tag{3.89}$$

$$\dot{k} \cong \frac{\partial \dot{k}}{\partial k}(k - k^*) + \frac{\partial \dot{k}}{\partial c}(c - c^*), \tag{3.90}$$

where all derivatives are considered at $k^* = k$, $c^* = c$. For simplicity purposes, let us substitute $k - k^* = \widetilde{k}$ and $c - c^* = \widetilde{c}$, while constancy of c^* and k^* implies that $\dot{\widetilde{k}} = \widetilde{k}$ and $\dot{\widetilde{c}} = \widetilde{c}$. Thus, we can write:

$$\dot{\widetilde{c}} \cong \frac{\partial \dot{c}}{\partial k}\widetilde{k} + \frac{\partial \dot{c}}{\partial c}\widetilde{c}, \tag{3.91}$$

$$\dot{\widetilde{k}} \cong \frac{\partial \dot{k}}{\partial k}\widetilde{k} + \frac{\partial \dot{k}}{\partial c}\widetilde{c}. \tag{3.92}$$

From Eq. (3.86) we read that $\dot{c} = \{[f'(k(t)) - g\theta - \rho]/\theta\}c$ and in combination with $k^* = k$, $c^* = c$ the derivatives in Eq. (3.91) follow:

$$\dot{\widetilde{c}} \cong \frac{f''(k^*)c^*}{\theta}\widetilde{k}, \tag{3.93}$$

and, similarly, from Eq. (3.87) we read that $\dot{k} = f(k) - (g + n)k - c$, so that derivatives in Eq. (3.92) yields:

$$\dot{\widetilde{k}} \cong [f'(k^*) - (g + n)]\widetilde{k} - \widetilde{c}. \tag{3.94}$$

Further, Eq. (3.86) implies that $f'(k^*) = \rho + \theta g$ and since $\rho - n - (1 - \theta)g = \beta$, we obtain:

$$\dot{\widetilde{k}} = \beta\widetilde{k} - \widetilde{c}. \tag{3.95}$$

The growth rate of $\widetilde{c}$ and $\widetilde{k}$ we can get by dividing Eq. (3.93) by $\widetilde{c}$ and (3.95) by $\widetilde{k}$:

$$\frac{\dot{\widetilde{c}}}{\widetilde{c}} \cong \frac{f''(k^*)c^*}{\theta}\frac{\widetilde{k}}{\widetilde{c}}, \tag{3.96}$$

$$\frac{\dot{\widetilde{k}}}{\widetilde{k}} \cong \beta - \frac{\widetilde{c}}{\widetilde{k}}, \tag{3.97}$$

which show that the growth rates depend on the ratio between $\widetilde{k}$ and $\widetilde{c}$. It means that the same rate of changes of $\widetilde{k}$ and $\widetilde{c}$ implies $\dot{\widetilde{c}}/\widetilde{c} = \dot{\widetilde{k}}/\widetilde{k}$ and the ratio between $\widetilde{k}$ and $\widetilde{c}$ is not changing either. For instance, if $\widetilde{k}$ and $\widetilde{c}$ are initially falling at the same rate, they continue to fall at that rate.

If we put $\mu = \dot{\widetilde{c}}/\widetilde{c}$, Eq. (3.96) states:

$$\frac{\widetilde{c}}{\widetilde{k}} = \frac{f''(k^*)c^*}{\theta} \frac{1}{\mu}, \tag{3.98}$$

and combining Eq. (3.97) with $\dot{\widetilde{c}}/\widetilde{c} = \dot{\widetilde{k}}/\widetilde{k}$ yields:

$$\mu = \beta - \frac{f''(k^*)c^*}{\theta} \frac{1}{\mu}. \tag{3.99}$$

Eliminating the last term and putting all terms to the left-hand side, we obtain:

$$\mu^2 - \beta + \frac{f''(k^*)c^*}{\theta} = 0, \tag{3.100}$$

where the roots of this quadratic equation are:

$$\mu_{1,2} = \frac{\beta \pm \left[\beta^2 - 4\frac{f''(k^*)c^*}{\theta}\right]^{\frac{1}{2}}}{2}. \tag{3.101}$$

From the stated above we can conclude that the economy converges to k^*, c^* only when $\mu < 0$, which requires:

$$\mu_1 = \frac{\beta - \left[\beta^2 - 4\frac{f''(k^*)c^*}{\theta}\right]^{\frac{1}{2}}}{2}, \tag{3.102}$$

while plugging μ_1 into Eq. (3.98) refers to the ratio of $\widetilde{k}$ and $\widetilde{c}$ where both evolve at the same rate μ_1. Now, we need to understand under which circumstances c and k converge to their balanced growth path values at rate μ_1. The dynamics can be captured through linearized equations for $\dot{c}$ and $\dot{k}$. Then, at $t = 0$ we have:

$$c = c^* + \frac{f''(k^*)c^*}{\theta\mu_1}(k - k^*), \tag{3.103}$$

and the converging process follows:

$$c(t) = c^* + e^{\mu_1 t}(c(0) - c^*), \tag{3.104}$$

$$k(t) = k^* + e^{\mu_1 t}(k(0) - k^*). \tag{3.105}$$

Additionally, Cobb-Douglas production function is adopted in order to keep comparability (regarding the speed of convergence) with the previous example of the Solow-Swan model. The simple form is $f(k) = k^\alpha$ with $f''(k^*) = \alpha(\alpha - 1)k^{*\alpha - 2}$. The balanced growth path determines consumption as the difference between output and break-even investments; hence, consumption per unit of effective labour corresponds to $c^* = k^{*\alpha-2} - (n+g)k*$. The rate μ_1 can be then expressed as:

$$\mu_1 = \frac{1}{2}\left(\beta - \left\{\beta^2 - \frac{4}{\theta}\alpha(\alpha-1)k^{*\alpha-2}\left[k^{*\alpha} - (n+g)k^*\right]\right\}^{\frac{1}{2}}\right), \tag{3.106}$$

where $\beta = \rho - n - (1-\theta)g$. From Eq. (3.84) we also know that $f'(k) = g\theta + \rho$, which in Cobb-Douglas terms implies $\alpha k^{*\alpha-1} = g\theta + \rho$. Expressing

$$k^* = \left(\frac{g\theta+\rho}{\alpha}\right)^{\frac{1}{\alpha-1}}, \tag{3.107}$$

and substituting into Eq. (3.106) generates:

$$\mu_1 = \frac{1}{2}\left(\beta - \left\{\beta^2 + \frac{4}{\theta}\frac{(1-\alpha)}{\alpha}(g\theta+\rho)[g\theta+\rho-\alpha(n+g)]\right\}^{\frac{1}{2}}\right), \tag{3.108}$$

which finally defines the rate of convergence.

For our purpose it is not necessary to provide detailed formal comparison between convergence rates in Ramsey-Cass-Koopmans and Solow-Swan models. The important conclusion is that both models demonstrate substantial converging forces. For simulations respecting adopted conditions, which also concretely show that Ramsey-Cass-Koopmans model evinces even more rapid convergence than in the case of Solow-Swan model, see e.g. Romer (2006: 69–70) or Heijdra and van der Ploeg (2002: 430–432).

3.4 Chapter Summary

The present chapter firstly underlines the importance of theory. It is clear, based on the empirical findings in the second chapter, that data need their interpretative framework, otherwise researchers face a mere disordered fraction of reality. Theory therefore provides logical explanation of the empirical dimension and reveals the underlying nature of researched phenomena.

In contrast to natural sciences, theory in social sciences is of a different kind since social scientists face a frequent problem of non-isolability. In explaining the logic of a given system through understanding the fundamental relationships among elements of the system, a theory in social sciences does not necessarily correspond to every particular aspect of reality but it is supposed to capture "totality" of the reality. Such kind of theory, which comprehend not only empirical surface, but also abstract nature of the system, is then capable of extrapolation to the future, which distinguishes a theory from a mere past-oriented statement based on empirical results.

The fact is that current economic theories, which potentially explain a variety of diverging tendencies, focus on particular determinants of unequal economic distribution. Simply put, there is no dominating economic theory that would explain, in general terms, the empirical findings presented in the second chapter as the intrinsic feature of the current economic system.

On the other hand, optimization in economic theory frequently leads to converging tendencies. In order to inspect converging theories in economics, and to point out at their limitations in explaining current economic distributions, we went into details of famous dynamic models of Solow-Swan and Ramsey-Cass-Koopmans. Despite both of these two models were formulated as explaining between-country convergence, their fundamental idea based on diminishing marginal returns and hence higher growth rates of the weaker players potentially constitute a framework for convergence in various agent-based theories. In other words, it is possible, on a higher level of abstractness, to apply logic of these two models on agent-based modelling and within-economy distribution.

In the first instance of the Solow-Swan model, where sustain growth is secured when the technological parameter is growing over time, the income grows only as long as capital grows. At the same time, capital reports diminishing marginal productivity and hence the capital will grow faster than income, resulting also in faster growth of depreciation than the growth of savings. The process of capital accumulation therefore has just temporary effect on the growth rate. As regards the long-run effect of increasing saving rate, the model generates higher levels of capital and income. In sum, the concept of conditional convergence, which is the concept coming from the Solow-Swan model primarily, tells that if economies share the same technology and fundamental determinants of capital accumulation (and hence the same steady-state), the poorer economy will converge to the steady-state more rapidly than the richer one.

In contrast to the Solow-Swan model, which assumes a fixed saving rate, the agent-based RCK model employs optimization between consumption and savings. RCK's agents therefore easily adopt smoothing patterns in consumption. Representative agent's discount factor therefore substitutes the saving rate in determining the rate of capital accumulation. By this, the RCK model substitutes exogenously given saving rate with preferences of the individuals in determining the equilibrium level of normalized output and consumption. Despite the convergence in the RCK is more complex issue than was the case of the Solow-Swan model, it was showed that under given assumptions the model also demonstrates converging tendencies. Respecting outlined conditions even leads to the rate of adjustment higher than in the case of the Solow-Swan model.

In order to provide just an intuitive counter-example to presented theories, we can mention the relationship between advanced and developing economies. Advanced economies with an abundance of capital naturally seek for the highest return, which is, in some cases, connected to developing countries with a low level of capital stock. This goes hand in hand with the neoclassical idea. The inflow of capital to developing countries often causes that the poor economy increases its output, which gives the impression of convergence measured by GDP. But if we focus on the disposable income of the poor economy, we have to subtract the outflow of capital, which is one of the most important issues for poorer economies. At the end, appreciated capital flights back to advanced economies and converging process is a mere misinterpretation based on GDP which does not reflect the existent flow of capital. When using national/disposable income as the critical measure, the diverging process is in sight, as well as it is closer to conclusions of Milanovic (2013) or Anand and Segal (2008) who argue that the importance of location in global inequality is on the rise.

These two models have established the theoretical background for convergence in economics. On the other side, empirical evidence indicates that rather diverging tendencies are gaining their ground. Upon a closer inspection we can see that converging forces come from the combination of two crucial assumptions: firstly, that we operate with identical economies (and their steady-states), and, secondly, that the marginal product is decreasing. If we use, mistakenly, these theories to explain the development of heterogenous economies, we would end up in a tautological trap. In other words, every single divergence can be explained through heterogeneity of economies/agents in a sense that each of them has a different steady-state to which it approaches. As an example, let us assume a big difference in equilibria of two economies. And despite the effect of diminishing marginal product, the richer economy may grow faster than the poor one since the rich one could be still farer from its steady-state than the poor economy.

Firstly, in the light of empirical findings (e.g. Thewissen et al. 2019), we must problematize the effect of diminishing marginal product. If we assume capital in the widest possible sense including human capital etc., it was clearly shown that the return of such capital is greater the greater is the capital stock. Employing standard Cobb-Douglas functions where α signifies decreasing returns to capital thus appears to be misleading to the explanation of various phenomena in economic distribution. It is easy to see that any kind of convergence springs from decreasing returns. This can be proved by setting $\alpha = 1$ i.e. constant returns, which would cause that convergence never happens.

Secondly, in order to understand the role of market mechanism in economic distribution, we will have to eliminate the effect of heterogeneous agents/economies. The reason is obvious since, as was demonstrated, every detected inequality is then ascribed to heterogeneity of researched subjects. Simply put, we need to accommodate diverging forces in economic distribution with the environment of identical agents, which is beyond the scope of presented neoclassical models.

References

Acemoglu D (2009) Introduction to modern economic growth. Princeton University Press
Anand S, Segal P (2008) What do we know about global income inequality? J Econ Lit 46(1):57–94
Barro RJ, Sala-i-Martín X (1992) Convergence. J Polit Econ 100(2):223–225
Barro RJ, Sala-i-Martín X (2004) Economic growth, 2nd edn. MIT Press, Cambridge
Blanchard O, Fischer S (1989) Lectures on macroeconomics. MIT Press, Cambridge
Gandolfo G (2010) Economic dynamics. Springer, Berlin

Heijdra BJ, van der Ploeg F (2002) The foundations of modern macroeconomics. Oxford University Press
Milanovic B (2013) The two faces of globalization: against globalization as we know it. World Dev 31(4):667–683
Maialeh R (2019) Generalization of results and neoclassical rationality: unresolved controversies of behavioural economics methodology. Qual Quant 53(4):1743–1761
Romer D (2006) Advanced macroeconomics, 3rd edn. McGraw Hill
Solow RM (1956) A contribution to the theory of economic growth. Q J Econ 70(1):65–94
Swan TW (1956) Economic growth and capital accumulation. Econ Rec 32(2):334–361
Thewissen S, Nolan B, Roser M (2019) Incomes across the distribution. https://ourworldindata.org/incomes-across-the-distribution. Accessed 24 Dec 2019
Uzawa H (1963) On a two-sector model of economic growth II. Rev Econ Stud 30(2):105–118

Chapter 4
Who Are Agents in Agent-Based Economic Models?

4.1 A Rational Decision-Making Process and Limits of the Behavioural Approach

This chapter demarcates a rational decision-making process of economic agents in neoclassical theory. On the contrary to the previous chapter, it is argued that general neoclassical approach can still be, despite widely discussed weaknesses, a viable tool to understand principal issues of economic distribution. In the light of the current trends in economic research, the chapter also discusses limits of behavioural approach. It is claimed that fragmental insights of behavioural research, which are increasingly gaining greater importance in economics over time, are of little help in comprehending general market principles and their link to economic inequality.

In general terms, by agents we understand economic units which interacts according to specified rules over space and time. Naturally, economic models treat agents variously. For instance, economists regularly differentiate between heterogeneous and representative agents; for the typical market equilibrium models we differentiate between households and firms, not to mention that current mainstream macroeconomics, which widely operates with dynamic stochastic general equilibrium (DSGE) models, regularly includes agents like governments and central banks and thus broadens the term of economic agents beyond strictly microeconomic terminology.

On the other hand, it is widely acknowledged that the foundational assumptions of neoclassical economics, operating with a rational agent, should be somehow challenged. The contentious debate on an individual's rationality from behavioural perspective includes e.g. Levitt and List (2007), Lee et al. (2009) or DellaVigna (2009). Current research heads towards context-dependence; idiosyncratic mistakes can be cancelled out by arbitrage, experience effects, or aggregation (see e.g. List 2004; Farber 2014). Some decisions however still include behavioural phenomena due to limits of arbitrage (Shleifer and Vishny 1997) and problems with debiasing

R. Maialeh, *Dynamic Models and Inequality*, Contributions to Economics,
https://doi.org/10.1007/978-3-030-46313-7_4

consumers (Gabaix and Laibson 2006) may lead to persisting anomalies in economic agents' decision-making. The mainstream critique, which is the behavioural one at the present time, puts the argument that economic models based on rational *homo oeconomicus* do not match observed data mainly from two reasons, which, according to Sen (1991, 1993), establish neoclassical rationality paradigm. Firstly, economic agents supposedly do not always maximize their utility; and, secondly, behaviour of economic agents exhibits high level of inconsistency. The present subchapter comes from Maialeh (2019) where outlined limits of behavioural approach are elaborated in more details.

Before we start the disputation about the relevance of behavioural critique and viability of neoclassical paradigm, we should firstly outline the theoretical background of the 'traditional' agent's decision-making process. To keep the general level of theorizing, let us start with a formal context of economic agent's behaviour. Such an economic agent purposefully acts according to expectations on future possible outcomes under the following conditions:

1. Probability of X is a non-negative real number, Ω is a non-empty finite set, then probability of a certain event is 1 and probability of an unrealizable event is 0, hence $P(X) \leq 1 \wedge P(\Omega) = 1 \wedge P(\emptyset) = 0 \Rightarrow 0 \leq P(X)1$.
2. If X_1, X_2 are mutually exclusive, then $P(X_1 \cup X_2) = P(X_1) + P(X_2)$, for a finite number of events we have $P\left(\cup_{i=1}^{k} X_i\right) = \sum_{i=1}^{k} P(X_i)$. Moreover, Bayesian agent assigns a subjective probability to any possible event from Ω. Under our specification it means that the agent has a certain degree of belief about everything and for that the set of probabilistic beliefs is coherent and complete.

Further, Kolmogorov axiomatic definition of probability (1), (2) is completed by conditional probability in order to capture probability of simultaneous occurrence of X_1, X_2. The economic agent therefore changes her beliefs, e.g. when exposed to new evidence, according to conditional probabilities:

3. $P(X_1 \cap X_2) = P(X_1)P(X_2 | X_1) = P(X_2)P(X_1 | X_2)$; for $X_1, X_2, \ldots, X_n$ we get $P \cap_{i=1}^{n} X_i = P(X_1)P(X_2|X_1)P(X_3|X_1 \cap X_2) \ldots P(X_n | \cap_{i=1}^{n-1} X_i)$.

   The agent thus decides on $\Omega = \{X_1, \ldots, X_n\}$, while assuming completeness:

$$\forall X_i, X_j \in \Omega : X_i \succ X_j \vee X_j \succ X_i \vee X_i \sim X_j. \tag{4.1}$$

Transitivity and hence constitutive element of consistency of choice is secured if

$$\forall X_i, X_j, X_k \in \Omega : X_i \succ X_j \wedge X_j \succsim \mathrm{X_k} \Rightarrow \mathrm{X_i} \succ \mathrm{X_k}. \tag{4.2}$$

General utility function is $u : \Omega \rightarrow \mathbb{R}$ and continuity axiom is defined as

$$\begin{aligned} &\forall X(u_0, u_1, \theta_0) \in \Omega : \exists Y : Y \sim X(u_0, u_1, \theta_0) \\ &\forall X(u_0, u_1, \theta_0), Y \in \Omega : \exists \theta_0 : Y \sim X(u_0, u_1, \theta_0) \end{aligned} \tag{4.3}$$

which implies that X_i is preferred to X_j while $u_0 = u_1$ iff

$$X_i(u_0, u_1, \theta_i) \succ X_j(u_0, u_1, \theta_i) : \theta_i > \theta_j. \tag{4.4}$$

For $X_i \succsim X_j$ and irrelevant alternative Z with probability of the occurrence $\theta_z \in (0, 1)$ the independence axiom states:

$$\theta_z X_i + (1 - \theta_z)Z \succsim \theta_z X_j + (1 - \theta_z)Z. \tag{4.5}$$

Based on these axioms, von Neuman-Morgenstern (vNM) utility function is defined as

$$u[X(u_0, u_1, \theta)] = (1 - \theta)u_0 + \theta u_1, \tag{4.6}$$

which subsequently establishes the ground for expected utility theory (EUT) (Maialeh 2019).

By assuming the neoclassical concept, we may rise the question whether this 'traditional' approach is still valid in the light of recent research. Especially behavioural economics has at its disposal a robust empirical evidence that supposedly contradicts this traditional approach. An illustrative example for all can be, for instance, consistency of choice. This necessary condition for a rational behaviour is supposed to be systematically violated and economic agents hence cannot be labelled as rational. Let us name e.g. crossing indifference curves in Knetsch (1990) and other violations of axiom of transitivity in Lee et al. (2009). Alongside with the simplifying statement that theoretical models cannot be falsified by mere contradicting sample of data, we should focus on purely theoretical critique of the neoclassical concept. One of the very few examples can be basic contraction consistency, also known as 'Property α' or 'the Chernoff condition', which serves as a theoretical background for many behavioural empirical findings (Maialeh 2019). It says that an alternative that is chosen from a set S and belongs to a subset T must be chosen from T as well. More formally:

$$[x \in C(S) \& x \in T \subseteq S] \Rightarrow x \in C(T).$$

In order to provide an example of how standard consistency conditions might be violated, Sen (1991) considers the following choices:

$$\begin{aligned} \{x\} &= C(\{x, y\}), \\ \{y\} &= C(\{x, y, z\}). \end{aligned}$$

Sen considers two individuals at a dinner table and a fruit basket with one remaining apple. Suppose the individual faces a choice between having the apple (y) and having nothing instead (x). The individual decides to behave decently and picks nothing (x) rather than the one apple (y). If the basket had contained two apples, the choice between having nothing (x), having the one apple (y) and having the added apple (z) *would have changed*. In that case, the individual could choose the one apple (y). Although not explicitly, Sen assumes that good behaviour is a part of individual's utility. Hence, it is concluded that the presence of another apple (z) makes one of the two apples choosable which supposedly violates consistency.

Simply put, consistency in neoclassical sense is violated when transitivity and independent alternative axioms do not hold. The added apple (z) however cannot be treated as the irrelevant alternative since it is a crucial game-changer for the decently behaving individual. In such cases we can neither employ independence axiom with irrelevant alternative Z (Eq. 4.5) and hence it would be too misleading to claim that the agent reports inconsistent and consequently non-rational behaviour.[1] The central counter-argument posits that consistency must be assessed strictly *ceteris paribus*, as can be seen from axiomatization above where we has to assess the decision within a given set of known alternatives Ω. Inconsistency in the provided example would mean that the agent, who repeatedly faces the same choice $\{x\} = C(\{x, y\})$, changes her mind and picks irregularly both x and y. This *ceteris paribus* requirement naturally applies to axiom of transitivity (Eq. 4.2) as well—if conditions of choice change, then it will lose its purpose, similarly as the independence axiom (Eq. 4.5) will get nonsensical if the added alternative may influence agent's utility. The Chernoff condition alone therefore does not represent the reliable criterion for consistently rational behaviour. An interesting debate in the broader context of Arrow's axiom and minimal consistency axiom is provided by Dalton and Ghosal (2011).

Based on these arguments, the agent in EUT would violate consistency iff (1) transitivity axiom (Eq. 4.2) under identical conditions of choice does not hold or if (2) the irrelevant alternative Z (Eq. 4.5) influences agent's decision-making. As regards (2), the irrelevancy of an alternative is derivable from agent's utility function, which, however, generally stays unknown to external evaluator. Otherwise we risk the above-mentioned situation, on which Sen clearly points out, that the agent maximizes her utility while she changes decisions. The fact that changing conditions cause changes in decision-making can be paradoxically a sign of rational behaviour—the agent adapts on the new conditions that may affect her utility and rationally pursue own goals through flexible changes in decision-making. Consistency under changing conditions should be therefore understood as a mental procedure through which the agent makes decisions that do not deviate from maximizing utility, rather than openly rigid decisions that may contradict own's utility—such rigid decisions definitely cannot be a part of rational behaviour within changing environment. Behavioural critique should therefore avoid the risk to set observable

[1]Compare with Sen (1993) who reached similar conclusion but out of neoclassical paradigm.

rigidity as a proxy for consistency, which is, without knowing utility function, unobservable.

If conditions of choice change only seemingly (in order to cause cognitive noise and to bring cognitive biases into play) and *de facto* stay unaffected, then we inspect cognitive limitations which is particularly the domain of behavioural approach as well. By this, behavioural approach challenges consistency in both ways (1, 2). Such approach however cannot distinguish whether the agent does not follow rational-choice procedure based on stated axioms or whether the suboptimal outcome stems from agent's cognitive limitations (Maialeh 2019).

Let us assume an extreme illustration (Maialeh 2019) based on widely discussed retirement policy which makes use of the fundamental trade-off between consumption and savings, or the problem of intertemporal choice respectively. The current research (e.g. Poterba 2014) demonstrates that many people may not reach a sufficient savings rate for retirement which leads policy-makers to increase household savings rate (Thaler and Benartzi 2004). The following example challenges the behavioural idea that cognitive biases, which may cause suboptimal outcomes, signifies that agent's utility is not maximized and hence such agent necessarily acts non-rationally. Thus, we have an agent who decides between present and future consumption; in optimum we get standard Euler equation:

$$u'(c_t) = E_t[\beta(1+r)u'(c_{t+1})], \beta = \frac{1}{1+\theta} \dots \in (1,0). \tag{4.7}$$

where $u'(c_t)$, $u'(c_{t+1})$ represent marginal utilities of present and future consumption, β is subjective discounting factor for transferring future values to the present, θ is marginal rate of time preference and r is interest rate. The agent rationally seeks long-run equilibrium $\theta = r$, which implies:

$$u'(c_t) = E_t[u'(c_{t+1})] \tag{4.8}$$

and hence the present value of present and future consumption is equal:

$$c_t = E_t[c_{t+1}], \tag{4.9}$$

which suggests consumption-smoothing preferences. Agent's preference over consumption sequences in infinite horizon is then captured by utility function:

$$U = E_t\left[\sum_{t=0}^{\infty} \beta^t u(c_t)|\Omega_0\right], \tag{4.10}$$

where Ω_0 represents a set of information available to the agent in $t = 0$. Now, let this set be affected e.g. by the bias detected by Baron et al. (1993) or Rottenstreich and Hsee (2001) which refers to agent's cognitive limitations to exactly compute probabilities. The objective state of the world is Ω_0^+ and the difference between Ω_0^+ and

Ω_0 represents agent's probability-based limitations to predict own's life expectancy. Given the consumption-smoothing preference and our assumption that agent's income in retirement does not suffice to cover consumption demands in retirement and labour income exceeds consumption when working, the only rational solution is to be enrolled to the "Save More Tomorrow" programme. However, the agent underestimates her personal risk of occurrence of a certain type of hereditary disease and after decades of participating in the programme the agent dies just before retirement. Was agent's decision to enter "Save More Tomorrow" programme rational? If such a situation is assessed on outcome-based criteria (*ex-post*), i.e. whether the agent maximized utility from consumption when alive, the agent can never be labelled as rational. The reason is very simple—the agent differed her current consumption in favour of consumption in retirement, but there will be no consumption in retirement. In other words, the agent chose inappropriate means to her long-term goal (maximize utility from consumption over the whole life), which is used by behavioural economists as a sign of non-rational behaviour. On the other hand, enrolment to the programme was at a given time and available information, i.e. *ex-ante*, the most rational act regardless the unlucky and unexpected outcome. This example shows that employing outcome-based criteria to rationality concepts exposes us to the risk that the one who *procedurally* behaves rationally but has bad luck could be assessed as less rational than the other one who may procedurally behave irrationally but have good luck. The example outlines that even though the agent uses the best available means to her ends, it is not guaranteed that agent's utility will be maximized. Therefore, behavioural attempts to prove systematic irrational behaviour, which is supposedly based on the discrepancy between preestablished ends and appropriate means, methodologically suffer with outcome bias similarly as researched by Gino et al. (2009). Outcome-based criteria, which inevitably entail both cognitive limitations (e.g. in computation probability) and pure randomness and unpredictability, simply put all uncontrollable factors, are thus highly problematic for assessing rational behaviour.

Without distinction whether the agent does not follow rational-choice procedure based on stated axioms or whether the suboptimal outcome stems from agent's cognitive limitations, behavioural results may report non-rational behaviour despite the agent intentionally follows rational decision-making process, but her cognitive limitations cause suboptimal or inconsistent decisions. That is because the agent simply cannot fully control the environment (due to agent's objective limitations), while the environment finally co-produces the outcome of her decisions. Put it differently, if behavioural approach requires to be accurate with description of empirical reality, it cannot at the same time posits completely unreal assumption that agents fully control their environment. A typical definition of rationality as instrumental one is especially important in economics—the agent is rational insofar as she adopts suitable means to her ends. As was seen, neoclassical agent is a Bayesian one—such agent optimizes on the basis of current beliefs. Contrarily, outcome-based assessment of rationality concerns *ex-post* rationality which is in contradiction with *ex-ante* approach of Bayesian agent in neoclassical economics

(Maialeh 2019). Based on these arguments we are about to continue with standard neoclassical approach to modelling agents' decision-making process.

The second reason why neoclassical agents are not considered as rational is that they supposedly do not always maximize their utility. There are, again, two main arguments for such claims but we will briefly discuss just one of them. The other one refers to misunderstanding of unselfish motives within the traditional concept of utility; for further elaboration on this debate see again Maialeh (2019). The crucial aspect denouncing utility maximizing strategy of neoclassical agents however relies on satisficing behaviour (Simon 1955, 1956). Simon's contribution concludes that satisficing behaviour differs from maximizing behaviour; or put it differently—that agents rather satisfice than optimize. It means that agents decide a satisfactory level that is good enough for each goal. Such a decision-making supposedly generates suboptimal outcome since the outcome do not correspond to the maximum level of satisfaction but rather to a sufficient level of satisfaction. Satisficing behaviour is thus probably the most challenging *monistic* cognitive strategy which confronts mainstream maximizing behaviour since it inspired a number of partial "save-time" heuristics, e.g. "fast and frugal heuristics" (Gigerenzer and Goldstein 1996; Goldstein and Gigerenzer 2002). Such heuristics are labelled as partial because they are just part of decision maker's repertoire of cognitive strategies, as opposed to monistic ones (satisficing vs. maximizing) which are supposed to determine agent's decisions alone.

Now, let us employ constraints in order to outline a similarity between satisficing and maximizing behaviour (Maialeh 2019). A similarity between these two cognitive strategies was already discussed by van Witteloostuijn (1988) who claims that if choice theoretic models are well-designed, which means that they introduce goal setting procedures, uncertainty, group decision making or computational disabilities, they might produce the same results. This is rather a laborious way to prove that these two cognitive strategies posit the same thing in two different languages. The following lines show that satisficing and maximizing must be the same *in principle*.

For this purpose, we investigate whether satisficing behaviour, a sequential process that stops the search when the predefined threshold is reached, is in contradiction with neoclassical assumption that agents generally try to achieve the best possible outcome from their decision-making. The example using neoclassical apparatus can be simple. Assume Doucouliagos' (1994) student who has the capacity to attain better grades but knowingly does not do so. Utility function of the student naturally contains the best possible grades but student's constraint, on the other hand, considers time and effort (say, price or disutility) that are required to be sacrificed in order to attain desired grades. The intuitive calculation is as follows: if the marginal subjectively perceived utility from a better grade exceeds marginal subjectively perceived disutility from sacrificed time and effort, then the student continues in improving her grades. If the marginal subjectively perceived disutility, conversely, exceeds marginal subjectively perceived utility, then continuation in improving student's grades decreases her net utility. At a certain subjectively defined point, pursuing better grades ceases to be the best alternative since net utility as a difference between gained utility and undergone disutility decreases. It follows that the student may maximize her utility (composed of the best possible grades) with grades which are not objectively the best. Nevertheless, utility is based on subjective perceptions. In a slightly altered way, when the agent expects a fixed level of utility for which she minimises expenditures, we may use another neoclassical textbook tool—Hicksian demand—which latently corresponds with Simon's (1956: 136) claim about a satisficing path "that will permit satisfaction at some specified level of all of its needs."

4.2 Internal and External Nature of the Agent: A Critical Approach

The following subchapter deals with internal motivations of the agent and the character of the external environment within which these motivations are pursued. In order to inspect fundamental principles of agents' behaviour in market society, we resort our attention to more philosophical insights. Since modern economic thought does not produce sufficiently influential, deep and critical reflection on the question of market society, the inspiration arises from prominent theorists in different scientific fields. Especially critical theorists' point of view, who historically have taken up the position of those who powerfully demystify the abstract mechanism of socio-economic order, is more than inspirational. The main value added of these theoretical stimuli is that they exceed a mere phenomenal side of the market mechanism, which is essential for our understanding of the fundamental market forces and their role in economic distribution.

For Adorno and Horkheimer (2002[1944]), the system is the form of knowledge which deals with facts; while facts consequently assist the subject in mastering nature and self-preservation becomes the constitutive principle of science. This opening statement inevitably affect the agent's nature in economic models, being both the product and the condition of material existence. As authors posit, "[t]he system's principles are those of self-preservation." (2002[1944]: 65) Natural components of humans are inseparable from any analysis dealing with human behaviour. They are always present, in any time and at any place. Economic models should therefore consider this biological moment, famously raised by Maslow (1943) who refers on homeostasis—an automatic mechanism of all living organisms which strives to preserve their natural living conditions. To be concrete, his first finding says that "physiological drive" is the strongest motive in human action. The second finding explains that unsatisfied physiological needs make other needs non-existing. Valuable philosophical foundations of the biological drive were also put by Spinoza: "*Conatus sese conservandi primum et unicum virtutis est fundamentum.* [The endeavour to preserve oneself is the first and only basis of virtue]" [1677] Plattner for instance summarizes Hobbesian, bourgeois view on human nature as follows: "All men are governed by selfish passions, above all the desire for their self-preservation, and no man has a greater right to what is necessary for his own preservation than does any other man. Each man is the sole judge of the best means to his own preservation; therefore, all men are naturally free. But men's selfish passions put them into perpetual conflict with one another. It is in this sense that Hobbes's natural man is evil. (...) [F]or object of men's strongest desire, self-preservation, is threatened by their very efforts to achieve it." (1979: 128) Materialistic moment of physical violence, resulting in self-preserving motivations, can be then easily connected to rational behaviour as "the legislating authority of any action" (Adorno and Horkheimer 2002[1944]: 22).

In Marx's (2009[1844]) is read that subjects of human instincts exist beyond and independently of human himself—man has to turn to 'the Outside' in order to reconcile his instincts and desires. These instinct imperatives therefore do not allow the agent to opt-out from these conditions that bind her to the Outside. In other words, agents are subjugated to market forces, while they experience success to the extent to which they follow market rules, which stay beyond control of agents. On the other hand, economic laws are socially constituted, and these laws only manifest themselves as laws of economic nature. Bonefeld however clarifies, that the fact that man has to eat says nothing about the mode of subsistence and what it entails. Therefore, society, not nature, is the point of critical departure (2014: 57). Agents are compelled to expenses (in the broadest possible sense) in order to gain access to the means of subsistence, for which they compete on the market. Agent faces over-determining structured framework. Such an agent is an investor, an entrepreneur of labour power seeking for access to the means of subsistence. As put by Bonefeld: "economic compulsion is a form of freedom that is experienced in and through a constant struggle to secure her living existence" (2014: 106). That is to say, known from the very Marxian times, that each agent has to expand her capital, so as to preserve it, only by means of progressive accumulation (2015[1867]).

Agents' rational behaviour is, in this sense, confronted by universal market power, while the prime criterion of success is their self preservation consisting in adaptation to objective rules of the market. The whole reproduces itself by imposing its universality on the social whole, whose self-preservation corresponds to its subordination to the whole. The subjectivity of an agent therefore tends to diminish as the objective laws are internalized into the rational behaviour of the agent.

Another important aspect is that economic agents are able to manage their resource allocation over time. While preconditions of any action are rooted in the past, conditions of agents' action are anchored in the present and consequences of their action reach into the future. Read economically, savings represent materialized activity of the past which come back to life in the present, actualized in the competitive struggle motivated by self-preservation. Motivation of the rational agent action is future-oriented.

The imperatives of the market mechanism are determining even for those in a privileged position. Reminding Adorno (2005[1951]), privileged classes have to follow the same own interest as others, otherwise they would not be able to possess their privileged position. The old-fashioned binary classification of society on workers and capitalists, which is still present in contemporary models, can easily transform into a common theoretical background where all agents are bounded to conditions of their reproduction. Disrespecting these conditions naturally means agents' extinction.

The success of an agent derives from her actual position and the distance to the critical level of self-preservation. The distance furnishes the agent with resources that can be used for the purpose of long-run survival. Intertemporal relatedness becomes almost paradoxical—what is not used to serve self-preservation is used to self-preservation, and the more an individual has above what he needs for her immediate existence the more likely she will reproduce herself in the future.

The *apparent* freedom of economic agents is a product of society's economic and social apparatus—the harshness of competitive society. Economic agents succumb to the universal mechanism of competition. The content of the self comes from society and the self-sufficient individual has become "a mere receptive organ of the market (. . .)" a shell without content. Economic agent accepts the conditions of her existence and aims to fulfil them (Adorno and Horkheimer 2002[1944]; Adorno 2005[1951]: 149; Horkheimer 1972[1937]). The pressure of adaptation annuls subjectivity and dominates the insights of specialized sciences from its meta-position.

It is important to understand that self-preservation of a particular agent depends on conditions of the objective. Economic success is then the function of agent's adaptation to the objective; i.e. to the market mechanism that governs allocation of all resources. At the same time, the success in such a hypothetical market society is based on providing countervalue, which means that the agent must perform in the market. Such an objectified agent modifies her performance in order to comply market requirements, while the reward from the market is the function of tightness between agent's performance and market requirements. In other words, the agent appropriates on the market the more, the more corresponds agent's action to market requirements. Market mechanism shape its elements (acting agents) to make them fit to the production; and their endowed subjectivity becomes a mere function of their reproduction. Economic progress is therefore conditioned with unavoidable adjustment of agents who appropriate resources on the market correspondingly to their affirmation.

For Kosík (1976), *homo oeconomicus* is exactly the subject who objectifies himself. The subject abstracts from his subjectivity and then metamorphoses into an object, a mere element determined by the system. A man becomes an abstract, analysable and mathematically describable unit, the real metamorphosis of man performed by capitalism which establishes and develops economics as a *science*, where the individual becomes the general, the stochastic, the lawful. In order to make such transformation, contemporary economics stands over individual purposes, becomes independent of them and the social relations among individuals (embedded in the market mechanism) transform themselves as an autonomous natural force over them. *Homo oeconomicus* is thus a functioning element of a system, whose essential features were defined in order to make the system running. *Homo oeconomicus* therefore does not answer "What is man?" but rather how the man should be to keep the system of economic relations in motion. Economics transforms, subjugates and adapts individuals to its objective mechanisms—methodology gets ontologized (Kosík 1976: 52–53).

Our approach to understanding economic inequality classifies economic gaps as a result of clashes between individual attributes and socioeconomic environment. The final economic distribution is merely the result of interplay between internal and external factors of any economic choice which the agent faces. For this purpose, we firstly formalized logical structure of agent's behaviour. It frames agents' utility maximizing decision-making process and outlines schemes of their action. Secondly, agents' action is happening within given socioeconomic conditions, so that understanding economic inequality requires also description of external forces which determines agents' steps. These external (and fundamentally underlying) forces are embedded in the reproduction process itself. They define mode of production of the whole socioeconomic system and establish conditions under which individualized agents pursue their interests. The question is how the ruling principle of socioeconomic reproduction in modern era—market mechanism—contributes to economic inequality.

Any economic model that has an ambition to explain economic inequality should therefore capture "the decisive substantive elements" (Horkheimer 1972[1937]: 234), the base of unchanging factors of the capitalist-market production process that is immanent to any particular phenomenon of the process; a structured dialectical whole from which any particular fact can be rationally comprehended (Kosík 1976).[2] In this sense, we are not so far from classical economists. Let us go with Adam Smith as an example: Stewart (Smith 1985: 22) interprets his approach as follows: In the absence of direct evidence, "when we are unable to ascertain how men have actually conducted themselves upon particular occasions" we must consider "in what manner they are likely to have proceeded, from the principles of their nature, and the circumstances of their external situation." He follows, that "[t]he known principles of human nature"; "the natural succession of inventions and discoveries"; "the circumstances of society"—these are the foundations on which rests Smith's thinking "whatever be the nature of his subject"; astronomy, politics, economics, literature, language. "In most cases, it is of more importance to ascertain the progress that is most simple, than the progress that is most agreeable to fact; for (. . .) the real progress is not always the most natural". This exactly corresponds to the idea of the desired model which strives to explain the general motion through single causal principle. The result is a uniform interpretation of all teleological aspects of the order without being a reductionist or making simplifications; where the unifying causal principle structures incoherent phenomenal *materia* and establishes its unity in diversity.

Contemporary economic research reflects all habitual, egoistic, altruistic, bigoted, logical and whatever actions of economic agents; however, research that would

[2]It is obvious that any theoretical model is unable to provide detailed explanation of a multitude of all stochastic particularities. By "any particular fact" we understand any fact that is explainable as a systemic in a sense it derives from the natural propensity of men in a given system.

focus on the very basic principles of agents' reproduction has almost disappeared. Theoretical analysis of inequality as the result of these basic principles of social reproduction is not incomplete, partial or one-sided analysis which generates results for this particular segment of social reality, on which causality of economic categories is further detected. In contrary, the process of inequality penetrates to the essence of the production process, i.e. of the process of creation and distribution of wealth in its all-embracing sense.

4.3 Chapter Summary

The aims of the fourth chapter were to inspect whether typical neoclassical agent-based modelling is a viable approach in researching general inequality trends and their linkages to market, especially in the light of still developing behavioural critique (Maialeh 2019). Secondly, we concerned the fundamental behavioural principles of economic agents organized by market mechanism. In the first instance we want to avoid a situation where the neoclassical approach, based on rational behaviour of agents, may be the source of unsatisfactory theoretical grasp of trends in economic distribution. The second part then defines fundamental but rather underlying principles of market mechanism and discusses how they affect rational behaviour of economic agents who pursue their own goals.

The first question reacts on a broad behavioural research that accuses mainstream models, extensively operating with the neoclassical paradigm of *homo oeconomicus*, that economic agents violate basic principles of rationality on which the neoclassical concept relies. Sen (1991, 1993) splits economic rationality into two main pillars: (1) consistency of choice and (2) utility maximizing behaviour. Both of these two pillars have to be met since neither an inconsistent agent trying to maximize her utility nor an agent who consistently makes steps against her utility maximization could be labelled as rational. Based on the formal presentation of the typical Bayesian decision-maker in neoclassical economics, it is argued that behavioural critique is *principally* unable to meet (mostly through experiments) the axiomatic formulation of the neoclassical transitivity and the irrelevancy of an alternative; and it rather focuses on particular cognitive limitations of agents. It is also showed that famous concept of satisficing behaviour does not disprove utility maximizing behaviour in neoclassical sense. Demonstrated on a simple example, it is clear that considering constraints changes the game drastically, while these constraints (or disutilities) are necessarily in play during any economic decision-making. Provided conclusions stay on the argument that if an agent has no utility-increasing reason to deviate from a "good enough" (satisficing) alternative, which means that the marginal utility of any better alternative outweighs the marginal disutility to reach such alternative, it necessarily implies that the agent's utility must be at the maximum.

The second subchapter of this chapter dealt with the conflict between internal agent's motivations and her external market environment. According to the reviewed literature, market logic narrows the direction of agents' action vectors immensely. Concretely, since perfectly operating market is a dynamical institution where reproduction of its elements is unsecure, the principle of self-preservation dominates all other thinkable agent's motives. This physiological drive (Maslow 1943), the first and only basis of virtue (Spinoza 1677), puts agents into perpetual conflict with one another. Here we come to the pillar of the market mechanism: the competition. In order to reproduce, economic agents have to turn to the external environment (market) from where they appropriate resources for reproduction. Hence, agents are forced, for the sake of their reproduction, to adopt market imperatives. The competitive struggle for scarce resources on the market therefore deprive agents of their preferences since their primary driving force pushes all unconsumed resources to be invested in the future ability of reproduction.

The fourth chapter is important mainly due to the following reasons. Firstly, it shows that procedural side of agent's rationality is principally immune to most of mainstream criticism. We do not praise the neoclassical concept at this place, but it is claimed that prevailing behavioural reproaches are unable to prove that agents do not maximize their utility or that they are not consistent in their choices; simply put, that they are not rational. All the detected deviations from supposedly rational procedure accentuates particular, psychologically specified phenomena which have a little impact on the explanation of general tendencies. That is to say that focusing on these particular deviations, which immanently through psychologization subjectivize the merit of the researched problem, may divert the attention from the general determining laws of market mechanism. Henceforth we will follow the traditional approach to agent's rationality and the typical agent-based modelling.

Secondly, the chapter presents a less common perspective on agents' interaction governed by market principles. If we search for the abstract essence of the market, it is worth to overcome the superficial division on buyers and sellers. The immanent and at the same time the most natural feature of the market mechanism is competition for scarce resources. As we will see in the following chapters, this principle stays behind the proclaimed 'naturality' of market principles that is also backed by the self-preserving imperative which determines the action vector of all economic agents. It also reverses the typical view where agents are competing among each other through their output delivered on the market, whether it be a given product in the case of a firm or labour competency in the case of a household. Understanding to economic inequality however requires grasping the process of resource appropriation. The outlined perspective therefore complements the traditional view of the market as a place supplied by agents via accentuating the process of how agents extract resources from the market for their reproductive purposes. Instead of freedom and preferential discourse, which is usually connected to market operations, the provided perspective underlines the determinative aspects of market mechanism.

To conclude, combining self-preservation and market competition pushes agents into the situation where "any slowdown or stagnation brings destruction" (Horkheimer 2012[1949–67]), which may consequently stimulate aggregate growth tendency of the whole economy. The subsequent chapters procedurally follow the standard neoclassical paradigm of rational agents. As regards the content of agents' behaviour, we have defined self-preservation as the prime internal factor that is about to assert against external environment, in our case within market competition. The task for the upcoming chapters is to reveal how resources of rationally behaving agents, whose interaction is governed by competitive markets, evolve over time and whether it can match empirical findings on economic inequality presented in the second chapter.

References

Adorno TW (2005[1951]) Minima moralia: reflections on a damaged life. Verso
Adorno TW, Horkheimer M (2002[1944]) Dialectic of enlightenment: philosophical fragments. Stanford University Press
Baron J, Granato L, Spranca M, Teubal E (1993) Decision making biases in children and early adolescents: exploratory studies. Merrill Palmer Q 39:23–47
Bonefeld W (2014) Critical theory and the critique of political economy: on subversion and negative reason. Bloomsbury Academic
Dalton P, Ghosal S (2011) Behavioral decisions and welfare. Netspar Discussion Papers 12/2011-097
DellaVigna S (2009) Psychology of economics: evidence from the field. J Econ Lit 47(2):315–372
Doucouliagos C (1994) A note on the evolution of homo economicus. J Econ Issues 28(3):877–883
Farber H (2014) Why you can't find a taxi in the rain and other labor supply lessons from cab drivers. NBER Working Paper No. 20604
Gabaix X, Laibson D (2006) Shrouded attributes, consumer myopia, and information suppression in competitive markets. Q J Econ 121(5):505–540
Gigerenzer G, Goldstein DG (1996) Reasoning the fast and frugal way: models of bounded rationality. Psychol Rev 103(4):650–669
Gino F, Moore A, Bazerman MH (2009) No harm, no foul: the outcome bias in ethical judgments. Harvard Business School NOM Working Paper No. 08-080
Goldstein DG, Gigerenzer G (2002) Models of ecological rationality: the recognition heuristic. Psychol Rev 109(1):75–90
Horkheimer M (1972[1937]) Critical theory. Herder and Herder, New York
Horkheimer M. (2012[1949–67]) Critique of instrumental reason. Verso, London
Knetsch JL (1990) Derived indifference curves. Working Paper, Simon Fraser University
Kosík K (1976) Dialectics of the concrete: a study on man and world. D. Reidel Publishing Company, Dondrecht
Lee L, Amir O, Ariely D (2009) Search of homo economicus: cognitive noise and the role of emotion in preference consistency. J Consum Res 36(2):173–187
Levitt S, List J (2007) What do laboratory experiments measuring social preferences reveal about the real world? J Econ Perspect 21(2):153–174
List J (2004) Neoclassical theory versus prospect theory: evidence from the market-place. Econometrica 72(2):615–625
Maialeh R (2019) Generalization of results and neoclassical rationality: unresolved controversies of behavioural economics methodology. Qual Quant 53(4):1743–1761
Marx K (2009[1844]) Economic and philosophic manuscripts. Progress Publishers, Moscow
Marx K (2015[1867]) The capital: a critique of political economy, vol I. Progress Publishers, Moscow
Maslow AH (1943) A theory of human motivation. Psychol Rev 50(4):370–396
Plattner MF (1979) Rousseau's state of nature: an interpretation of the discourse on inequality. Northern Illinois University Press

Poterba J (2014) Retirement security in an aging population. Am Econ Assoc 104(5):1–30
Rottenstreich Y, Hsee CK (2001) Money, kisses, and electric shocks: on the affective psychology of risk. Psychol Sci 12:185–190
Sen A (1991) On ethics and economics. Wiley, New York
Sen A (1993) Internal consistency of choice. Econometrica 61(3):495–521
Shleifer A, Vishny RV (1997) The limits of arbitrage. J Financ 52(1):35–55
Simon HA (1955) Behavioral model of rational choice. Q J Econ 69(1):98–118
Simon HA (1956) Rational choice and the structure of the environment. Psychol Rev 63 (2):129–138
Smith A (1985) Lectures on rhetoric and belles lettres. In: Bryce JC (ed) Vol. IV of The Glasgow edition of the works and correspondence of Adam Smith. Liberty Fund, Indianapolis
Spinoza B [1677] Ethics, 4, prop. 22, cor
Thaler R, Benartzi S (2004) Save more tomorrow: using behavioral economics to increase employee saving. J Polit Econ 112(1):164–187
van Witteloostuijn A (1988) Maximising and satisficing opposite or equivalent concepts? J Econ Psychol 9(3):289–313
John A. List, (2004) Neoclassical Theory Versus Prospect Theory: Evidence from the Marketplace. Econometrica 72 (2):615-625
Dalton P, Ghosal S (2011) Behavioral Decisions and Welfare. CentER Discussion Paper, 2010–2022

Chapter 5
Models of Subsistence Consumption

As was showed in the fourth chapter, the fundamental aspect of agents' behaviour relates to self-preservation. Despite there are various options how to comprehend self-preservation in economics, we can generally understand it as expending a certain amount of resources in order to reproduce to the next period. This idea closely relates to a range of economic literature that is dedicated to subsistence consumption. The difference between using the term 'reproduction' instead of 'subsistence' is here rather semantical and it is not meant to be crucial for our further analysis. Nevertheless, in our sketchy understanding, reproduction more directly links to the dynamic processes, while subsistence has rather static connotations. This is potentiated by the fact that for most relevant articles it is common to consider subsistence consumption as constant. Nevertheless, we will use these terms throughout this book interchangeably with a preference to use the term 'subsistence consumption', following the practice of the field of study where this book is written.

Reproduction traditionally signifies a kind of renewal which is divided into three main categories of Marxian theory. Firstly, simple reproduction refers to a process such that at the end of it the agent remains the same both in terms of quantity and quality. Extended reproduction then refers to a process whereby the agent undergoes only quantitative changes. And finally, an agent who goes through expanded reproduction has developed qualitatively, i.e. moved forward on an upper level of economic development. In the light of the previous parts, our understanding of reproductive consumption naturally inclines to extended reproduction since simple reproduction, as is widely known, does not accommodate economic growth. Therefore, by considering constant subsistence we revive simple reproduction which, however, in the context of dynamic processes would mean an economic degeneration.[1]

This does not devalue theories based on subsistence; conversely, it is one of the very few concepts which reflects the *necessity* in economic agent's behaviour. The

[1]Recall how Horkheimer (2012 [1949–1967]) referred to stagnation as destruction.

R. Maialeh, *Dynamic Models and Inequality*, Contributions to Economics,
https://doi.org/10.1007/978-3-030-46313-7_5

focus on necessity escapes traditional domination of economic modelling based on preferences—it allows to properly capture the crucial differences, for instance between *willingness* to save (invest) and *ability* to save (invest). Such theoretical insights are the more important if we consider empiricalizing trends in economic research over recent decades. Aggregate numbers alone can hardly uncover motivations and underlying forces; e.g. households' saving rate of a certain amount may be the result of prodigal behaviour as well as of harsh austerity measures. The incorporation of reproductive and subsistence consumption into economic models transforms not only interpretation of results, but also fundamental settings of economic models. For instance, preferences based on widely used constant intertemporal elasticity of substitution (CIES) assumes that all disposable resources can be saved. Most of economic agents are then put into artificial system of preferential ranking between present and future consumption; similar examples on the relationship between consumption and savings can be made even more directly. As regards macro-level, we might mention Jones (1985) who claims that saving rates in post-war economies were low as real income was close to subsistence level.

In a historical perspective, subsistence consumption was formulated in various ways and contexts. Starting with Nelson (1956) and his theory of 'low-level equilibrium trap', it is shown that up to a certain level of income we observe dissaving due to constant level of necessary consumption. In the context of capital formation and population growth, the model suggests a tentative hypothesis that continuous economic growth could take place only through exploitation or other forms of subjection; examples provided on the international level refer to colonies and subject states.

A more focused paper was provided by Christiano (1989) who modified neoclassical model with subsistence consumption in order to explain post-war growth path in Japan. Important advances were reached by using Stone-Geary preferences (e.g. Rebelo 1992; King and Rebelo 1993; Easterly 1994 or Sarel 1994). An interesting idea was postulated by Azariadis (1996) who combined overlapping generations model (OLG) with endogenously determined subsistence level of consumption. In this framework, subsistence consumption is seen, among others, behind poverty traps in both convex and nonconvex economies with complete market structures. An indirect connection to subsistence consumption may be seen in Ogaki et al. (1996). Authors come up with conclusion that sensitivity to the interest rate depends on the country's income level. Concretely, richer economies are more sensitive on changes of the interest rate, while poorer countries less. Their hypothesis that the saving rate and its sensitivity to the interest rate is an increasing function of income further has strong empirical support. A possible explanation is that the income of poorer economies is too close to a subsistence level so that no matter how low the interest rate is, savings are determined by the difference between low income and relatively high subsistence consumption. Generally, it was shown that the performance of economic models improves as they are subsistence-augmented. For instance, Strulik (2010) shows on the example of AK model that the evolution of saving and growth rates over time is independent from the size of subsistence consumption, which underlines generalizability of this approach.

Subsistence consumption can be smoothly added into two-asset portfolio-choice models. The model composed by Achury et al. (2012) explains typical features which relate to inequality issues. Namely, it focuses on (i) the higher saving rates of the rich; (ii) on the greater share of personal wealth held in risky assets by the rich; and (iii) on the higher volatility of consumption of the wealthier. In this line of models, we can also find valuable contributions of Zimmerman and Carter (2003) or more recent Shin et al. (2018). We should not also forget Steger (especially 2000) whose work helped to understand the importance of subsistence consumption in development economics. In sum, all of these papers somehow indicate that considering subsistence consumption often oppose converging tendencies that are traditionally embedded in mainstream economic models. A comprehensive literature review on the topic up to mid-1980s was elaborated by Sharif (1986).

5.1 Linear Growth Model with Subsistence Consumption and Stone-Geary Preferences

The following part intentionally omit the level of subsistence consumption. The reason is very simple—in order to detect the influence of underlying market forces on inequality, one must abstract from particular economic conditions and focus on general laws of motion. It also allows to clarify the role of subsistence consumption in itself. Naturally, considering a certain level of necessary consumption restricts an ability to save which consequently has an impact on potential growth of the economic agent. In terms of income, the closer to the level of subsistence consumption the agent is, the more important is the role of subsistence consumption.

Subsequent analysis (Steger 2000) is based on the representative agent who maximizes its lifetime utility. Intertemporal consumption decision-making which considers subsistence consumption frequently starts with intertemporal Stone-Geary utility function, which is a generalization of the Cobb-Douglas utility function. The function was firstly developed by Klein and Rubin (1947–1948) and econometrically applied by Geary (1950) and Stone (1954).[2]

The subsistence level of consumption $\overline{c} > 0$ is the lower bound constant and consumption $c \geq \overline{c}$ represents well-being; hence we get twice continuously differentiable and strictly concave ($u'(c) > 0, u''(c) < 0$) instantaneous utility function:

$$U[\{c(t)\}] = \int_0^\infty \frac{\left(c(t) - \overline{c}\right)^{1-\theta}}{1-\theta} e^{-(\rho-n)t} dt, \tag{5.1}$$

where intertemporal preferences are given by the sum of the discounted instantaneous utility. Further, θ represents a preference parameter, ρ is the individual time

[2]Stone was the first who estimated the linear expenditure system.

preference and n is the growth rate of population. This intertemporal utility function is, above that, non-homothetic and implies that elasticity of consumption expenditures with respect to income is less than one. Another reason why to use intertemporal Stone-Geary utility function is that consumption is additively separable, so that we could transform an infinite horizon problem into a recursive two-period problem. The utility functional converges to a finite value when $\rho > n$. It can be also seen that if subsistence consumption is ignored (i.e. $\overline{c} = 0$), the utility function would correspond to the usual CIES function. However, this assumption may be neglected only when modelling economies with income well above their subsistence level. The difference between income and subsistence consumption is then big enough to make subsistence consumption theoretically irrelevant. If we consider only consumption above the level of subsistence consumption $(c - \overline{c})$, the instantaneous Stone-Geary utility function implies a constant elasticity of the marginal utility:

$$\eta(c - \overline{c}) \equiv -\frac{u''(c - \overline{c})(c - \overline{c})}{u'(c - \overline{c})} = \theta. \tag{5.2}$$

On the other hand, the elasticity of the marginal utility with respect to consumption reads:

$$\eta(c) \equiv -\frac{u''(c)c}{u'(c)} = \frac{\theta c}{c - \overline{c}} \tag{5.3}$$

The instantaneous Stone-Geary utility function implies a variable intertemporal elasticity of substitution (IES) for two immediate points in time:

$$\sigma(c) \equiv -\frac{u'(c)}{u''(c)c} = \frac{c - \overline{c}}{\theta c}. \tag{5.4}$$

From above we read that $\sigma(c) = 0 \Leftrightarrow c = \overline{c}$, which means that the economy cannot transfer consumption in time. This means that intertemporal considerations are in play only for the fraction of consumption $c \geq \overline{c}$. IES also increases with consumption and asymptotically converges to θ^{-1} as $c \to \infty$.

To start, let us assume a low-income economy with Stone-Geary preferences in an infinite time horizon. The dynamic problem of optimal control is concave with a bounded control set:

$$\max_{\{c(t)\}} \int_0^\infty \frac{(c(t) - \overline{c})^{1-\theta}}{1 - \theta} e^{-(\rho - n)t} \mathrm{d}t,$$

$$\text{s.t.}\quad \dot{k}(t) = Ak(t) - (\delta + n)k(t) - c(t),$$

$$k(0) = k_0, k(t) \geq 0,$$

$$\bar{c} \leq c(t) \leq Ak(t). \tag{5.5}$$

Gross output is a linear function of capital; $y = Ak$, where k is the stock of human and physical capital[3] and A is a constant technology parameter. Both θ and n are considered as constant. All variables are expressed in per capita terms and t represents the time index. The optimal solution is reached through the Lagrangian and current-value Hamiltonian:

$$\mathcal{L}(c, k, \lambda, v_1, v_2) = H(c, k, \lambda) + v_1[Ak - c] + v_2(c - \bar{c}). \tag{5.6}$$

$$\mathcal{H}(c, k, \lambda) = u(c - \bar{c}) + \lambda[Ak - (\delta + n)k - c], \tag{5.7}$$

where v_1, v_2 denote the dynamic Lagrangian multipliers. The Hamiltonian is concave and thus necessary conditions are also sufficient for a maximum. The application of the maximum principle leads to FOCs, while the optimal trajectory must satisfy the transversality condition: $\lim\limits_{t\to\infty} e^{-(\rho-n)t}\lambda(t)k(t) = 0$. Concretely, respecting Eq. (5.5) yields:

$$\frac{\partial \mathcal{L}}{\partial \lambda} = k(t) = Ak(t) - (\delta + n)k(t) - c(t). \tag{5.8}$$

$$\dot{\lambda} = \lambda(\rho - n) - \frac{\partial \mathcal{L}}{\partial k} = \lambda[\rho + \delta - A] - v_1 A, \tag{5.9}$$

$$\frac{\partial \mathcal{L}}{\partial c} = (c(t) - \bar{c})^{-\theta} - \lambda - v_1 + v_2 = 0, \tag{5.10}$$

$$v_1(Ak(t) - c(t)) = 0, v_1 \geq 0, \tag{5.11}$$

$$v_2(c(t) - \bar{c}) = 0, v_2 \geq 0. \tag{5.12}$$

To continue, we derive the *Keynes-Ramsey rule* of optimal consumption for a linear technology and Stone-Geary preferences:

$$\frac{\dot{c}(t)}{c(t)} = \frac{c(t) - \bar{c}}{\theta c(t)}(A - \rho - \delta). \tag{5.13}$$

[3]Operating with human and physical capital under one broad definition of capital stock can be seen already in Rebelo (1991). This definition of capital will be useful in the last chapter of this book.

Combining the *Keynes-Ramsey rule* (Eq. 5.13) with the instantaneous Stone-Geary utility function (Eq. 5.5) we get the linear system of differential equations that governs the dynamics of the economy. Considering FOCs for (Eq. 5.5), for consumption (control variable) we have:

$$\dot{c} = c(t)\theta^{-1}(A - \rho - \delta) - \overline{c}\theta^{-1}(A - \rho - \delta), \tag{5.14}$$

and for capital (state variable) we already have:

$$\dot{k}(t) = Ak(t) - (\delta + n)k(t) - c(t), \tag{5.15}$$

The solution for the control variable is:

$$c(t) = \overline{c} + \exp\left[\theta^{-1}(A - \rho - \delta)t\right]b, \tag{5.16}$$

where b is a constant of integration with respect to transversality condition. From the first-order differential equation in k we read:

$$\dot{k}(t) = (A - \rho - \delta)k - \overline{c} + \exp\left[\theta^{-1}(A - \rho - \delta)t\right]b. \tag{5.17}$$

The homogenous part is then solved as:

$$k(t) = k(0)e^{(A-\rho-\delta)t} \tag{5.18}$$

and the solution to the non-homogenous part $\left(\widetilde{k}(t)\right)$ reads:

$$\widetilde{k}(t) = -e^{(A-\rho-n)t}\int\left[\overline{c} + be^{\theta-1(A-\rho-\delta)t}\right]e^{-(A-\rho-n)t}dt. \tag{5.19}$$

The integration finally gives:

$$\widetilde{k}(t) = \frac{\overline{c}}{A-\rho-n} - \frac{b}{\theta^{-1}(A-\rho-\delta) - A + \rho + n}e^{\theta-1(A-\rho-\delta)} - a_0e^{(A-\rho-n)t} \tag{5.20}$$

where a_1, a_2 are arbitrary constants for which applies $a_0 = a_1 + a_2$; for more details on the analysis see Gandolfo (2010, 163–184). By following superposition principle for linear systems, the solution to the first-order differential equation in k is:

$$k(t) = (k(0) - a_0)e^{(A-\rho-\delta)t}$$
$$+\frac{\overline{c}}{A-\rho-n} - \frac{b}{\theta^{-1}(A-\rho-\delta) - A + \rho + n} e^{\theta-1(A-\rho-\delta)t}. \quad (5.21)$$

The general transversality condition is altered according to Barro and Sala-i-Martín (1995) into the form:

$$\lim_{t\to\infty}\left[k(t)e^{-(A-n-\delta)t}\right] = 0. \quad (5.22)$$

Plugging the solution to the first-order differential equation in k into the transversality condition yields:

$$\lim_{t\to\infty}\left\{(k(0) - a_0) + e^{-(A-n-\delta)t}\frac{\overline{c}}{A-\delta-n}\right.$$
$$\left.+\frac{b}{A-\delta-n-\theta^{-1}(A-\rho-\delta)}e^{-[(A-\delta-n)-\theta^{-1}(A-\rho-\delta)]t}\right\} = 0. \quad (5.23)$$

The infinite horizon utility naturally requires: $A-\delta-n-\theta^{-1}(A-\rho-\delta) > 0$ In the first step, the transversality condition requires $k(0) - a_0 = 0$ Further, if $A - \delta - n > 0$ then the second term of the equation in the infinite horizon asymptotically vanishes, as well as the third one, which follows the growth path given by $A-\rho-\delta > 0$. The optimal solution is then:

$$c(t) = \overline{c} + be^{\theta-1(A-\rho-\delta)t} \quad (5.24)$$

$$k(t) = \frac{\overline{c}}{A-\delta-n} + \frac{b}{A-\delta-n-\theta^{-1}(A-\rho-\delta)}e^{\theta-(A-\rho-\delta)t}. \quad (5.25)$$

Since the initial value of capital is predetermined (Eq. 5.5), the corresponding value of the consumption can be gained through the policy function which allows the formulation of the stable arm of the saddle-path. Combining Eqs. (5.24) and (5.25) yields policy function in the form:

$$c(t) = \overline{c} + z\left[k(t) - \overline{k}\right] \quad (5.26)$$

where

$$z \equiv A - \delta - n - \theta^{-1}(A-\rho-\delta) > 0,$$

which demonstrates the optimal choice of the control variable (c) as a function of the state variable (k). Further, putting Eqs. (5.24) and (5.26) yields:

$$b = (c(t) - \overline{c})e^{\theta - 1(A-\rho-\delta)t} = z(k(t) - \overline{k})e^{\theta - 1(A-\rho-\delta)t}. \quad (5.27)$$

This implies that there is a unique optimal choice of consumption for each value of capital which satisfies FOCs. Respecting Eqs. (5.24) and (5.25), the asymptotic growth rate of consumption and capital follows:

$$\lim_{t\to\infty}\frac{\dot{c}}{c} = \lim_{t\to\infty}\frac{\dot{k}}{k} = \theta^{-1}(A - \rho - \delta), \quad (5.28)$$

which secures that the optimal trajectory asymptotically approaches the balanced growth path. The transversality condition is satisfied and the final solution of the differential equation system is:

$$c(t) = \overline{c} + [c(0) - \overline{c}]e^{\theta - 1(A-\rho-\delta)t}, \quad (5.29)$$

$$k(t) = \overline{k} + [k(0) - \overline{k}]e^{\theta - 1(A-\rho-\delta)t}, \quad (5.30)$$

where

$$\overline{k} \equiv \frac{\overline{c}}{A - \delta - n}$$

and

$$A - \delta - n > 0.$$

The provided solution also tells that there are three possible dynamic equilibria. The first one relates to the subsistence level of both consumption and capital. If consumption and capital correspond to their subsistence levels, the net saving rate $s = 0$ and income just suffices to cover necessary consumption($\overline{c}$) and reduction of capital due to depreciation (δk) and population growth (nk). Hence, we have $\dot{c} = 0, c = \overline{c}$ In this case, economic agents are not *willing to* (Steger 2000) postpone consumption since the net marginal product of capital is lower than the time preference rate. The long-run solution of the steady state corresponds to subsistence described by Eq. (5.5).

The second equilibrium corresponds to the situation in which the marginal product of capital equals the time preference rate. The economy then operates with zero growth and with capital and consumption slightly above subsistence. In this situation, we have $\dot{c} = 0, c > \overline{c}$.

Thirdly, an asymptotic balanced-growth equilibrium is considered. It corresponds to a situation of unbounded growth $c \to \infty$ which presumes that the net marginal product of capital exceeds the time preference rate. The growth rates of consumption and capital then converge to values given by Eq. (5.28).

In order to provide a comprehensive interpretation for all mentioned dynamic equilibria, the policy function can be stated in the form:

$$c = (A - \delta - n)k - \theta^{-1}(A - \rho - \delta)(k - \overline{k}). \tag{5.31}$$

It clearly shows that whenever $k = \overline{k}$ or the net marginal product of capital equals the time preference rate, consumption is chosen at the level when the capital is constant, $\dot{k} = (A - \delta - n)k - c = 0$.

5.1.1 *Transitional Dynamics*

The following part focuses on the saving rate in the context of subsistence. Based on the policy function, the net saving rate is given by the relation between net investment and net income:

$$s = \frac{A - \rho - \delta}{(A - \delta - n)\theta} \frac{k - \overline{k}}{k}. \tag{5.32}$$

It reads that zero net saving rate corresponds to a constant stock of capital which equals its subsistence level. The net saving rate is positive as far as $A - \rho - \delta > 0$ and initial level of capital stock $k(0)$ is greater than its subsistence level k. In that case, the saving rate monotonically converges to its dynamic equilibrium:

$$s^* = \frac{A - \rho - \delta}{(A - \delta - n)\theta}. \tag{5.33}$$

Conversely, the net saving rate is negative whenever $A - \rho - \delta < 0$ and coverges to its dynamic equilibrium $s^* = 0$; the condition $k(0) > \overline{k}$ applies.

Equation (5.33) allows to connect the model with the analysis in the previous part. The *ability* to save, which can be defined as the difference between the current income and the subsistence level of consumption/income, corresponds to unconsumed resources that can be saved and invested; simply put resources usable in competition struggle. This ability is given by $\left(k - \overline{k}\right)/k$, while

$$\lim_{k \to \overline{k}} \frac{k - \overline{k}}{k} = 0, \tag{5.34}$$

$$\lim_{k \to \infty} \frac{k - \overline{k}}{k} = 1. \tag{5.35}$$

The *willingness* to save is then given by the remaining part of the saving rate; $(A - \rho - \delta)/(A - \delta - n)\theta$. It is then clear that high-income economies have relatively lower requirements on subsistence consumption, while low-income economies have, conversely, relatively higher requirements on subsistence consumption. If we divide the influence on the saving rate, the initial ability to save defines the initial level of the saving rate and the subsequent path, while the willingness to save is behind the asymptotic value of the saving rate. Another fact is that the growth rate of income varies positively with the distance between the current and the balanced-growth-equilibrium state of the economy. Put it differently, an increasing saving rate generates more investment which consequently causes increasing growth rate of capital which equals the growth rate of income.

Evidently, the relation between the initial stock of capital and its subsistence level plays the crucial role. The linear model naturally displays a constant marginal and average product of capital and hence the investment rate fully translates into the growth rate of income. The non-converging tendency thus comes from the conclusion that the growth rate of income is rising with the level of income on a unique balanced-growth path.

Based on usual calibration of parameter values,[4] low-income economies with relatively high subsistence level are necessarily burdened with enormously low-speed convergence. Using Stone-Geary utility function with subsistence consumption determines declining elasticity of marginal utility in the level of consumption. It followingly causes that savings rates and economic growth rates are jointly rising with economic development, which is given by the share of subsistence consumption on total resources. This fact corresponds to the empirical literature showing that saving rates—the decisive factor of growth—increases with income on both micro (Dynan et al. 2004) and macro (Loayza et al. 2000) levels, which contributes to an explanation of persisting inequalities.

5.1.2 Does the Level of Subsistence Matter?

The aim of this part is to show that the evolution of saving rates and growth rates is independent of the size of subsistence needs which implies systematic impact of the whole issue of subsistence. This is important in order to expose economic inequality exclusively in the light of market mechanism and its fundamental *principles*, not by particular setups of parameters that allow manipulation. This is especially important if we consider that the level of subsistence consumption permits a fair degree of freedom.

Then, we again reconsider (and slightly simplify) the linear AK growth model with subsistence consumption. In line with Strulik (2010), we define a representative agent with instantaneous Stone-Geary utility:

[4] $A = 0.1,\ \theta = 3,\ \rho = 0.01,\ \delta = 0.02,\ n = 0.03,\ \bar{c} = 2$, for more details see Steger (2000).

$$\max_{\{c\}} \int_0^\infty \frac{(c-\overline{c})^{1-\theta}}{1-\theta} e^{-\rho t} dt, \tag{5.36}$$

$$\text{s.t.} \qquad \dot{k} = Ak - c, \qquad \text{where } A > \rho.$$

The parameter $\overline{c}$ again denotes subsistence consumption, c is consumption, ρ is time preference, and θ is the ultimate elasticity of marginal utility when $c \to \infty$, which decreases as the distance between c and $\overline{c}$ gets larger. Thus, the greater the distance is, the less urgent subsistence consumption is and the lower is the effective rate of time preference. Such process inevitably leads to increasing share of savings with increasing income. For simplicity we assume a linear production function with standard productivity parameter A which is greater than time preference rate in order to allow for positive balanced growth.

The FOCs of the stated problem are computed as in the previous example; concretely we get the following conditions:

$$(c-\overline{c})^{1-\theta} \tag{5.37}$$

$$\lambda A = \lambda \rho - \lambda \tag{5.38}$$

with λ as the costate variable of the associated current-value Hamiltonian. This costate variable is eliminated through log-differentiating Eq. (5.37) with respect to time and plugging into Eq. (5.38), which gives:

$$(A-\rho)(c-\overline{c}) = \theta\dot{c} \qquad \text{where} \qquad \dot{c} = c'(k)\dot{k}. \tag{5.39}$$

Considering the linear production function, we get:

$$(A-\rho)(c-\overline{c}) = \theta c'(k)(Ak-c). \tag{5.40}$$

Strulik (2010) solves this non-homogeneous differential equation using the method of undetermined coefficients:

$$c = \frac{(A-\rho)\overline{c}}{\theta A} + \left[\frac{A(\theta-1)}{\theta} + \frac{\rho}{\theta}\right] k, \tag{5.41}$$

where the second term on the right side refers to constant shares of optimal consumption on income. However, the first term on the right side changes this interpretation in the already familiar sense that increasing income pushes consumption upward, but the share of consumption on income decreases which results in increasing saving rate.

In order to analyse dynamics of the economy, we introduce the consumption-capital ratio $x = c/k$, which evolves according to

$$\dot{x} = \frac{(\dot{c}k + c\dot{k})}{k^2} = \dot{k}\frac{(c'(k) - x)}{k}. \tag{5.42}$$

In combination with $c'(k)$ derived from Eq. (5.41) and with $\dot{k}$ from Eq. (5.36), it yields the economy described by the following differential equation:

$$\dot{x} = (A - x)\left[\frac{A(\theta - 1)}{\theta} + \frac{\rho}{\theta} - x\right]. \tag{5.43}$$

Based on Eq. (5.43), we are allowed to formulate partial results: There exists a unique steady state of stagnation at $A = x$. Additionally, there exists a unique balanced growth path along which the economy grows at rate $(A - \rho)/\theta$, while:

$$x \equiv x^* = \frac{A(\theta - 1)}{\theta} + \frac{\rho}{\theta}, \tag{5.44}$$

which implies that the balanced growth path is locally stable, in contrast with the unstable steady state of stagnation.[5]

From Eq. (5.43) we can already see that the *level* of subsistence consumption does not play a role. For completeness, once we obtain the path of $x(t)$, it is easy to derive the path of income growth per capita:

$$g_y(t) = A - x(t), \tag{5.45}$$

and the path of the savings rate:

$$s(t) = 1 - \frac{c(t)}{y(t)} = 1 - \frac{x(t)}{A}, \tag{5.46}$$

where y refers to income. Further, consumption grows along the balanced growth path at rate $g_c{}^* = A - x^* \Rightarrow x^* = A - g_c$, and similarly for the savings rate $s^* = 1 - x^*/A \Rightarrow A = g_c{}^*/s^*$. In combination with Eq. (5.44), the system dynamics (Eq. 5.43) is rewritten as:

$$\dot{x} = \left(\frac{g_c{}^*}{s^*} - x\right)\left[g_c{}^*\left(\frac{1}{s^*} - 1\right) - x\right]. \tag{5.47}$$

The consumption-capital ratio is therefore determined by the growth rate and the savings rate along the balanced growth path. When we define the path of the ratio (x

---

[5]For the proof see Strulik (2010:766).

(t)), the paths of savings and growth will be $s(t) = 1 - x(t)/A$ and $g_\nu(t) = A - x$ respectively. It follows that the dynamics of the system is independent not only on subsistence consumption, but it allows us to leave time preference ρ and elasticity of marginal utility θ unspecified as well, which neutralizes particularity of individual settings and supports generality of the theoretical outcome.

It should be also noted that any change of subsistence consumption immanently includes a change of the capital stock. Referring to the steady state of stagnation, from $x = A$ we have $k = \overline{c}/A$ and hence the dynamics with respect to the reference point $(\overline{c}, \overline{c}/A)$ remains unaffected. For this purpose, Strulik (2010) undertakes the transformation of variables $\widetilde{c} = c - \overline{c}, \widetilde{k} = k - \overline{c}/A$. The former problem is then transformed into:

$$\max_{\{c\}} \int_0^\infty \frac{\widetilde{c}^{1-\theta}}{1-\theta} e^{-\rho t} \mathrm{d}t,$$

$$\text{s.t.} \qquad \dot{\widetilde{k}} = A\widetilde{k} - \widetilde{c}. \tag{5.48}$$

Corresponding policy function $\widetilde{c}\left(\widetilde{k}\right)$ is derived from the FOCs to this altered problem through the Euler equation:

$$\frac{\dot{\widetilde{c}}}{\widetilde{c}} = \frac{A-\rho}{\theta} \Rightarrow \widetilde{c}\left(\widetilde{k}\right) = \left[\frac{A(\theta-1)}{\theta} + \frac{\rho}{\theta}\right]\widetilde{k}. \tag{5.49}$$

It is now obvious that the choice of $\overline{c}$ must influence absolute levels of consumption and income. However, we can also clearly see that the policy function, and as a consequence the consumption-capital ratio, the saving rate and the growth rate, are independent from the level of $\overline{c}$. The augmented AK model therefore provides the immensely important conclusion that economic rates evolve irrespective of the country- or individual-specific subsistence level. This modification shows that incorporating subsistence consumption can still produce general theoretical conclusions.

5.2 Portfolio Choice with Time-(In)variant Subsistence and Heterogeneous Agents

Now it is evident that incorporating subsistence consumption brings the issue of income, consumption and savings into a new light. The following subchapter focuses on explaining selected stylized facts which are empirically relevant and important in the current trends of economic distribution. Namely, we are going to uncover the intuitively positive relationship between lifetime income and saving rates (e.g. Dynan et al. 2004). Further, we are curious about mechanisms that are behind lower fraction of risky assets in poor stockholding households (e.g. Wachter and Yogo 2010), as well as why rich stockholders have more volatile consumption than the rest (e.g. Malloy et al. 2009). Examining these questions will deepen our insight into agent-based perspective on the main variables that form the current trends in inequality—income (wealth), savings and consumption.

To hit these research questions, we use the model of Achury et al. (2012) that is based on a typical two-asset model (Merton 1969, 1971). From now, we also assume a certain level of inequality; i.e. that economic agents will be divided into two groups—'poor' and 'rich'.

5.2.1 Time-Invariant Subsistence

Firstly, we have a typical Stone-Geary utility function with time-invariant subsistence:

$$u(c(t)) = \frac{(c(t) - \chi)^{1-\frac{1}{\eta}} - 1}{1 - \frac{1}{\eta}}, \tag{5.50}$$

where

$$\chi, \eta > 0.$$

The agent is placed in continuous time $t \in [0, \infty)$, with initial wealth holdings $k_0 > 0$ and a fraction of agent's wealth allocated in the risky asset ϕ, while the rest of agent's wealth is allocated in the risk-free asset. The aim of the following part is to inspect decision rules and dynamics of agent's wealth.

The agent follows the consumption path $(c(t))_{t \geq 0}$ and the path of portfolio composition $(\phi(t))_{t \geq 0}$ that maximize agent's expected utility:

$$E_0 \left[\int_0^{\infty} \frac{(c(t) - \chi)^{1-\frac{1}{\eta}} - 1}{1 - \frac{1}{\eta}} e^{-\rho t} dt \right], \tag{5.51}$$

$$\text{s.t.} \quad dk(t) = \left\{ \left[\phi(t)R + (1 - \phi(t))r^f \right] k(t) - c(t) \right\} dt + \sigma \phi(t) k(t) dz(t),$$

where $\rho, \chi, \eta > 0$.

Except already introduced variables, this budget constraint is defined by the mean rate of return of the risky asset (R), the risk-free rate (r^f) and a Brownian motion defined by $dz(t) = \varepsilon(t)\sqrt{dt}$, where $\varepsilon(t) \sim N(0, 1)$.

The Hamilton-Jacobi-Bellman equation (HJB) is:

$$\rho J(K) = \max_{\{c \geq 0, \phi\}} \left\{ \frac{(c-\chi)^{1-\frac{1}{\eta}} - 1}{1 - \dfrac{1}{\eta}} + J'(K)\{[\phi R + (1-\phi) r^f]k - c\} + \frac{(\sigma \phi k)^2}{2} J''(K) \right\} \tag{5.52}$$

and FOCs are then:

$$J'(k) = (c - \chi)^{-\frac{1}{\eta}}, \tag{5.53}$$

$$\phi = \frac{J'(k)}{-J''(k)k} \frac{R - r^f}{\sigma^2}. \tag{5.54}$$

In order to secure interior solutions, we have to adopt two assumptions. Firstly, initial conditions are subjected to:

$$k_0 > \frac{\chi}{r^f}, \tag{5.55}$$

which secures that all agents have well-defined problems and the interior solution exists. Further, parameter η must be strictly below the strictly positive value $\overline{\eta}$. Hence, the second assumption states:

$$0 < \eta < \overline{\eta} \equiv \frac{1 - \dfrac{r^f - \rho}{\dfrac{1}{2}\left(\dfrac{R - r^f}{\sigma}\right)^2} + \left\{ \left[\dfrac{r^f - \rho}{\frac{1}{2}\left(\frac{R-r^f}{\sigma}\right)^2} \right]^2 + 2\dfrac{r^f - \rho}{\frac{1}{2}\left(\frac{R-r^f}{\sigma}\right)^2} + 1 \right\}^{\frac{1}{2}}}{2} \tag{5.56}$$

from which we confirm that for σ, ρ, R, $r^f > 0$ we have $\overline{\eta} > 0$. The solution of the HJB equation under the given assumptions we get through a guess on the functional form of the value function:

$$J(k) = a + b\frac{(k - \omega)^{1-\frac{1}{\eta}}}{1 - \frac{1}{\eta}}, \tag{5.57}$$

which gives:

$$J'(k) = b(k - \omega)^{-\frac{1}{\eta}} \tag{5.58}$$

and

$$J''(k) = -\frac{1}{\eta} b(k - \omega)^{-\frac{1}{\eta}-1}. \tag{5.59}$$

Putting Eq. (5.58) together with Eq. (5.53), we get:

$$c = b^{-\eta}k + \chi - b^{-\eta}\omega \tag{5.60}$$

and substituting Eqs. (5.58) and (5.59) into Eq. (5.54) gives:

$$\phi = \eta \frac{R - r^f}{\sigma^2}\left(1 - \frac{\omega}{k}\right). \tag{5.61}$$

Further, substituting Eqs. (5.57)–(5.61) into the HJB (Eq. 5.52) yields:

$$\begin{aligned} \rho a + \rho b \frac{(k-\omega)^{1-\frac{1}{\eta}}}{1 - \dfrac{1}{\eta}} &= \frac{b^{1-\eta}(k-\omega)^{1-\frac{1}{\eta}}}{1 - \dfrac{1}{\eta}} - \frac{1}{1 - \dfrac{1}{\eta}} + \\ +b(k-\omega)^{-\frac{1}{\eta}} &\left[\eta\left(\frac{R - r^f}{\sigma}\right)^2 \left(1 - \frac{\omega}{k}\right)k + r^f k - b^{-\eta}k - \chi + b^{-\eta}\omega\right] - \\ &- \frac{1}{2\eta}\left(\eta \frac{R - r^f}{\sigma}\right)^2 b(k-\omega)^{1-\frac{1}{\eta}}. \end{aligned} \tag{5.62}$$

When dividing Eq. (5.62) by $b(k - \omega)^{1-\frac{1}{\eta}}$ and putting $a = 1/\left(\rho \frac{\rho}{n}\right)$, we get:

$$\left[\frac{\rho - b^{-\eta}}{1 - \dfrac{1}{\eta}} - \frac{\eta}{2}\left(\frac{R - r^f}{\sigma}\right)^2\right]k - \left[\frac{\rho - b^{-\eta}}{1 - \dfrac{1}{\eta}} - \frac{\eta}{2}\left(\frac{R - r^f}{\sigma}\right)^2\right]\omega = (r^f - b^{-\eta})k + b^{-\eta}\omega - \chi. \tag{5.63}$$

Now, we must find b and ω such that k and the constant terms in Eq. (5.63) are equal zero. Hence:

$$\frac{\rho - b^{-\eta}}{1 - \frac{1}{\eta}} - \frac{\eta}{2}\left(\frac{R - r^f}{\sigma}\right)^2 = r^f - b^{-\eta}, \tag{5.64}$$

and expressing $b^{-\eta}$ produces:

$$b^{-\eta} = \rho\eta + (1-\eta)r^f - \frac{\eta(\eta-1)}{2}\left(\frac{R-r^f}{\sigma}\right)^2. \tag{5.65}$$

If $k = 0$ (as required), we get:

$$\left[\frac{\rho - b^{-\eta}}{1-\frac{1}{\eta}} - \frac{\eta}{2}\left(\frac{R-r^f}{\sigma}\right)^2\right]\omega = -b^{-\eta}\omega + \chi,$$

which in combination with Eq. (5.64) yields:

$$\left(r^f - b^{-\eta}\right)\omega = -b^{-\eta}\omega + \chi, \tag{5.66}$$

and thus

$$\omega = \frac{\chi}{r^f}. \tag{5.67}$$

Plugging Eq. (5.67) into Eq. (5.60) then gives the decision rule for consumption:

$$c = b^{-\eta}k + \chi\left(1 - \frac{b^{-\eta}}{r^f}\right) \tag{5.68}$$

and after substituting Eq. (5.65) it is:

$$c = \left[\rho\eta + (1+\eta)r^f - \frac{\eta(\eta-1)}{2}\left(\frac{R-r^f}{\sigma}\right)^2\right]k + \chi\eta\frac{r^f - \rho + \frac{\eta-1}{2}\left(\frac{R-r^f}{\sigma}\right)^2}{r^f}. \tag{5.69}$$

Setting

$$\xi = \rho\eta + (1-\eta)r^f - \frac{\eta(\eta-1)}{2}\left(\frac{R-r^f}{\sigma}\right)^2, \tag{5.70}$$

and

$$\psi = \chi\eta\frac{r^f - \rho + \frac{\eta-1}{2}\left(\frac{R-r^f}{\sigma}\right)^2}{r^f}, \tag{5.71}$$

the final form of the decision rule for consumption is:

$$c^* = C(k) = \xi k + \psi. \tag{5.72}$$

Further, it is needed to verify whether the second assumption does not collide with our requirement on $\xi > 0$. From Eq. (5.69) it implies:

$$\eta^2 - \left[1 - \frac{r^f - \rho}{\frac{1}{2}\left(\frac{R-r^f}{\sigma}\right)^2}\right]\eta - \frac{r^f - \rho}{\frac{1}{2}\left(\frac{R-r^f}{\sigma}\right)^2} < 0 \tag{5.73}$$

and the discriminant with respect to η is:

$$\left[\frac{r^f - \rho}{\frac{1}{2}\left(\frac{R-r^f}{\sigma}\right)^2}\right] + 2\frac{r^f - \rho}{\frac{1}{2}\left(\frac{R-r^f}{\sigma}\right)^2} + 1 > 0 \tag{5.74}$$

with two real roots with opposite signs different from zero. Since $0 < \eta < \overline{\eta}$ and with respect to η given by Eq. (5.73), the positive root of the quadratic polynomial is represented by $\overline{\eta}$.

The decision rule for portfolio choice is then:

$$\phi^* = \Phi(k) = \eta\frac{R - r^f}{\sigma^2}\left(1 - \frac{\frac{\chi}{r^f}}{k}\right), \tag{5.75}$$

and it determines that the portfolio share of risky assets is strictly positive in increasing wealth. Finally, the value function is given by:

$$J(k) = -\frac{1}{\rho - \frac{\rho}{\eta}} + \xi^{-\frac{1}{\eta}}\frac{\left(k - \frac{\chi}{r^f}\right)^{1-\frac{1}{\eta}}}{1 - \frac{1}{\eta}}. \tag{5.76}$$

Secondly, we concern the dynamics of the agent's wealth. It must be secured that discretionary lifetime resources $k - \chi/r^f$ are strictly positive in equilibrium; i.e.:

$$k^*(t) > \frac{\chi}{r^f}, \forall t \geq 0. \tag{5.77}$$

Substituting the decision rule for consumption ($C(k)$) and the portfolio choice ($\Phi(k)$) into the budget constraint (Eq. 5.51) yields:

$$dk = \eta\left[\frac{\eta + 1}{2}\left(\frac{R - r^f}{\sigma}\right)^2 + r^f - \rho\right]\left(k - \frac{\chi}{r^f}\right)dt + \eta\left(\frac{R - r^f}{\sigma}\right)\left(k - \frac{\chi}{r^f}\right)dz, \tag{5.78}$$

and applying Itô's lemma gives:

$$d\ln\left(k - \frac{\chi}{r^f}\right) = \eta\left[\frac{1}{2}\left(\frac{R - r^f}{\sigma}\right)^2 + r^f - \rho\right]dt + \eta\left(\frac{R - r^f}{\sigma}\right)dz. \tag{5.79}$$

If we apply Itô's stochastic integral (where $z(0) = 0$ and $z(t) = \int_0^t dz(s)$) on Eq. (5.79), we get the dynamics of wealth:

$$k^*(t) - \frac{\chi}{r^f} = \exp\left\{\eta\left[r^f - \rho + \frac{1}{2}\left(\frac{R - r^f}{\sigma}\right)^2\right]t + \eta\left(\frac{R - r^f}{\sigma}\right)z(t)\right\}\left(k_0 - \frac{\chi}{r^f}\right) \tag{5.80}$$

which respects both formulated assumptions.

In order to define the evolution of the saving rate, we substitute the decision rule for consumption and for portfolio choice into the budget constraint, which yields the equilibrium savings at time t in the form:

$$S^*(t) = \varsigma\left(k^*(t) - \frac{\chi}{r^f}\right) \tag{5.81}$$

where

$$\varsigma = \eta\left[\frac{\eta + 1}{2}\left(\frac{R - r^f}{\sigma}\right)^2 + r^f - \rho\right]. \tag{5.82}$$

The corresponding saving rate is:

$$s^*(t) = \frac{S^*(t)}{\phi^*(t)(R - r^f)k^*(t) + r^f k^*(t)} \tag{5.83}$$

and after substituting $\Phi(k)$ from the decision rule for portfolio choice we get:

$$s^*(t) = \frac{\varsigma}{\eta\left(\frac{R - r^f}{\sigma}\right)^2 + \frac{r^f}{1 - \frac{\chi}{k^*(t)}}} \tag{5.84}$$

implying that

$$\frac{ds^*(t)}{dk^*(t)} > 0 \Leftrightarrow \varsigma > 0 \Leftrightarrow \eta > \underline{\eta} \equiv -1 - \frac{r^f - \rho}{\frac{1}{2}\left(\frac{R - r^f}{\sigma}\right)^2}. \tag{5.85}$$

If the right-hand inequality does not hold, i.e. $\eta \leq \underline{\eta}$, then savings must be negative since $\varsigma < 0$. All this means that under adopted assumptions, the saving rate will be increasing with wealth iff the above applies, which further satisfies necessary and sufficient conditions for the outlined evolution of the saving rate. Complementarily, from Eq. (5.80) we can easily derive that the household's wealth grows at a strictly positive rate iff:

$$\frac{\eta+1}{2}\left(\frac{R-r^f}{\sigma}\right)^2+r^f-\rho>0. \tag{5.86}$$

The economic interpretation of this problem says that the household strives to mitigate the pressure of subsistence needs while a growing trajectory of the household's expected wealth depends on strictly increasing saving rate. Naturally, it is harder for poorer households to generate higher saving rates since consuming lower fraction of their wealth is restricted by the level of subsistence needs that must be met. Intertemporal decisions of the poorer households are therefore generally burdened with lower possibility to reach higher saving rates and hence to follow the trajectory of increasing wealth.

Under such circumstances and if wealth of all agents goes up, wealth inequality among agents increases over time as well. Considering the dynamics of wealth (Eq. 5.80) and two agents with unequal level of wealth, i.e. a rich agent is wealthier than a poor one ($k_{r,0}>k_{p,0}$), we get:

$$\frac{k_r^*(t)-\frac{\chi}{r^f}}{k_p^*(t)-\frac{\chi}{r^f}}=\frac{k_{r,0}-\frac{\chi}{r^f}}{k_{p,0}-\frac{\chi}{r^f}}. \tag{5.87}$$

Rearranging the term leads to:

$$\frac{k_r^*(t)}{k_p^*(t)}=\frac{k_{r,0}-\frac{\chi}{r^f}}{k_{p,0}-\frac{\chi}{r^f}}-\frac{\chi}{r^f}\frac{k_{r,0}-k_{p,0}}{k_{p,0}-\frac{\chi}{r^f}}\frac{1}{k_p^*(t)} \tag{5.88}$$

which implies that increasing wealth of the poor agent over time is accompanied by increasing relative wealth inequality. As regards the technical side of the problem, the model is incompatible with any steady-state stationary distribution of relative wealth. However, as will be also shown in the following chapters, it does not disqualify the model from our general conclusions.

Additionally, the decision rule for consumption (Eq. 5.72) combined with the dynamics of wealth (Eq. 5.80) gives:

$$E[C(k^*(t))]=\xi E[v(t)]\left(k_0-\frac{\chi}{r^f}\right)+\xi\frac{\chi}{r^f}+\psi \tag{5.89}$$

where

$$v(t) \equiv \exp\left\{\eta\left[r^f - \rho + \frac{1}{2}\left(\frac{R - r^f}{\sigma}\right)^2\right]t + \eta\left(\frac{R - r^f}{\sigma}\right)z(t)\right\}. \quad (5.90)$$

From the decision rule for consumption we also know that:

$$\psi = \chi\left(1 - \frac{\xi}{r^f}\right), \quad (5.91)$$

which together implies:

$$E[C(k^*(t))] = \xi E[v(t)]\left(k_0 - \frac{\chi}{r^f}\right) + \chi. \quad (5.92)$$

The coefficient of variation[6] (or relative standard deviation) is:

$$CV_{C(k^*(t))} = \frac{\xi\{\mathrm{Var}[v(t)]\}^{\frac{1}{2}}}{\xi E[v(t)] + \frac{\chi}{k_0 - \frac{\chi}{r^f}}} \quad (5.93)$$

where

$$\{\mathrm{Var}[v(t)]\}^{\frac{1}{2}}; E[v(t)] > 0, \quad (5.94)$$

which implies that

$$\frac{dCV_{C(k^*(t))}}{dk_0} > 0. \quad (5.95)$$

Now, by substituting the decision rules for consumption and for portfolio choice into the budget constraint we gain the volatility of consumption growth through:

$$dk = \theta\left(k - \frac{\chi}{r^f}\right)dt + \eta\left(\frac{R - r^f}{\sigma}\right)\left(k - \frac{\chi}{r^f}\right)dz, \quad (5.96)$$

where

$$\eta\left[\frac{\eta + 1}{1}\left(\frac{R - r^f}{\sigma}\right)^2 + r^f - \rho\right] = \theta. \quad (5.97)$$

[6] As was explained in the opening chapter, the coefficient of variation can be also used directly as a measure of economic inequality.

In order to discover the relationship between the coefficient of variation of consumption and initial wealth, as well as the relationship between the variance of the growth rate of consumption and current wealth, we have:

$$C(k^*(t)) = \xi k^*(t) + \psi = \xi\left(k^*(t) - \frac{\chi}{r^f}\right) + \chi \tag{5.98}$$

and applying Itô's lemma again yields:

$$\begin{aligned} d\ln\left(C(k^*)\right) = & \left\{\xi\theta\frac{\widehat{k}^*}{\xi\widehat{k}^* + \chi} - \frac{1}{2}\left[\xi\eta\left(\frac{R - r^f}{\sigma}\right)\right]^2\left(\frac{\widehat{k}^*}{\xi\widehat{k}^* + \chi}\right)^2\right\}dt \\ & + \xi\eta\left(\frac{R - r^f}{\sigma}\right)\frac{\widehat{k}^*}{\xi\widehat{k}^* + \chi}dz \end{aligned}, \tag{5.98}$$

where

$$\widehat{k}^* = k^* - \frac{\chi}{r^f}. \tag{5.100}$$

This implies that the growth rate of consumption is increasing in current wealth since:

$$\mathrm{Var}(d\ln(C(k^*))) = \left[\xi\eta\left(\frac{R - r^f}{\sigma}\right)\right]^2\left(\frac{\widehat{k}^*}{\xi\widehat{k}^* + \chi}\right)^2 dt \tag{5.101}$$

is an increasing function of k^*. Based on this, we can conclude that the coefficient of variation of consumption is strictly increasing with initial wealth and it is expected that the rich have more volatile consumption than is the case of the poor.

5.2.2 Time-Variant Subsistence

In order to analyse the problem with time-variant subsistence consumption, the Stone-Geary function takes the form:

$$u\left(c(t), \overline{C}(t)\right) = \frac{\left(c(t) - \gamma\overline{C}(t)\right)^{1-\frac{1}{\eta}} - 1}{1 - \frac{1}{\eta}}, \tag{5.102}$$

where $\gamma \in (0, 1)$ and $\overline{C}$ denotes average consumption corresponding to the average initial wealth $\overline{K}_0$ on a given territory. The expected utility function then follows:

$$E_0\left[\int_0^\infty \frac{\left(c(t)-\gamma\overline{C}(t)\right)^{1-\frac{1}{\eta}}}{1-\frac{1}{\eta}}e^{-\rho t}\mathrm{d}t\right]. \tag{5.103}$$

Similarly, the utility function follows the idea that consumption of a particular agent is influenced by consumption standards of the rest of agents. In order to secure interior solutions, γ is restricted such that all agents have consumption $c(t) > \gamma\overline{C}(t)$. Agents face the similar budget constraint:

$$dk(t) = \{[\phi(t)R + (1-\phi(t))r^f]k(t) - c(t)\}dt + \sigma\phi(t)k(t)dz(t), \tag{5.104}$$

where the difference is that the value function is of the form $J(k,\overline{K})$ since it does not depend only on agent's current level of wealth $k(t)$, but also on $\overline{K}$. This means that the agent with k must also take into consideration the dynamics of the average agent's constraint (with wealth holdings $\overline{K}$), although the agent with k does not control $\overline{C}(t)$ or $\overline{K}(t)$. The constraint is then:

$$d\overline{K}(t) = \{[\overline{\Phi}(t)R + (1-\overline{\Phi}(t))r^f]\overline{K}(t) - \overline{C}(t)\}dt + \sigma\overline{\Phi}(t)\overline{K}(t)dz(t) \tag{5.105}$$

and after putting together with the HJB equation of households with holdings k, we get:

$$\begin{aligned}\rho J(k,\overline{K}) = \max_{\{c\geq 0,\,\phi\}} \Bigg\{ & \frac{\left(c-\gamma\overline{C}\right)^{1-\frac{1}{\eta}}-1}{1-\dfrac{1}{\eta}} \\ & + J_k(k,\overline{K})\{[\phi R + (1-\phi)r^f]k - c\} \\ & + J_{\overline{K}}(k,\overline{K})\{[\overline{\Phi}R + (1-\overline{\Phi})r^f]\overline{K} - \overline{C}\} + \frac{(\sigma\phi k)^2}{2}J_{kk}(k,\overline{K}) \\ & + \frac{\left(\sigma\overline{\Phi}\overline{K}\right)^2}{2}J_{\overline{K}\overline{K}}(k,\overline{K}) + \sigma^2\phi k\overline{\Phi}\overline{K}J_{\overline{K}k}(k,\overline{K})\Bigg\}\end{aligned} \tag{5.106}$$

where J_x and J_{xx} denote first and second derivatives with respect to variable $x \in \{k, \overline{K}\}$ and the same applies for the cross-derivative. Again, we have to adopt a restriction on parameter γ so that the interior solution is detectable. Concretely, $k_0/\overline{K}_0 > \gamma$, where the numerator is the initial wealth of the poorest household and the denominator is the average initial wealth. FOCs for the stated problem are as follows:

$$\left(c-\gamma\overline{C}\right)^{-\frac{1}{\eta}} = J_k(k,\overline{K}), \tag{5.107}$$

$$\phi = \frac{R - r^f}{\sigma^2} \frac{J_k(k, \overline{K})}{-J_{kk}(k, \overline{K})k} + \overline{\Phi} \frac{J_{\overline{K}k}(k, \overline{K})\overline{K}}{-J_{kk}(k, \overline{K})k}. \tag{5.108}$$

Let our guess for the value function be:

$$J(k, \overline{K}) = a + b\frac{k - \gamma\overline{K}^{1-\frac{1}{\eta}}}{1 - \frac{1}{\eta}}, \tag{5.109}$$

and hence it implies:

$$J_k(k, \overline{K}) = b(k - \gamma\overline{K})^{-\frac{1}{\eta}}, \tag{5.110}$$

$$J_{kk}(k, \overline{K}) = -\frac{b}{\eta}(k - \gamma\overline{K})^{-\frac{1}{\eta}-1}, \tag{5.111}$$

$$J_{\overline{K}}(k, \overline{K}) = -\gamma b(k - \gamma\overline{K})^{-\frac{1}{\eta}}, \tag{5.112}$$

$$J_{\overline{K}\,\overline{K}}(k, \overline{K}) = -\frac{\gamma^2 b}{\eta}(k - \gamma\overline{K})^{-\frac{1}{\eta}-1}, \tag{5.113}$$

$$J_{k\overline{K}}(k, \overline{K}) = \frac{\gamma b}{\eta}(k - \gamma\overline{K})^{-\frac{1}{\eta}-1}. \tag{5.114}$$

The first FOC (Eq. 5.107) with Eq. (5.110) together yields:

$$c = b^{-\eta}(k - \gamma\overline{K}) + \gamma\overline{C} \tag{5.115}$$

and the second FOC (Eq. 5.108) with Eqs. (5.110), (5.111) and (5.114) give:

$$\phi = \eta\frac{R - r^f}{\sigma^2}\left(1 - \gamma\frac{\overline{K}}{k}\right) + \overline{\Phi}\gamma\frac{\overline{K}}{k}. \tag{5.116}$$

Plugging Eqs. (5.115) and (5.116) into the budget constraint results in:

$$dk(t) = \left[\eta\left(\frac{R-r^f}{\sigma}\right)^2 - b^{-\eta} + r^f\right]k$$
$$+\gamma\left[b^{-\eta} + (R-r^f)\overline{\Phi} - \eta\left(\frac{R-r^f}{\sigma}\right)^2\right]\overline{K} - \gamma\overline{C}\,dt \tag{5.117}$$
$$+\left[\eta\frac{R-r^f}{\sigma}k + \gamma\left(\sigma\overline{\Phi} - \eta\frac{R-r^f}{\sigma}\right)\overline{K}\right]dz,$$

which fully captures the equilibrium law of motion of wealth among rich and poor. Whether the solution (based on our guess) is consistent with the stated problem, we need to check constancy of b. Since the equation implies linear aggregation of the equilibrium law of motion of wealth among rich and poor, we are allowed to substitute $\overline{K}$ and $\overline{\Phi}$ in Eq. (5.117). Hence, the portfolio choice of the average household is:

$$\overline{\Phi} = \eta\frac{R-r^f}{\sigma^2} \tag{5.118}$$

and after substituting it back into Eq. (5.117) we receive:

$$\phi = \overline{\Phi} = \eta\frac{R-r^f}{\sigma^2}, \forall k > 0. \tag{5.119}$$

Further, linearly aggregated Eq. (5.115) yields:

$$c = b^{-\eta}k, \forall k > 0. \tag{5.120}$$

By setting $a = -1/[\rho(1-1/\eta)]$ and substituting Eqs. (5.109) through (5.116) into HJB (Eq. 5.106), we get:

$$\frac{\rho - \frac{1}{\eta}b^{-\eta}}{1-\frac{1}{\eta}} - r^f = (R-r^f)\frac{\phi k - \gamma\overline{\Phi K}}{k-\gamma\overline{K}} - \frac{\sigma^2}{2\eta}\left(\frac{\phi k - \gamma\overline{\Phi K}}{k-\gamma\overline{K}}\right)^2. \tag{5.121}$$

The solution to the stated problem (Eq. 5.106) is the decision rule for consumption:

$$c^* = C(k,\overline{K}) = \xi k \tag{5.122}$$

where, again,

$$\xi = \rho\eta + (1-\eta)r^f - \frac{\eta(\eta-1)}{2}\left(\frac{R-r^f}{\sigma}\right)^2. \tag{5.123}$$

The decision rule for portfolio choice is then:

$$\phi^* = \Phi\left(k,\overline{K}\right) = \eta\frac{R-r^f}{\sigma^2}, \tag{5.124}$$

and the value function is given by

$$J\left(k,\overline{K}\right) = -\frac{1}{\rho-\frac{\rho}{\eta}} + \xi^{-\frac{1}{\eta}}\frac{\left(k-\gamma\overline{K}\right)^{1-\frac{1}{\eta}}}{1-\frac{1}{\eta}}. \tag{5.125}$$

When interpreting the results, it is worth to note that the dynamics of wealth follows a geometric Brownian motion with the same coefficients regardless agents' initial conditions. The solution to HJB equation (5.106) then implies that the coefficient of variation of personal consumption, the variance of the growth rate of consumption, and thus the saving rate and the portfolio composition are the same across wealth groups. Time-variant subsistence consumption generates a stationary relative distribution of wealth with different IES across the wealth groups throughout the whole equilibrium path.

To summarize, if all agents are subjected to the same market shocks, which—in our case—follow a random walk, the inequality in the distribution of relative wealth would be increasing over time. In case of time-invariant subsistence, poor agents escape poverty very slowly due to low saving rates which reflect high disutility of consuming less when close to the subsistence level. The economic situation of poor agents, determined by the closeness to the subsistence level, naturally implies lower shares of risky assets since even the less risky assets with lower expected returns may contribute to escaping the subsistence level, but only when expected wealth exhibits a strictly positive growth rate. Contrarily, time-variant subsistence reflects, based on the outlined external habits (in our case 'keeping up with the Joneses'), that the subsistence level is rising. As the result, since subsistence needs grow together with aggregate consumption, poor agents are under pressure of increasing consumption which forces them to not lower the saving rate or take fewer risks. Finally, the poor end up with the same saving rates and portfolio shares despite lower IES.

5.3 Portfolio Management of Heterogeneous Agents Under Risk and Inequality Consequences

Asset and consumption smoothing strategies in the context of risk and subsistence needs can obviously vary between poor and rich agents. The following analysis therefore assumes that agents differentiate between safe savings instruments (conservative assets) with lower profitability and more risky assets with higher returns. Another important feature incorporated into the analysis is incompleteness of financial markets and credit constraints. This significantly modifies agents' capacities to manage market shocks and smooth consumption; see e.g. Deaton (1991, 1992).

In the following case, we explore portfolio management of agents initially distributed over a two-dimensional asset space where agents' strategies bifurcate between rich and poor. For this purpose, we use the model of Zimmerman and Carter (2003). In order to grasp the general market mechanism, the model has to exceed its former context of rural households in developing countries. Our reinterpretation is supposed to bring findings of the model on a higher level of abstractness with higher generalizability. Still, the environment of the model supposes that wealthier agents smooth their consumption through relatively high-return portfolios, drawing down assets as a consequence of possible income shocks. Poorer agents with conservative portfolio (also in accordance with Dercon 1998), on the other hand, smooth income through destabilizing consumption in order to preserve their asset base, which makes risk management relatively expensive for initially poorer agents.

As regards the model itself, authors formulate a dynamic stochastic model of asset accumulation under covariant risk, asset market constraints and subsistence constraints. Agents are endowed with heterogeneous levels of wealth which is allocated in both "productive" (Rosenzweig and Wolpin 1993) and "non-productive" (Deaton 1991) assets (also "buffer assets"). The non-productive assets M are risk-free with low return and productive assets T are risky with high return. Further, high-return assets tend to report higher level of variance of returns and *vice-versa*. It is assumed that the two-asset model captures the full set of portfolio choices and since agents face borrowing constraints the holdings of both assets must be non-negative. Prices of the non-productive assets tend to rise with positive income shock and fall with negative shock. Agents are aware of these tendencies and have rational beliefs about mean prices and the covariation between prices and income shocks, which, in fact, explains the demand through expected future covariance of prices and income shocks. Hence, agents follow:

$$\begin{aligned} &F(T_{it}, M_{it}, \theta_{it}, \theta_{et}) = \theta_{it}\theta_{et}D(T_{it})^{\sigma} + \mu M_{it}, \\ \text{s.t.} \quad &F(T_{it}, M_{it}, \theta_{it}, \theta_{et}) - P_{Tt}(T_{it+1} - T_{it}) - (M_{it+1} - M_{it}) \geq c_t \end{aligned} \tag{5.126}$$

where T_{it} is i's agent holding of the productive asset in period t; M represents non-productive assets; D is a productivity parameter; σ is an output elasticity parameter which denotes decreasing returns and μ is the rate of return of non-productive assets. Further, θ_i is an idiosyncratic shock that affect i's agent only, and θ_e is an external covariant shock that affects all agents. As regards the budget constraint, it is clear that it accommodates both consumption and investments choice as well as portfolio composition choice. The price of the productive asset is P_T.

In our settings, agents maximize the present-value utility over the infinite horizon. This additively separable function takes the form:

$$\max_{\{\underline{c_{i0}}, \underline{T_{i1}}, \underline{M_{t1}}\}} E_0 \left\{ \sum_{t=0}^{\infty} \beta^t u(c_{it}) | \phi(P_{Tt}, \theta_{et} | \Omega_0) \right\}$$

$$\begin{aligned} C_S &= \{C_S, C_{S+1}, C_{S+2}, \ldots\} \\ T_S &= \{T_S, T_{S+1}, T_{S+2}, \ldots\} \\ M_S &= \{M_S, M_{S+1}, M_{S+2}, \ldots\} \end{aligned} \quad (5.127)$$

where $\phi(P_{Tt}, \theta_{et}| \Omega_0)$ is the joint distribution of the fully endogenous asset prices and the covariant shocks, while assuming normal distribution of both prices and income shocks.

We can also claim that the covariance increases with the number of agents who allocate their assets to subsistence consumption,[7] which depends on three effects: (i) on how low average consumable asset stocks are relative to the variation of income; (ii) on the price elasticity of demand for productive assets; and (iii) on the relative size of the contribution of covariant shocks in total income shocks.

To complete the issue of subsistence level of consumption, Zimmerman and Carter (2003) overcome few assumptions made by Rosenzweig and Wolpin (1993). Firstly, authors do not employ subsistence insurance. The aim of subsistence insurance was that, regardless of income, consumption does not fall below epsilon above the subsistence level. Authors also do not assume that a subsistence shortfall in a given period has no impact on subsequent periods. Since both of these two assumptions considerably distorted dynamics of the subsistence, the presented utility is defined as:

$$u(c_{it}) = \begin{cases} (c_{it}/R)^{\varepsilon} \text{if}\, c_{it} \geq R \,\text{and}\, c_{is} \geq R \forall s \in \{1, 2, \ldots t-1\}, \text{where}\ \varepsilon < 1 \\ 0, \qquad \text{otherwise} \end{cases} \quad (5.128)$$

where R_0 is the subsistence level, and ε is the utility curvature parameter.

In a dynamic sense, agents take into account statistical properties (mean and variability) of future asset prices with regards to their portfolio composition. Further, by considering the subsistence level we remind another intertemporal element;

[7]If the agent does not meet the subsistence level and operates below, her utility from that time on equals zero.

concretely, future utility is influenced by the consumption choices in the current period which means that the problem of dynamic choice is inseparable in time. Such models must be solved simultaneously for all time periods. However, due to computational difficulty when solving time-inseparable models with many time periods, we employ a state variable that represent effects of past decisions on the current and future states. Let the state variable L_S be zero if the agent has had no consumption in the past (i.e. in periods $s-1$, $s-2$, ..., $s-n$) and be one if otherwise, while the irreversibility of $L_{S+1}=0$ simplify the model into a convenient form.

The essential intertemporal dilemma is therefore between present and future consumption, while the future consumption relies on accumulated assets. By following the already mentioned additively separable problem (Eq. 5.127), the solution for the outlined trade-off will be found through splitting it into two parts, one for the present and one for the future consumption:

$$\max_{\{\underline{c_0},\underline{T_1},\underline{M_1}\}} E_0\left\{\sum_{t=0}^{\infty}\beta^t u(c_t)|\phi(P_{Tt},\theta_{et}|\Omega_t)\right\}$$
$$=\max_{\{c_0,T_1,M_1,L_1\}}\left\{u(c_0)+\beta L_1 E_0\left\{\max_{\{\underline{c_1},\underline{T_2},\underline{M_2},\underline{L_2}\}}\left\{\sum\nolimits_{t=1}^{\infty}\beta^t u(c_t)|\phi(P_{Tt},\theta_{et}|\Omega_t)\right\}\right\}\right\} \tag{5.129}$$

s.t. (Eqs. 5.126–5.128) ($\forall t$) given T_0, M_0, θ_{i0}, θ_{e0}.

Equation (5.129) captures the typical trade-off between current consumption and foregone current consumption in favour of investment. The value function in the future is hence:

$$J^*(T_0,M_0,L_0)\equiv L_0E_0\left\{\max_{\{\underline{c_0},\underline{T_1},\underline{M_1},\underline{L_1}\}}\sum_{t=0}^{\infty}\beta^t u(c_t)\right\}, \tag{5.130}$$

where the left side determines the maximum expected present value from assets (T_0, M_0) and the state variable (L_0). Equation (5.129) is then rewritten as:

$$\max_{\{\underline{c_0},\underline{T_1},\underline{M_1},\underline{L_1}\}}\{u(c_0)+\beta J^*(T_1,M_1,L_1)\} \tag{5.131}$$

$$\text{for}\quad t=0$$

$$\text{given}\quad T_0,M_0,\theta_{i0},\theta_{e0}$$

Since agents distribute their resources among consumption, productive and non-productive assets, the portfolio choice problem is solved through:

Table 5.1 Model parametrization

Parameter	Notation	Value
Productivity (per unit of the productive asset)	D	650
Output elasticity (decreasing returns)	σ	0.95
Return on non-productive assets	μ	0.00
Subsistence level	R_0	800
Discount factor	β	0.95
Utility curvature	ε	0.10

Source: Zimmerman and Carter (2003)

$$\frac{J_1^*(T_{s+1}, M_{s+1}, L_{s+1})}{P_{Ts}} = J_2^*(T_{s+1}, M_{s+1}, L_{s+1}) \tag{5.132}$$

and the trade-off between consumption and investment through:

$$u'(C_S) = \beta \frac{J_i'(T_{s+1}, M_{s+1}, L_{s+1})}{P_{Ts}} \tag{5.133}$$

where $u'(C_S)$ represent marginal utility from consumption and J_i' is the first derivative of J^* with respect to the i-th argument. We can see that if consumption is greater than the subsistence level, i.e. $L_{s+1} = 1$, the problem is relatively straightforward. On the other hand, if $L_{s+1} = 0$, then both derivatives (u', J') are zero except at the discontinuous point $C_S = R_0$. In that situation, agents decide which of these two solutions ($L_{s+1} = 1$ and $L_{s+1} = 0$) generates higher utility.

The reason why the model must undergo numerical procedure is that it does not produce a closed-form solution. That is because J depends not only on the agent's own assets, but also on assets of all agents and their effects on prices and rational expectations on prices. The aim of the simulation is to capture the decisive market forces in economies characterized by subsistence constraints, covariant risk and thin asset markets.

Zimmerman and Carter (2003) run the simulation on data collected in Burkina Faso. For our purpose, however, it is important to look at simulation's inputs more generally. The simulation includes 100 agents with relatively egalitarian initial distribution of productive and non-productive assets. Agents produces according to Eq. (5.127) and solve the optimization problem (Eq. 5.126) through allocating their resources to consumption and to productive and non-productive accumulation or decumulation. The price of the productive assets corresponds to supply and demand in every of 35 simulated time periods which implies a time series of endogenous prices.[8] The model is parametrized as follows (Table 5.1):

[8]For further details including the proof of numerical estimation of the true value function see Zimmerman and Carter (2003).

Table 5.2 Shock structure

	Covariance shock (θ_e)		
Idiosyncratic shock (θ_i)	Low (p = 0.3)	Medium (p = 0.4)	High (p = 0.3)
Low (p = 0.2)	$\theta_i = 0.90$	$\theta_i = 0.80$	$\theta_i = 0.70$
	$\theta_i\theta_e = 0.675$	$\theta_i\theta_e = 0.800$	$\theta_i\theta_e = 0.875$
Medium (p = 0.6)	$\theta_i = 1.00$	$\theta_i = 1.00$	$\theta_i = 1.00$
	$\theta_i\theta_e = 0.75$	$\theta_i\theta_e = 1.00$	$\theta_i\theta_e = 1.25$
High (p = 0.2)	$\theta_i = 1.10$	$\theta_i = 1.20$	$\theta_i = 1.30$
	$\theta_i\theta_e = 0.825$	$\theta_i\theta_e = 1.20$	$\theta_i\theta_e = 1.625$

Source: Zimmerman and Carter (2003)

Further, the average endowment of the productive asset is 3.5 and average year income is thus 2137. It means that the subsistence level reaches 37% of average income. The risk parametrization is as follows (Table 5.2):

To conclude with parametrization of the model, it is worth to note that even when parameters varied by 5–10%, the numerical values would not change substantively.

With regards to an initial distribution of agents across the two-dimensional asset space, numerical analysis shows that agents follow one of three types portfolio strategies. These are (i) permanent loss of utility, (ii) conservative portfolio strategy and (iii) entrepreneurial portfolio strategy. The first is characterized by a zero-wealth position and no income that could be allocated to asset investment. The second portfolio strategy consists of low-yield and short-term asset management primarily focused on asset protection and asset smoothing. Finally, the third portfolio strategy focuses on assets with higher yields and converting them into a high-liquidity form in order to mitigate effects of shocks and to smooth agent's consumption.

The Table 5.3 illustrates group averages in two portfolio regimes—conservative portfolio strategy followed by agents in the lower half of the wealth distribution and entrepreneurial portfolio strategy followed by agents in the upper half of the wealth distribution. Both groups of agents were affected by a 250-year vector of random shocks.

The Table 5.3 shows that despite all agents were initially endowed with the same proportion of productive and non-productive assets, conservative portfolio strategy reports significantly lower levels of wealth than is the case of entrepreneurial portfolio strategy. As regards the portfolio compositions, conservative portfolio strategists hold in average 37.1% of their portfolio's value in non-productive assets, meanwhile entrepreneurial portfolio strategists hold non-productive assets only in 0.8% of their portfolio's value in average.

The effect of decreasing returns on productive assets causes that despite the maximum expected return is higher for poorer agents, the achieved mean rate of return of poorer agents (5.3%) is lower than that of richer agents (5.9%). Above that, poorer agents with conservative portfolios pay an 18% premium in terms of foregone rate of return on wealth to achieve smoother income, while richer agents loose only 0.4%. This difference indicates willingness of the poorer agents to pay for insurance, which is also present in line with Rosenzweig and Binswanger (1993) who came up

Table 5.3 Characteristics of optimal stable portfolios

	Conservative portfolio (poor agents)	Entrepreneurial portfolio (rich agents)
Portfolio value, composition and returns		
Value of portfolio (final period price)	21,013	125,427
Portfolio composition (% of non-productive in value of portfolio)	37.1	0.8
Expected rate of return	5.3%	5.86%
Cost of risk coping		
Maximum possible expected rate of return	6.3%	5.88%
Percent of maximum possible return foregone	18	0.4
Income smoothing		
Coefficient of variation of income	20%	25%
Consumption smoothing		
Coefficient of variation of consumption	13.5%	8.4%
Asset smoothing		
Coefficient of variation of productive assets	0.7%	7%
Coefficient of variation of non-productive assets	1.3%	66%

Source: Zimmerman and Carter (2003)

with an intuitive finding that poor agents are willing to forego potential income in favour of less-risky investment strategy. It also shows that it is relatively "more expensive" to be poor.

Another fact is that entrepreneurial portfolio strategy generates smoother consumption (variation coefficient equals 8.4%) than is the case of conservative portfolio strategy (with variation coefficient 13.5%). These results are obtained despite the riskier portfolio reports higher variability of income than the safer one. Poorer agents therefore tend to shift from productive assets to non-productive assets in order to smooth income since returns to productive assets are burdened with greater risks. The results also outline that poor agents rather manipulate consumption to protect assets than the other way around, which demonstrates their longer-term goal settings. This stays in contradiction to a frequent assertion that poorer agents do not generate sufficient level of savings in order to grow due to their impatience in consumption.

The presented dynamic model with subsistence level therefore stands against common concave utility idea that agents always want to smooth their consumption as much as possible. As can be seen, the conservative portfolio exhibits higher coefficient of variation of consumption than coefficient of variation of assets (0.7% and 1.3% for productive and non-productive assets respectively). The opposite situation is with rich agents who are relatively safe above the subsistence level. These agents have similar coefficient of variation of consumption as poor agents, however, their coefficient of variation in asset stocks is significantly higher. The distance from a subsistence level actually enables rich agents to bear some degree of asset price risk so that they can afford to keep their consumption level through productive assets.

The decisive category for the development of inequality between given groups of agents lies in simulating accumulation trajectories. Agents can be thus grouped into three classes: The first class of agents stock out over the course of the simulation. The effect of subsistence level draws this group of agents down, even though these agents were initially endowed with both productive and non-productive assets. The second class of agents, initially endowed with between 1.5 and 4 units of productive assets,[9] readjust their portfolios in favour of non-productive assets. Such readjustment naturally drag-down the average rate of return on agents' overall asset portfolio. Understandably, lower return on assets goes hand in hand with lower risk. The third class of agents, initially endowed with more than four units of productive assets, increase their stock of productive assets while holding low level of non-productive assets. Comparatively greater wealth of these agents makes them immune from any subsistence threat and hence their risk aversion is reduced to standard curvature of their utility function.

What is important is the group formation which is initially based on probability. However, after several periods, agents' long-run portfolio positions become more clearly classified and agents form respective clusters. As a consequence, income mobility across these clusters becomes quite rare. It should be also noted that rich agents with more than four units of productive assets continually accumulate wealth despite the effect of decreasing returns. Their wealth (portfolio value) is based almost exclusively on productive assets, but at the expense of the poor, who are "forced" to hand over productive assets to the rich. This, of course, affects total productivity of a given economy, which can be potentially improved through redistribution. The model demonstrates a positive relationship between initial wealth and rate of return on wealth. In the context of the presented model, initial asset inequalities reproduce and deepen themselves over time. The dynamic perspective also signifies that agents may use time and savings to accumulate wealth, but the dominating effect of market dynamics on initially poorer agents is rather of a threat than of an opportunity.

5.4 Chapter Summary

The aim of this chapter was to inspect self-preservation in economic models. Our interest thus inevitably gravitated to subsistence consumption; the topic which was already concerned in various subfields of economics. It is evident that assuming a certain level of necessary consumption restricts an ability to save, which usually constrains any potential growth of the economic agent. The subsistence consumption is then the more binding the closer is the agent's income. It is then clear that high-

[9]Bear on mind that the average endowment of the productive asset is 3.5.

income agents have relatively low requirements on subsistence consumption, while low-income agents have, conversely, relatively high requirements on subsistence consumption. This inevitably causes that richer agents are more sensitive on changes of the interest rate, while poorer agents less. In other words, it was shown that the saving rate and its sensitivity to the interest rate is an increasing function of income which already has strong empirical support.

Subsistence consumption also plays an important methodological role. It enables to abstract from typical 'preference fetishism' and put an emphasize on the basic necessity which is immanent to any agent operating on the market. By using this approach, we are directed to differentiate between willingness and ability in agent's decision-making. A concrete application on the saving rate then refers to the initial ability to save as the decisive factor for the initial level of the saving rate and the subsequent path, while the willingness to save is behind the asymptotic value of the saving rate.

In order to incorporate subsistence consumption, and hence self-preservation imperatives of economic agents, the Stone-Geary preferences are the first choice to define utility function in agent-based models. Using Stone-Geary utility function with subsistence constraints determines declining elasticity of marginal utility in the level of consumption. It followingly causes that savings rates and economic growth rates are jointly rising with economic development, which is given by the share of subsistence consumption on total resources. This fact corresponds to the empirical literature showing that saving rates—the decisive factor of growth—increases with income on both microeconomic and macroeconomic level. The models presented in this chapter, which use this special type of utility function, then conclude that the divergent tendency comes from the growth rate of income that is rising with the level of income on a unique balanced-growth path. Generality and theoretical relevance of the subsistence idea was then unveiled when the evolution of saving rates and growth rates is independent of the size of subsistence level.

Subsistence consumption was also considered in frequently used portfolio management framework. The first model of this kind says that the household strives to mitigate the pressure of subsistence needs while a growing trajectory of the household's expected wealth depends on strictly increasing saving rate. It uses the fact that it is harder for poorer households to generate higher saving rates since consuming lower fraction of their wealth is restricted by the level of subsistence needs. Intertemporal decisions of the poorer households thus suffer with lower possibility to reach higher saving rates and hence to follow the trajectory of increasing wealth. The portfolio choice scheme also shows that increasing wealth of the poor agent over time is accompanied by increasing relative wealth inequality.

Further, there were presented group averages in two portfolio regimes—conservative portfolio strategy followed by poorer agents and entrepreneurial portfolio strategy followed by richer agents. A greater distance from the subsistence level actually enables richer agents to bear some degree of asset price risk so that they can afford to keep their consumption level through productive assets. Conversely, poorer agents are rather dominated by their risk aversion due to closeness to the subsistence level.

Despite all agents were initially endowed with the same proportion of productive and non-productive assets, conservative portfolio strategy reports significantly lower levels of wealth than is the case of entrepreneurial portfolio strategy. Conservative portfolio strategists also hold in average more than third of their portfolio's value in non-productive assets, meanwhile entrepreneurial portfolio strategists hold non-productive assets only less than 1% of their portfolio's value in average.

It is also revealed that despite the effect of decreasing returns on productive assets, the achieved mean rate of return of poorer agents is lower than that of richer agents. Above that, poorer agents with conservative portfolios loose almost one fifth in terms of foregone rate of return on wealth in order to achieve smoother income, while richer agents in fact do not lose anything.

If we have a look on the group formation, which is initially based on probability, after several periods we see that agents' long-run portfolio positions become more clearly classified and agents form respective clusters. As a consequence, income mobility across these clusters becomes quite rare. The second model on portfolio management also displays that agents with initially greater amount of productive assets continually accumulate wealth despite the effect of decreasing returns, while mobility across groups of agents becomes extremely rare. The impetus for divergence thus lies in the higher risk aversion of those who are close to the subsistence level, which causes low returns on their assets. On the contrary, richer agents in a safe distance from the subsistence level may afford to invest to high-return assets which speed-up their accumulation even further.

In sum, all presented models in various ways indicate that considering subsistence consumption often oppose converging tendencies that are traditionally embedded in mainstream economic models.

References

Achury C, Hubar S, Koulovatianos C (2012) Saving rates and portfolio choice with subsistence consumption. Rev Econ Dyn 15(1):108–126

Azariadis C (1996) The economics of poverty traps, Part One: Complete markets. J Econ Growth 1:449–486

Barro RJ, Sala-i-Martín Y (1995) Economic growth. McGraw-Hill, New York

Christiano L (1989) Understanding Japan's saving rate: the reconstruction hypothesis. Federal Reserve Minneapolis Quart Rev Spring:10–15

Deaton A (1991) Saving and liquidity constraints. Econometrica 59:1221–1248

Deaton A (1992) Understanding consumption. Oxford University Press, Oxford

Dercon S (1998) Wealth, risk and activity choice: cattle in Western Tanzania. J Dev Econ 55:1–42

Dynan KE, Skinner J, Zeldes S (2004) Do the rich save more? J Polit Econ 112:397–444

Easterly W (1994) Economic stagnation, fixed factors, and policy thresholds. J Monet Econ 33:525–557

Gandolfo G (2010) Economic dynamics. Springer

Geary RC (1950) A note on "A constant-utility index of the cost of living". Rev Econ Stud 18 (2):65–66

Horkheimer M (2012[1949–67]) Critique of instrumental reason. Verso, London

Jones R (1985) Report. Japan Economic Institute

King RG, Rebelo S (1993) Transitional dynamics and economic growth in the neoclassical model. Am Econ Rev 83:908–931
Loayza N, Schmidt-Hebbel K, Serven L (2000) What drives private saving across the world? Rev Econ Stat 82:165–181
Malloy CJ, Moskowitz TJ, Vissing-Jorgensen A (2009) Long-run stockholder consumption risk and asset returns. J Financ 64:2427–2480
Merton RC (1969) Lifetime portfolio selection under uncertainty: the continuous-time case. Rev Econ Stat 51:247–257
Merton RC (1971) Optimum consumption and portfolio rules in a continuous-time model. J Econ Theory 3:373–413
Nelson R (1956) A Theory of the low-level equilibrium trap in underdeveloped economies. Am Econ Rev 46(5):894–908
Ogaki M, Ostry JD, Reinhart CM (1996) Saving behaviour in low- and middle-income developing countries: a comparison. IMF Staff Pap 43(1):38–71
Rebelo S (1991) Long-run policy analysis and long run growth. J Polit Econ 99:500–521
Rebelo S (1992) Growth in open economies. Carn-Roch Conf Ser Public Policy 36:5–46
Rosenzweig MR, Binswanger HP (1993) Wealth, weather risk and the composition and profitability of agricultural investments. Econ J 103:56–78
Rosenzweig MR, Wolpin KI (1993) Credit market constraints, consumption smoothing, and the accumulation of durable production assets in low-income countries: investment in bullocks in India. J Polit Econ 101:223–244
Sarel M (1994) On the dynamics of economic growth. IMF Working Paper 138
Sharif M (1986) The concept and measurement of subsistence: a survey of the literature. World Dev 14:555–577
Shin YH, Koo JL, Roh KH (2018) An optimal consumption and investment problem with quadratic utility and subsistence consumption constraints: a dynamic programming approach. Math Model Anal 23(4):627–638
Steger T (2000) Economic growth with subsistence consumption. J Dev Econ 63:343–361
Stone R (1954) Linear expenditure systems and demand analysis: an application to the pattern of British demand. Econ J 64(255):511–527
Strulik H (2010) A note on economic growth with subsistence consumption. Macroecon Dyn 14 (5):763–771
Wachter JA, Yogo M (2010) Why do household portfolio shares rise in wealth? Rev Financ Stud 23:3929–3965
Zimmerman FJ, Carter M (2003) Asset smoothing, consumption smoothing and the reproduction of inequality under risk and subsistence constraints. J Dev Econ 71(2):233–260

Chapter 6
Models of Competition

Theories of economic inequality frequently concern individual characteristics as the prime determinant of economic distribution. This chapter therefore accentuates partly overlooked but important structural feature of the market mechanism, namely competition among economic agents. It is the ruling principle of allocation of resources which keeps the dynamics of the whole market system. As will be explained in more details, the dynamics of the market system based on competition subsequently results in growth stimulating tendencies. The chapter therefore considers selected competition theories in order to depict important perspectives on competing agents in the context of the main driving forces of economic growth in modern economies. At the end, the task is to connect competitive structures and economic distribution. Understandably, we include just a small fraction of theories accentuating competition. On the other hand, presented models unveil the founding pillars of competitive processes which influence economic distribution at the end. Hence, we automatically abstract from various particular aspects that are usually present in extended versions of growth and competition models. By following this strategy, again, we elevate these models on a higher level of abstractness which eliminates various possible sorts of selectivity. A higher perspective also allows to formulate models for different types of agents, from individuals and households to firms and national states.

Contemporary context of economic environment, characterized by a considerable level of monopolization, may favour distinguishing between competitive and monopolized capitalism. There is a long tradition of authors dealing with these questions, in modern economic history let us name for example Paul A. Baran or Paul Sweezy. The latter refers to a "hierarchy of profit rates", where the highest profit rates belongs to monopolized spheres of the economy, while the lowest ones are gained on the most competitive markets (Sweezy 1968). Following this intuition, highly competitive markets should rather even out economic distribution among agents. Ought we therefore pursue a highly competitive environment in order to moderate inequality? And what about intensity of competition—is it always rising

R. Maialeh, *Dynamic Models and Inequality*, Contributions to Economics,
https://doi.org/10.1007/978-3-030-46313-7_6

with the quantity of agents? A simple Bertrand oligopoly model suggests that the answer is not that straightforward.

There are several studies which touch the relationship between markets and inequality, and which focus on different possible connections. Namely, Baker and Salop (2015) examined the relationship between inequality and market power with the conclusion that markets tend to raise the return to capital and hence contribute to the progression and perpetuation of inequality. In a similar fashion we read e.g. a paper from Rognlie (2015) who demonstrates his findings on a new multisector model of factor shares; not to mention the seminal work of Comanor and Smiley (1975) who focus on the influence of monopoly power on distribution of wealth. Among others, we could also mention Furman and Orszag (2015) who posit that lack of competition may explain a fair portion of the increase in inequality. A positive relationship between market power and inequality was detected earlier e.g. by Creedy and Dixon (1999).

Competitive markets themselves, and of course an optimal allocation of resources, are then guaranteed by a large number of agents, typically profit maximising producers and utility maximising consumers. This concept is usually enriched with perfect mobility of all resources and assumptions such as perfect information and no externalities. Competition thus pushes quantities and prices from their perpetual disequilibria towards an equilibrium, similarly as gravitation brings all the mass and energy towards one another. But how this generalizing principle can contribute to our understanding of economic inequality? This will be the question for the following subchapters which show how different perspectives, based on innovation stimuli, market power and appropriation ability, are crucial for the economic distribution within competitive markets.

6.1 Competition in the Schumpeterian Growth Model

Unlike mainstream models such as Solow-Swan or AK model, which in their default set up assume stability and perfect competition, Schumpeterian approach is of a different kind. Its otherness rises from rejection of steady-state equilibrium as the normative aspect of economic analyses, which automatically introduces inherent instability into economic systems. Schumpeterian economic system also accentuates another fundamental attribute of the market mechanism, namely innovations. Innovation stimuli are inseparable parts of the resource allocation on competitive markets. Economic agents through innovation processes, to which they are pushed by market competitive pressures, improve their competitiveness and their ability to reproduce. Naturally, high innovation activity is supposed to increase the output of the economy which establishes important connection between competition, innovation and growth. The aim of the following model is to depict innovations as the natural outcome of competitive pressures, where growth is the necessary side-product of a higher technological level caused by innovation activities.

These questions were brought to contemporary economics largely thanks to Philippe Aghion. The following lines examine the seminal model on growth with creative destruction (Aghion and Howitt 1992). The source of growth in this model stems from vertical (i.e. productivity-improving) innovations on competitive markets. This type of innovations makes the model close to Schumpeter's 'creative destruction', where a new technology (or a 'new combination' in Schumpeterian language) on one hand becomes the engine of economic growth, but also destroys obsolete technologies of the past on the other hand.

The basic model assumes three types of inputs: (i) inputs used directly to produce output (*M*); (ii) inputs that can be used either in producing intermediates or in innovation processes (*N*); and (iii) inputs used exclusively in innovation processes (*R*). Assuming constant returns and fixed quantity of *M*, we can define the production function as:

$$y = AF(x), \tag{6.1}$$

where *y* represents the flow of output, *x* is the flow of intermediate product and *A* its productivity. As usual, the production function follows $F' > 0$ and $F'' < 0$. Production of intermediates states:

$$x = L, \tag{6.2}$$

with *L* as the flow of *N* inputs used to produce intermediates.

Research and development sectors produce innovations at the Poisson rate $\lambda\phi(n, R)$, where *n* is the flow of *N* inputs used in the innovation process, ϕ signifies concave production function with constant returns, and λ is a constant parameter. The aim of the innovation process is to produce new intermediates that will increase the productivity parameter *A*. The innovation rate depends only upon the present value of *n*, which allows to write $\phi(0, R) = 0$, while $\phi(n, 0) = n$. This implies that the economy without *N* inputs in the innovation process cannot innovate its intermediates and hence it cannot grow.

We assume continuous time$\tau \geq 0$, while $t = 0, 1$ etc. represents the interval starting with the *t*-th innovation ending at $t + 1$. The length between *t* and $t + 1$ is random and prices and quantities during the interval are constant. In cases of successful innovation, productivity of inputs, concentrated in the parameter *A*, increases by the factor $\gamma > 1$ For simplicity, we abstract from lags in the diffusion of new technology and the most competitive intermediate always dominates the market. When putting A_0 as the initial level of intermediate's productivity, it posits:

$$A_t = A_0\gamma^t; t \in [0, \infty). \tag{6.3}$$

This process enables the innovator to gain a certain monopoly power (to use Schumpeterian terms), or, simply put, to reach a competitive advantage over other competitors on the market. Such a competitive advantage lasts until the next successful innovation occurs and the intermediate production is thus the only imperfectly competitive market. The model can be depicted as follows (Scheme 6.1):

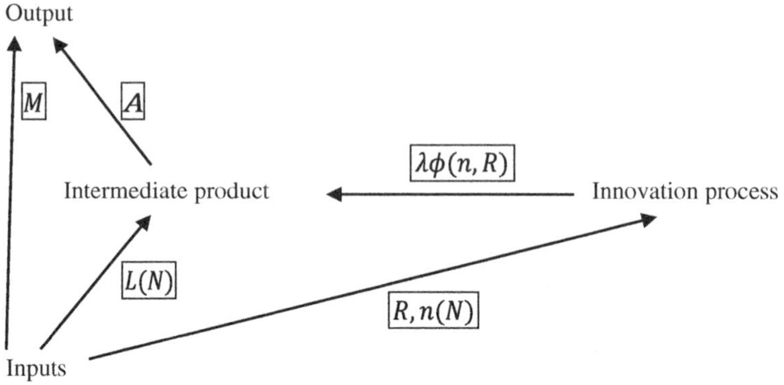

Scheme 6.1 Schumpeterian model of economic growth. Source: Own elaboration, based on Aghion and Howitt (1992)

In case of drastic innovations (Tirole 1988), the innovator is not affected by the previous intermediate product due to her monopoly power. The goal of such innovator is to maximise the expected present value of profits over the interval from the successful implementation of the innovation until a new innovation occurs.

Now, let x_t be the flow of the intermediate product created during interval t. Due to perfectly competitive markets, the innovator charges the price p_t equal to the marginal product:

$$p_t = A_t F'(x_t). \tag{6.4}$$

Since w_t is the price of N inputs, the innovator's objective is to choose x_t such that:

$$\max\,(A_t F'(x_t) - w_t)x_t, \tag{6.5}$$

while taking w_t and A_t as given. The "productivity-adjusted costs" are given by $\omega_t \equiv w_t/A_t$, and the "marginal revenue function" is defined as $\widetilde{\omega}(x) \equiv F'(x) + xF''(x)$. Assuming that the latter is downward-sloping and satisfies Inada conditions; formally we write:

$$\widetilde{\omega}'(x) < 0, \forall x > 0,$$

$$\lim_{x\to 0} \widetilde{\omega}(x) = \infty,$$

$$\lim_{x\to\infty} \widetilde{\omega}(x) = 0. \tag{6.6}$$

The innovator then chooses x_t according to FOCs:

$$\omega_t = \widetilde{\omega}(x_t), \tag{6.7}$$

or

$$x_t = \widetilde{x}(\omega_t), \tag{6.8}$$

where $\widetilde{x}$ is the function $\widetilde{\omega}^{-1}$. The flow of innovator's profit is given by:

$$\pi_t = A_t\widetilde{\pi}(\omega_t), \tag{6.9}$$

where $\widetilde{\pi}(\omega) \equiv -(\widetilde{x}(\omega))^2F''(\widetilde{x}(\omega))$. Values of $\widetilde{x}$ and $\widetilde{\pi}$ are strictly positive and strictly decreasing $\forall\omega_t > 0$. A simple and familiar example which fits to our conditions is the Cobb-Douglas function in the form $F(x) = x^\alpha$, $0 < \alpha < 1$. Thus, we get the following set of equations:

$$p_t = \frac{W_t}{\alpha}, \tag{6.10}$$

$$\pi_t = w_t x_t\left(\frac{1-\alpha}{\alpha}\right), \tag{6.11}$$

$$x_t = \left(\frac{\omega_t}{\alpha^2}\right)^{\frac{1}{\alpha-1}}. \tag{6.12}$$

The innovation process is independent of innovation processes of other competitors. So, the objective is to maximize the flow of expected profits from the innovation process by optimizing the amount of two factors (z, s) employed in the process. Therefore, the decision-maker follows:

$$\max\left(\lambda\phi(z,s)V_{t+1} - w_t z - w_t^s s\right). \tag{6.13}$$

The term V_{t+1} denotes the value of the t + 1st innovation, which can be also interpreted as the expected present value of the flow of monopoly profits π_{t+1} generated by the t + 1st innovation over exponentially distributed time period with parameter $\lambda\varphi(n_{t+1})$. Finally, w_t^s is the price of R input. Kuhn-Tucker conditions for Eq. (6.13) state:

$$w_t \geq \varphi'(n_t)\lambda V_{t+1}, n_t \geq 0 \tag{6.14}$$

with at least one equality, and where $\varphi(n_t) \equiv \phi(n_t, R)$, while

$$\varphi(0) = 0, \varphi'(n) > 0, \varphi''(n) \leq 0, \forall n \geq 0. \quad (6.15)$$

Therefore, we have:

$$V_{t+1} = \frac{\pi_{t+1}}{r + \lambda\varphi(n_{t+1})}, \quad (6.16)$$

where r denotes the interest rate and $\lambda\varphi(n_{t+1})$ accounts for the element of creative destruction which decreases the expected value of the flow of monopoly profits. Here, the crucial aspect of the model comes to the light—the model says that the successful innovator (monopolist) is not motivated to start another innovation process since the value of the next innovation is strictly less than the value of the next innovation to all other actors except the monopolist; formally $V_{t+1} - V_t < V_{t+1}$. Agents on the market thus take turns in the monopoly position which naturally mitigates diverging tendencies that could be based on a 'success breeds success' principle.

An important problem for the decision-maker is to decide what fraction of N input to devote to producing intermediates with the initial level of productivity and what fraction of N input to dedicate to innovation process that enhances the level of intermediates productivity. The equilibrium is found through the set of already known Eqs. (6.7), (6.9), (6.14) and (6.16) combined with the condition $N = x_t + n_t$. Then, it yields:

$$\frac{\gamma\tilde{\pi}(\tilde{\omega}(N - n_{t+1}))}{r + \lambda\varphi(n_{t+1})} \leq \frac{\tilde{\omega}(N - n_t)}{\lambda\varphi'(n_t)}, \quad (6.17)$$

with $n_t \geq 0$. Assuming a strictly decreasing, positive-valued function $\psi : [0, N) \rightarrow \mathbb{R}^+$, we derive the flow of N inputs used in the innovation process during interval t as:

$$n_t = \psi(n_{t+1}). \quad (6.18)$$

Then, based on Eq. (6.17), we simply define "marginal cost" $c(n_t)$ and "marginal benefit" $b(n_{t+1})$ of the innovation process:

$$c(n_t) \equiv \frac{\tilde{\omega}(N - n_t)}{\lambda\varphi'(n_t)}, \quad (6.19)$$

$$b(n_{t+1}) \equiv \frac{\gamma\tilde{\pi}(\tilde{\omega}(N - n_{t+1}))}{r + \lambda\varphi(n_{t+1})}. \quad (6.20)$$

Reminding the terms (Eq. 6.6) and (Eq. 6.15), marginal cost c must be strictly increasing and marginal benefit b strictly decreasing, while $c(n_t) \to \infty \Leftrightarrow n_t \to N$. These properties of c and b sign that a unique stationary equilibrium exists.

As we can also see, the relationship between current and future innovation processes is negative. Firstly, higher innovation activities in the future discourages present innovation activities by reducing the flow of expected profits $\widetilde{\pi}(\widetilde{\omega}(N - n_{t+1}))$ due to rising future costs on production factors. Secondly, higher innovation activities in the future increases the creative destruction $\lambda\varphi(n_{t+1})$, which consequently shortens the monopolistic period of the future successful innovator and thus the value of the innovation.

The stationary equilibrium is reached when n_t is constant, i.e. as the solution to $\widehat{n} = \psi(\widehat{n})$ This naturally requires that there are no impulses for a change within a sequence $\{n_t\}_0^\infty$ satisfying Eq. (6.18) $\forall t \geq 0$. We can prove that $c(0) = [(\widetilde{\omega}N)/(\lambda\varphi'(0))] < b(0) = [\gamma\widetilde{\pi}(\widetilde{\omega}(N))]/r \Rightarrow \widehat{n} > 0$; and thus:

$$\frac{\widetilde{\omega}(N - \widehat{n})}{\lambda\varphi'(\widehat{n})} = \frac{\gamma\widetilde{\pi}(\widetilde{\omega}(N - \widehat{n}))}{r + \lambda\varphi(\widehat{n})}. \tag{6.21}$$

The fact that $\widehat{n} > 0$ implies a positive Poisson rate $\lambda\varphi(\widehat{n}) > 0$ and thus innovations occur and the economy experiences growth. Conversely, $c(0) \geq b(0) \Rightarrow \widehat{n} = 0 \Rightarrow \lambda\varphi(0) = 0$, i.e. without innovations there is no growth.

Now, let us assume a linear innovation process $\varphi(n) \equiv n$ within Cobb-Douglas framework $F(x) = x^\alpha$. Based on Eqs. (6.10)–(6.12), the Eq. (6.21) transforms into:

$$1 = \frac{\lambda\gamma\left(\frac{1-\alpha}{\alpha}\right)(N - \widehat{n})}{r + \lambda\widehat{n}}, \tag{6.22}$$

and with the condition for $\widehat{n} > 0$:

$$\frac{\lambda\gamma\left(\frac{1-\alpha}{\alpha}\right)N}{r} > 1. \tag{6.23}$$

These equations based on the Cobb-Douglas form define monopoly power in the Lerner's sense as $1 - \alpha$. Equation (6.22) reads that increasing market power (decreasing α) increases $\widehat{n}$ for all $\widehat{n} > 0$. The second equation in the Cobb-Douglas form (Eq. 6.23) demonstrates that the condition $\widehat{n} > 0$ is satisfied iff there is a certain market power. This requires α to be:

$$\alpha^* \equiv \frac{\lambda\gamma N}{\lambda\gamma N + 1} < 1. \tag{6.24}$$

The reason is that market power under this critical value would generate too low profits from the next innovation, even though creative destruction in the next period will not be in play.

If we dedicate our attention back to more general matters, comparative statics of Eq. (6.21) says that decreasing interest rate increases the present value of profits from successful innovation and hence the marginal benefit of the innovation process. It also reads that the greater is the scale of the innovation, the greater is the size of next interval's monopoly profits relative to this interval's productivity. Of course, this increases the marginal benefit of the innovation process as well. Thirdly, increasing endowment of inputs N reduces the marginal cost of innovation through lowering the price of these inputs, and, at the same time, increases the marginal benefit of innovation. Lastly, increasing parameter λ (which indicates innovation boom) on the one hand increases the future rate of creative destruction and thus decreases the marginal benefit of innovations. On the other hand, increasing λ results in more productive units within innovation processes, which decreases the marginal cost of innovations. The latter effect dominates the effect of increasing creative destruction.[1] To sum up, the stationary equilibrium of inputs in innovation processes $\widehat{n}$ increases with decreasing rate of interest r; increasing size γ of each innovation; increasing amount of N input; and increasing parameter λ.

In order to assess driving forces of inequality, we need to capture balanced growth. The output during t follows:

$$y_t = A_t F(N - \widehat{n}), \tag{6.25}$$

implying:

$$y_{t+1} = \gamma y_t. \tag{6.26}$$

The time path of the logarithm of the output $\ln y(\tau)$ is a random step-function starting at $\ln y_0 = \ln F(N - \widehat{n}) + \ln A_0$ with each step of the constant size $\ln\gamma > 0$, and with the time between each step $\{\Delta_1, \Delta_2, \ldots\}$ a sequence of independent and identical variables exponentially distributed with parameter $\lambda\varphi(\widehat{n})$. In combination with Eq. (6.21) it determines the non-stationary stochastic process behind the concerned output. For simplicity, Aghion and Howitt (1992) assumes discrete observations; then Eq. (6.26) yields:

$$\ln y(\tau + 1) = \ln y(\tau) + \varepsilon(\tau), \tau = 0, 1, \ldots \tag{6.27}$$

with $\varepsilon(\tau)$ as $\ln\gamma$ multiplied by the number of innovations between τ and $\tau + 1$. Hence, we are able to formulate a sequence of independent and identical variables Poisson distributed with parameter $\lambda\varphi(\widehat{n})$:

[1]To problematize this statement in the context of the average growth rate see Aghion and Howitt (1992) Appendix 1.

$$\left\{\frac{\varepsilon(0)}{\ln\gamma}, \frac{\varepsilon(1)}{\ln\gamma}, \ldots\right\}, \tag{6.28}$$

which allows to reinterpret Eq. (6.27) as:

$$\ln y(\tau+1) = \ln y(\tau) + \lambda\varphi(\widehat{n})\ln\gamma + e(\tau), \tau = 0, 1, \ldots \tag{6.29}$$

where $e(\tau)$ is independent and identically distributed, defined as $e(\tau) \equiv \varepsilon(\tau) - \lambda\varphi(\widehat{n})\ln\gamma$, with

$$E(e(\tau)) = 0, \mathrm{Var}\, e(\tau) = \lambda\varphi(\widehat{n})(\ln\gamma)^2. \tag{6.30}$$

Based on Eqs. (6.29) and (6.30) we see that the discrete sequence of observations on the logarithm of output follows a random walk with constant positive drift. The average growth rate and the variance of the growth rate are thus defined as follows:

$$AGR = \lambda\varphi(\widehat{n})\ln\gamma, \tag{6.31}$$

$$VGR = \lambda\varphi(\widehat{n})(\ln\gamma)^2. \tag{6.32}$$

Both the average growth rate and the variance of the growth rate increase with higher "arrival" parameter of innovations, with the size of innovations, with the greater endowment of N input, and—in the case of Cobb-Douglas setup—with the level of market power. On the other hand, increasing interest rate causes drops in the average growth rate and the variance of the growth rate.

This basic endogenous model with drastic innovations assumes that economic growth stems from competition within innovation processes. For simplicity, it is assumed that each innovation creates an economy-wide monopoly in the production of intermediate goods. Successful innovation generates monopolistic rent, which belongs to the innovator until a new innovation occurs. The model shows off three different levels of tradeable objects. These are connected to classified inputs which can be used directly to produce the output, or to increase agent's competitiveness through the innovation process, and, finally, to produce intermediate product. Hence, there is a trade-off between producing output for rather immediate needs and increasing competitiveness for a longer-term perspective, which, however, depends on the parameters linked to the innovation process. This necessarily leads to the key connection, already outlined in the previous chapters, between agents' growth potential and possibilities to innovate. It is then clear that variance in growth potential is decisive factor of inequality dynamics and that agents competing through the innovation processes contribute to increasing aggregate output.

6.2 Monopoly Power and Inequality

In the previous subchapter we have learned that economic agents are pushed by competitive pressures to strive for a monopolistic rent. This inevitably creates a space for economic inequality, but the Schumpeterian model assumes that innovative incentives are stronger for all agents except for the monopolist. Thus, the principle of creative destruction secures that monopolists are rotating on a given market.

From a certain point of view, market power can be defined as the ability to setup prices (and hence to influence revenues) above the level of perfectly competitive markets (i.e. marginal costs). As a consequence of such market power, both poor and rich agents will suffer with higher prices of purchased goods. On one hand, already proven disproportionate holdings of corporate assets (Gans et al. 2019), naturally in favour of the rich, will compensate these higher expenditures of rich agents. On the other hand, poor agents could not expect such a counter-balancing effect of increased profits.[2] Then, it suggests itself that increasing competition should lead to lowering inequality.

The importance of mark-ups in market analyses is underlined by the fact that mark-ups (measured as the value above marginal costs) were steadily rising from 21% in 1980 to nearly 61% in 2014, with a sharp increase in 1980s and 1990s, stagnating during 2000s and then rapid rise since the Great Recession. Additionally, this sharp increase is highly selective since it is almost exclusively caused by rising mark-ups in firms with the already highest mark-ups. To be more concrete, the median of the mark-up distribution remains barely unchanged while the top of the distribution is described by a fat upper tail (De Loecker et al. 2019). As was already shown in the second chapter, the outlined development of mark-ups quite fairly copies the development of economic inequality.

To have a more direct connection between market power and economic inequality, we consider the model developed by Ennis et al. (2019) which tries to build a bridge between two strands of literature. Namely, it stresses evidences on increasing inequality in most of developed countries and simultaneous rise in market concentration accompanied by increasing mark-ups. Higher market shares then allow to utilize this better market position to setup higher prices with higher mark-ups. Thus, the model aims to capture the effect of higher prices (that stems from excessive market power) on different wealth-groups of agents. It is based on actual income, wealth and consumption expenditure distributions with the following assumptions:

(i) Market power for each given economy can be approximated by the difference between the average mark-up (across all sectors) and a minimum mark-up that

[2]This assumption is crucial for our subsequent considerations. It is based on the latest research that calculates this distribution for the United States, using data from the Survey of Consumer Finances and the Consumer Expenditure Survey. The statistics reveal that the top 20% consumed approximately as much as the bottom 60% but had 13 times as much corporate equity in 2016 (Gans et al. 2019).

reflects the best-practices of most competitive economies. The method is designed to recognise that a significant level of mark-up is needed to cover necessary returns on investment and legitimate sources of market power such as patents and trademarks.

(ii) The marginal propensity to save (ŭ60;′) remains constant across wealth groups. Despite this assumption stays in contrast to previous findings, it simplifies the solution to the model. It must be noted that relaxing this assumption will only increase the magnitude of the redistributive effect that is identified.

(iii) Market power gains are distributed in proportion to the current net wealth distribution (f_i). This mirrors the fact that corporate income and capital gains are distributed via business ownership, so that those with the largest wealth shares (whether in the form of corporate shares, bonds, pension fund entitlements, dwellings, land or others) will, proportionally, appropriate a bigger share of the profits than those with lower wealth shares.

(iv) The price of different baskets of goods will be inflated by market power in an equal percentage. This implies that market power equally influences products for the poor and products for the rich. To the extent that the poor are more exposed to monopolisation, the model provides conservative, lower-bound estimates.

Of course, there are several questions regarding stated assumptions which are put aside. For instance, low mark-ups can be sign of a highly competitive market, but also it might indicate declining industry. Another example can be the impact of dead weight loss on inequality within monopolistic markets since it harms both business owners and consumers. Lastly, we could confront the assumption that greater market power always leads to higher prices. As an exception from this assumption we could name a competitive oligopoly market. Such market could, on one hand, end up in a price war, naturally in favour of customers, but on the other hand it may give rise to enormous costs related to acquiring customers. But these costs typically do not enter the price setting on a monopoly market. Oligopoly market thus could produce at even higher prices but with lower mark-ups than a monopoly market.

As regards notation of the model, Y denotes the total income, F is net wealth, C represents aggregate consumption expenditure, W is the labour income and R is the capital income. Upper indexes m and c refer to the monopolistic and competitive steady states. This is because the model considers the steady state with observed monopolistic distributions of wealth, income and consumption expenditures, as well as a hypothetical steady state with competitive distributions of wealth, income, consumption expenditures and reduced mark-ups. The economic growth rate is as usual g, the average saving rate of the economy is $\bar{s}$; s' is the marginal propensity to save, α_K and α_L denote the shares of capital and labour income in the monopolistic steady state. Finally, μ is the mark-up given by the difference between price and marginal costs.

The model is simplified in a way that market power only affects the price, which is consequently the only determinant of the difference between monopolistic and competitive equilibrium. Thus, wealth, income and consumption in competitive and monopolistic environment are defined as follows:

$$F^m = \mu F^c, Y^m = \mu Y^c, C^m = \mu C^C. \tag{6.33}$$

Further, aggregate output is the sum of labour and capital incomes. The national income identity states:

$$Y^j = W + R^j, \text{where } j = c, m. \tag{6.34}$$

As can be seen, the move from monopolistic market to the competitive one does not affect labour income. The relation between R^m and R^c is derived from Eqs. (6.33) and (6.34). Firstly, we have:

$$R^c = Y^c - W, \tag{6.35}$$

and dividing Eq. (6.33) by μ yields:

$$Y^c = \frac{Y^m}{\mu}, \tag{6.36}$$

which in combination with Eq. (6.35) gives:

$$R^c = \frac{Y^m}{\mu} - W. \tag{6.37}$$

After combining Eqs. (6.34) and (6.37) we get:

$$R^c = \frac{W + R^m}{\mu} - W, \tag{6.38}$$

while multiplying W by μ/μ, the final rearrangement then produces $Y^c = W + R^c$, where:

$$R^c = W\frac{(1-\mu)}{\mu} + \frac{R^m}{\mu}. \tag{6.39}$$

The income of a given population group i is in both steady states given as follows:

$$y_i^m Y^m = W_i + f_i^m R^m \tag{6.40}$$

$$y_i^c Y^c = W_i + f_i^c \left[\frac{(1-\mu)}{\mu} W + \frac{R^m}{\mu} \right], \tag{6.41}$$

where W_i is the labour income of i-th population group and lower case letters denote the shares of wealth and income of a particular population group. Similarly, as was the case of aggregate labour income, the nominal level of the labour income W_i remains constant across the considered steady states. In order to define variations of wealth and income shares caused by market power, we have to subtract in the first step Eqs. (6.40) and (6.39):

$$y_i^m Y^m - y_i^c Y^c = W_i + f_i^m R^m - W_i - f_i^c \left(\frac{1-\mu}{\mu} + \frac{R^m}{\mu} \right). \tag{6.42}$$

After eliminating W_i and making use of Eq. (6.33) we have:

$$y_i^m Y^m - y_i^c \frac{Y^m}{\mu} = f_i^m R^m + f_i^c W - f_i^c \frac{(W + R^m)}{\mu}. \tag{6.43}$$

Using Eq. (6.34) for $j = m$ implies:

$$y_i^m Y^m - y_i^c \frac{Y^m}{\mu} = f_i^m (Y^m - W) + f_i^c W - f_i^c \frac{Y^m}{\mu}. \tag{6.44}$$

Multiplying by μ and dividing by Y^m generates:

$$\mu y_i^m - y_i^c = \mu f_i^m (1 - \alpha_1) + \mu f_i^c \alpha_L - f_i^c, \tag{6.45}$$

where $\alpha_L = W/Y^m$ is the labour share of income. After rearranging the terms, we have:

$$y_i^m - y_i^c = y_i^m (1-\mu) + \mu f_i^m (1 - \alpha_L) - f_i^c (1 - \mu \alpha_L), \tag{6.46}$$

and after adding and subtracting $f_i^m (1-\mu)$ to the right-side, we get:

$$y_i^m - y_i^c = y_i^m (1-\mu) - f_i^m (1-\mu) + f_i^m [1 - \mu + \mu (1 - \alpha_L)] - f_i^c (1 - \mu \alpha_L). \tag{6.47}$$

Final rearrangement then gives:

$$y_i^m - y_i^c = (\mu - 1)(f_i^m - y_i^m) + (1 - \mu \alpha_L)(f_i^m - f_i^c) \tag{6.48}$$

which is the desired equation that captures wealth and income variations as a consequence of market power.

Aggregate consumption function takes the standard Keynesian form:

$$C^j = \overline{C}^j + (1 - s')Y^j, \text{where } j = c, m. \tag{6.49}$$

Hence, the relation between average saving rate of the economy and the marginal propensity to save follows:

$$\frac{Y^m - C^m}{Y^m} = \overline{s} = s' - \frac{\overline{C}}{Y}. \tag{6.50}$$

The Eq. (6.50) follows empirical evidences and reads that for positive values of autonomous consumption the marginal propensity to save is greater than the average saving rate. Further, it is assumed that the average saving rate is non-negative since the ratio of autonomous consumption to income remains sufficiently small.

To continue, c_i is the consumption share of i-th population group so that the consumption expenditures on competitive and monopolistic markets follow:

$$c_i^c C^c = \overline{C}_i^c + (1 - s')y_i^c Y^c \tag{6.51}$$

$$c_i^m C^m = \overline{C}_i^m + (1 - s')y_i^m Y^m, \text{where } \mu \overline{C}_i^c = \overline{C}_i^m. \tag{6.52}$$

It can be seen that even though we adopted an assumption on identical reaction of all agents on variations in income, the model allows saving rates to vary across population groups due to group-specific terms $\overline{C}_i^m$ and $\overline{C}_i^c$. Multiplying Eq. (6.41) by μ and subtracting it from Eq. (6.52) yields:

$$c_i^m C^m - \mu c_i^c C^c = \overline{C}_i^m - \mu \overline{C}_i^c + (1 - s')y_i^m Y^m - (1 - s')\mu y_i^c Y^c, \tag{6.53}$$

Following Eq. (6.33) and bearing on mind that autonomous consumption remains constant on both competitive and monopolistic markets regardless changes of income or wealth (hence, $\overline{C}_i^m = \mu \overline{C}_i^c$), it gives:

$$c_i^m C^m - c_i^c C^m = \overline{C}_i^m - \overline{C}_i^m + (1 - s')y_i^m Y^m - (1 - s')y_i^c Y^m, \tag{6.54}$$

and after basic alterations we get:

$$\left(c_i^m - c_i^c\right) C^m = (1 - s')\left(y_i^m - y_i^c\right) Y^m. \tag{6.55}$$

In order to isolate the change in consumption expenditures on the competitive and monopolistic market, we divide the equation by C^m:

$$c_i^m - c_i^c = \frac{(1 - s')\left(y_i^m - y_i^c\right) Y^m}{C^m}. \tag{6.56}$$

Since $1 - \overline{s} = C^m / Y^m$, we have:

$$c_i^m - c_i^c = \frac{(1 - s')(y_i^m - y_i^c)Y^m}{(1 - \overline{s})Y^m} \tag{6.57}$$

and final rearranging produces:

$$c_i^m - c_i^c = \frac{1 - s'}{1 - \overline{s}}(y_i^m - y_i^c), \tag{6.58}$$

which describes reactions in consumption shares on income share changes, depending on the marginal propensity to save and the average saving rate.

The final part before solving the model deals with wealth dynamics; concretely how savings (simply defined as the difference between income and consumption) influence aggregate wealth in equilibrium. Let us have the difference equation:

$$F_{t+1} = F_t + Y_t - C_t, \tag{6.59}$$

which says that accumulated wealth equals the wealth in the previous time period plus aggregate savings ($=Y_t - C_t$). Considering the exogenous rate of growth g, the solution of the difference equation is $F_{t+1} = F_t(1 + g)$ and generally we have:

$$F^j = \frac{Y^j - C^j}{g}, \tag{6.60}$$

where again $j = c, m$. In steady state, the solution must fit to any population group:

$$f_i^c F^c = \frac{y_i^c Y^c - c_i^c C^c}{g} \tag{6.61}$$

$$f_i^m F^m = \frac{y_i^m Y^m - c_i^m C^m}{g}. \tag{6.62}$$

If we multiply Eq. (6.61) by mark-up μ and subtract it from Eq. (6.62), the term takes the form:

$$f_i^m F^m - \mu f_i^c F^c = \frac{y_i^m Y^m - \mu y_i^c Y^c - c_i^m C^m + \mu c_i^c C^c}{g}, \tag{6.63}$$

and considering Eq. (6.33) again yields:

$$f_i^m F^m - \mu f_i^c F^c = \frac{y_i^m Y^m - y_i^c Y^m - c_i^m C^m + c_i^c C^m}{g}. \tag{6.64}$$

When isolating common factors and using the steady state solution of wealth dynamics (Eq. 6.60) we get:

$$f_i^m - f_i^c = \frac{Y^m\left(y_i^m - y_i^c\right) - C^m\left(c_i^m - c_i^c\right)}{Y^m - C^m}. \tag{6.65}$$

Further, since we already know that $C^m = (1 - \overline{s})Y^m$, it implies:

$$f_i^m - f_i^c = \frac{Y^m(y_i^m - y_i^c) - Y^m(1 - \overline{s})(c_i^m - c_i^c)}{Y^m - (1 - \overline{s})Y^m}. \tag{6.66}$$

If we divide the right side by Y^m, after final rearrangement we get:

$$f_i^m - f_i^c = \frac{(y_i^m - y_i^c)}{\overline{s}} - \frac{(1 - \overline{s})(c_i^m - c_i^c)}{\overline{s}}. \tag{6.67}$$

The whole model is solved through equilibrium dynamics of wealth, income and consumption shares, i.e. Eqs. (6.67), (6.58) and (6.48). The system of these three equations is solved in the following steps: firstly, plugging Eq. (6.58) into Eq. (6.67) yields:

$$f_i^m - f_i^c = \frac{(y_i^m - y_i^c)}{\overline{s}} - \frac{1 - \overline{s}}{\overline{s}} \frac{1 - s'}{1 - \overline{s}} (y_i^m - y_i^c). \tag{6.68}$$

After simplifying the term $f_i^m - f_i^c = s'/\overline{s}\left(y_i^m - y_i^c\right)$ and plugging it into Eq. (6.48), we receive:

$$y_i^m - y_i^c = (\mu - 1)\left(f_i^m - y_i^m\right) = (1 - \mu\alpha_L)\frac{s'}{\overline{s}}\left(y_i^m - y_i^c\right). \tag{6.69}$$

Simple rearrangement yields:

$$y_i^m - y_i^c = \frac{(\mu - 1)\left(f_i^m - y_i^m\right)}{1 - \frac{s'}{\overline{s}}(1 - \mu\alpha_L)} \tag{6.70}$$

and combining it with $f_i^m - f_i^c = s'/\overline{s}\left(y_i^m - y_i^c\right)$ again gives:

$$f_i^m - f_i^c = \frac{\frac{s'}{\overline{s}}(\mu - 1)\left(f_i^m - y_i^m\right)}{1 - \frac{s'}{\overline{s}}(1 - \mu\alpha_L)}, \tag{6.71}$$

which clearly capture the redistributive effects of market power on income (Eq. 6.70) and wealth (Eq. 6.71). If we assume a certain lower bound which corresponds to the situation when $\overline{s} = s'$, the solution of the model then would be:

$$f_i^c - f_i^m = y_i^c - y_i^m = \frac{L(y_i^m - f_i^m)}{\alpha_L}, \tag{6.72}$$

with L as the Lerner index measuring monopoly power.

To have an empirical insight into the problem, Ennis et al. (2019) use data for eight advanced economies (Canada, France, Germany, Japan, Korea, Spain, United Kingdom and United States) to calibrate the model. Despite their numerical analysis does not entail more sophisticated econometric approach, it provides a vivid insight and uncovers some of general market tendencies. These data[3] focus on the following:

(i) Wealth and income shares based on the relation between i-th share of income (y_i) and i-th share of wealth (f_i). Market power therefore contributes to accumulation of gains if $f_i > y_i$; and, conversely, i-th group of agents with $f_i < y_i$ will experience decline in both wealth and income.

(ii) Market power measured by mark-ups. Naturally, the greater the mark-ups are, the less competitive the market is. However, it is not considered that complete eradication of mark-ups is the policy goal. Hence, actual mark-ups are compared with the lowest sector specific mark-ups observed across the eight economies in order to detect excessive mark-ups. The model is then able to simulate what the wealth distribution would be if the excess mark-up were not exist.

(iii) Income share of labour which reflect the fraction of labour gains (mostly wages) on total income. The measure is adjusted for self-employment which comes under labour income as well.

(iv) Marginal propensity to save and average saving rate which influence the scale of the impact of market power on inequality.

The main results of the model suggest that in average from 12% to 21% of the wealth of the top 10% is linked to market power. Another measure that can be adopted on the issue relies in manipulation of mark-ups. It shows that a 1% decrease in mark-ups in the UK increases the wealth of the bottom 20% by approximately 22%. In the absence of market power, the income of the bottom 20% in average economy is supposed to rise between 14% and 19%. According to provided estimates on the average economy, market power increases the wealth of the top 10% by between 12% and 21%, while it reduces the income of the bottom 20% by at least 11%. It is then intuitive that market power transfer economic power from consumers (in proportion to the income they earn) to business owners (in proportion to the wealth or capital they hold). In absolute terms, the most vulnerable are those with high incomes and low business ownership.

Similar results were already reached by Ennis and Kim (2016), whose paper is inspired by Comanor and Smiley (1975). On the other hand, using the similar approach on their data, Gans et al. (2019) found out that eliminating market power

---

[3]For data sources and more details on methods see Ennis et al. (2019).

would improve the income share of the bottom 60% from 19% to 21% and simultaneously it would decrease the income share of the top 20% from 64% to 61%. Based on these findings, market power does not seem to be the greatest driver of inequality.

To conclude, the analysis shows that higher profits in average improve the economic situation of a tiny group at the top of economic distribution while the vast majority tends to stagnate or to be even worse off. Potential surplus as a measure of increased profits due to unregulated market power therefore tend to be highly unequally distributed. To conclude, there is a detectable pattern which shows that market power contributes to accumulation of resources at the top and decumulation of resources at the bottom. These two factors inevitably lead to widening the gap between rich and poor, despite it could be hardly labelled as the only factor that boost inequality.

6.3 A Biomathematical Model of Resource Appropriation

Economic theory is not the only discipline which deals with units competing for scarce resources. A very fruitful perspective on competition can be found in mathematical biology. Unlike competitive models in economics, biomathematical approaches to competition look at the problem from a different perspective which is frequently based on the ability to usurp scarce resources from the outside in order to reproduce. It is often asserted that competition is a natural environment to human beings, something that is embedded in our genetic code. The following subchapter therefore deals with this very natural approach where economic agents are endowed with behavioural properties which are common for any biological entity.

In biology we distinguish various forms of competition; for instance, intraspecific and interspecific competition, depending on whether competing units are of the same species (intraspecific) or not (interspecific). Intuitively, modelling perfect competition in economics may use of knowledge in intraspecific models, while economic models integrating heterogeneity of agents can draw inspiration from interspecific models. According to Park (1962), competition can also have interfering or exploitative character. In the first case, competing units strive to exclude each other from a given environment. The exploitative character of competition occurs when one or more species appropriate scarce resources at the expense of other species. The last important types of competition are scramble competition and contest competition (Nicholson 1954). To start with the latter, the agent with the highest competitive ability monopolizes all resources, i.e. such competitive environment produces the winner and losers at a given time. On the contrary, scramble competition refers to situations where all competitors enjoy equal share of a limited resource so that increasing number of competitors decreases resources per unit, which basically corresponds to Malthusian understanding of population growth.

This source of knowledge has already produced many inspirational models[4] that could possibly, after careful reformulations, enrich economic theory in the question of resource distribution. The most viable model for our purpose turned out to be Hassell (1975). His population model, in combination with Beverton and Holt (1957) and Ricker (1954), was re-examined by Anazawa (2019) who interlinks reproduction of certain population with resource inequality.

Anazawa's model follows basic Hassell's setup which defines the expected value of the population size N in $t + 1$ as a function of the population size in t However, for the purpose of this book, we reinterpret the model in order to underline the dynamics of capital reproduction as the necessary condition for agents' reproduction. Assume to have N agents and each agent can obtain only a fixed size of resource units (u) at a given time. The total amount of resources (R) is constant and given by the size of resource units and number of such resource units (M); hence $R = uM$. Each unit of resources is randomly appropriated by an agent and the total number of resource units obtained within the competition struggle follows a binomial distribution. The agent thus obtains m resource units with probability:

$$p_m(M) = \left(\frac{1}{N}\right)^m \left(1 - \frac{1}{N}\right)^{M-m} \binom{M}{m}, \tag{6.73}$$

where $m \leq M$. The variance of the actual amount of resources obtained by an agent (um) then follows:

$$\mathrm{Var}(um) = uR\left(1 - \frac{1}{N}\right)\frac{1}{N}. \tag{6.74}$$

This reads that the variance is proportional to the size of the resource unit appropriable at a time, and hence increasing u is connected with increasing inequality in resource distribution. Individual reproduction also relies on the subsistent level of required resources (s). The probability of successful reproduction then refers to:

$$Q(M) = \sum_{m=s}^{M} p_m(M). \tag{6.75}$$

Following the 'population' character of the Hassell model, λ denotes the expected number of new individuals produced per reproductive individual. Transformed into economic language it means that if each agent is understood as a materialized capital, the reproduction of the agent, mediated by the reproduction of capital connected to that agent, depends on additional resources obtained from the outside (market). In other words, the agent successfully reproduces to the extent that her capital reproduces. This can be expressed as $N = \theta K$, where K is the amount of capital and θ

[4]Let us name for instance Lotka-Volterra population model (Lotka 1925; Volterra 1926) or Tilman model (1982) who established resource-ratio hypothesis.

denotes a positive transmission parameter which translates capital reproduction into reproduction of agents. Thus, λ can be interpreted as a reproductive parameter of capital. Provided reinterpretation should not be at the expense of clarity since the aim is to present principles of resource allocation, which are, in this particular case, purely random regardless the character of reproducing unit. Then, the expected amount of capital in the subsequent period follows:

$$f(K) = \lambda KQ(M), \tag{6.76}$$

which also indicates reproductive potential of the population of agents. If the value of R is unknown, to define the expected amount of capital in the next period requires at least probability distribution to be known. Assume an exponential distribution[5] with the probability density:

$$q(R) = \frac{e^{-\frac{R}{\overline{R}}}}{\overline{R}}, \tag{6.77}$$

with $\overline{R}$ as the expected value of R. The total number of resource units M follows a geometric distribution:

$$P_M = \left(1 - e^{-\frac{u}{\overline{R}}}\right)e^{-\frac{uM}{\overline{R}}}. \tag{6.78}$$

Combining the distribution with Eq. (6.76) yields:

$$f(K) = \sum_{M=0}^{\infty} \lambda KQ(M)P_M. \tag{6.79}$$

Since $p_m(M) = 0 \Leftrightarrow m > M$, the upper bound in Eq. (6.75) can be changed as follows:

$$Q(M) = \sum_{m=s}^{\infty} p_m(M), \tag{6.80}$$

and then substituted into Eq. (6.79) yields:

$$f(K) = \lambda K \sum_{M=0}^{\infty} \sum_{m=s}^{\infty} p_m(M)P_M. \tag{6.81}$$

Rearranging the term gives:

[5]For more details on the distribution type choice see Anazawa (2019:4–5).

$$f(K) = \lambda K \sum_{m=s}^{\infty} \widehat{p}_m, \tag{6.82}$$

where

$$\widehat{p}_m = \sum_{M=0}^{\infty} p_m(M) P_M \tag{6.83}$$

is the probability of obtaining m resource units with geometrically distributed M (Eq. 6.78). Again, since $p_m(M) = 0 \Leftrightarrow m > M$, and substituting $e^{-u/R} = a$, then putting together Eqs. (6.73) and (6.78) with (6.83) gives:

$$\widehat{p}_m = \sum_{M=m}^{\infty} (1-a)a^M \left(\frac{1}{K}\right)^m \left(1 - \frac{1}{K}\right)^{M-m} \frac{M!}{m!(M-m)!}. \tag{6.84}$$

To simplify the following computations, we put $M - m = M$; hence:

$$\widehat{p}_m = \sum_{M=m}^{\infty} (1-a)a^{M'+m} \left(\frac{1}{K}\right)^m \left(1 - \frac{1}{K}\right)^{M'} \frac{(M'+m)!}{m!M'!}. \tag{6.85}$$

The expansion formula is in the form:

$$(1-x)^{-k-1} = \sum_{n=0}^{\infty} x^n \frac{(n+k)!}{k!n!}, \tag{6.86}$$

where $|x| < 1$. Applying the formula to Eq. (6.85), we get:

$$\widehat{p}_m = \left[\frac{1}{(a^{-1}-1)K}\right]^m \left[1 + \frac{1}{(a^{-1}-1)K}\right]^{-m-1}. \tag{6.87}$$

Combining Eq. (6.87) with Eq. (6.82) yields:

$$f(K) = \lambda K \sum_{m=s}^{\infty} \left[\frac{1}{(a^{-1}-1)K}\right]^m \left[1 + \frac{1}{(a^{-1}-1)K}\right]^{-m-1}. \tag{6.88}$$

Substituting back the reproduced capital for the reproduced agents and summing with respect to m yields the Hassell model. After final rearrangements, we get:

$$f(N) = \frac{\lambda N\theta^{-1}}{\left[1 + N\theta^{-1}(e^{-\frac{u}{R}} - 1)\right]^{s}}, \tag{6.89}$$

where $s = s'/u$ with s' as the actual subsistent level of required resources and $N = \theta K$. The model depicts how the population of agents evolves with regards to reproduction of capital. It confirms that the larger is the exponent s, i.e. the smaller is u (and the greater is s'), the lower is inequality.

The level of inequality then oscillates between two extremes described by special cases of the model. Firstly, when the size of resource units u is sufficiently large, an agent then reproduces with s equal unity and the model becomes Beverton-Holt (1957):

$$f(N) = \frac{\lambda N\theta^{-1}}{1 + N\theta^{-1}(e^{-\frac{u}{R}} - 1)}, \tag{6.90}$$

which corresponds to maximally unequal distribution of resources. On the contrary, the size of resource units u limitedly approaching to zero yields the Ricker model (1954):

$$f(N) = \lambda N\theta^{-1} \exp\left(-\frac{s' N\theta^{-1}}{\overline{R}}\right), \tag{6.91}$$

which, by contrast, corresponds to perfectly equal distribution.

As was already the case of previously presented models on subsistence consumption, we could parallelly think of varying resource units required for reproduction (s) among agents. Assuming p_s as the probability that an agent requires s resource units for reproduction, a 'capital formation' then follows:

$$f(K) = \sum_{s=0}^{\infty} \lambda K\left[1 + K(e^{-\frac{u}{R}} - 1)\right]^{-s} p_s. \tag{6.92}$$

It suggests itself to apply certain conditions. Still following Anazawa (2019), we propose that $s < s_0 \Rightarrow p_s = 0$ and for $s \geq s_0$ the difference $s - s_0$ follows a negative binomal distribution:

$$p_s = \frac{\Gamma(s - s_o + k)}{\Gamma(k)\Gamma(s - s_o + 1)} \left(\frac{\delta}{k}\right)^{s - s_0} \left(1 + \frac{\delta}{k}\right)^{-s + s_0 - k}, \tag{6.93}$$

where s_0, $k > 0$ and $\delta = \overline{s} - s_0 (> 0)$, while $\overline{s}$ is the mean of s and k is a shape parameter. The variance (σ^2) of s thus negatively relates to k and positively to δ, since $\sigma^2(s) = \delta + \delta^2/k$. The case of $\delta \to 0$ implies that $\sigma^2(s) = 0$ and thus s stays constant.

Equation (6.92) can be rewritten into the form of expected value $E[X(s)]$ of a function $X(s)$ of a random variable s:

$$f(K) = E\left[\lambda K\left[1 + K\left(e^{-\frac{u}{R}} - 1\right)\right]^{-s}\right], \tag{6.94}$$

and then altered as:

$$f(K) = \lambda K\, G\left(1 + K\left(e^{-\frac{u}{R}} - 1\right)^{-s}\right), \tag{6.95}$$

where $G(z) \equiv E[z^s]$ represents a probability-generating function of s. Based on the properties of Eq. (6.93), the respective generating function is:

$$E\left[z^{s-s_0}\right] = \left[1 + (1 - z)\frac{\delta}{k}\right]^{-k}. \tag{6.96}$$

The generating function of s is defined as $G(z) = z^{s_0} E\left[z^{s-s_0}\right]$ which in combination with Eq. (6.96) yields:

$$G(z) = z^{s_0}\left[1 + (1 - z)\frac{\delta}{k}\right]^{-k}, \tag{6.97}$$

and substituted into Eq. (6.95) yields:

$$f(K) = \frac{\lambda K}{\left[1 + K\left(e^{-\frac{u}{R}} - 1\right)\right]^{s_0}}\left[\frac{1 + K\left(e^{-\frac{u}{R}} - 1\right)}{1 + \left(1 + \frac{\delta}{k}\right)K\left(e^{-\frac{u}{R}} - 1\right)}\right]^{k}, \tag{6.98}$$

while an additional condition $k = s_0$ gives the Hassel model:

$$f(K) = \frac{\lambda K}{\left[1 + \left(1 + \frac{\delta}{k}\right)K\left(e^{-\frac{u}{R}} - 1\right)\right]^{k}}. \tag{6.99}$$

The effect of varying s is mirrored in k since $\sigma^2(s) = \delta + \delta^2/k$ and $\delta + k = \overline{s}$. The first of the two variables constituting the mean of resource units for reproduction is determined as:

$$k = \frac{\overline{s}}{1 + \frac{\sigma^2(s)}{\overline{s}}} = \frac{\overline{s}'}{u + \frac{\sigma^2(s)'}{\overline{s}'}}, \tag{6.100}$$

where $\sigma^2(s)'$ and $\overline{s}'$ represent the mean and variance of resource units for reproduction $s' = su$. It can be seen that k, determined by these two statistical characteristics, reflects both varying actual level of required resources for reproduction and inequality in distribution of resources. Concretely, higher variance of s' is supposed to mitigate inabilities of agents to reproduce during capital appropriation process.

To complete the analysis, the second variable constituting the mean of resource units for reproduction reads:

$$\delta = \frac{\sigma^2(s)}{1 + \frac{\sigma^2(s)}{\bar{s}}} = \frac{\frac{\sigma^2(s)'}{u}}{u + \frac{\sigma^2(s)'}{\bar{s}'}}. \tag{6.101}$$

The last but highly important part of the model refers to varying reproductive parameter of capital λ (fecundity parameter in population models). The importance stems from the connection between how much of additional capital is obtained and how much of resources was allocated to the process of obtaining additional capital. Assume the reproductive parameter of capital as a function of allocated resource units m:

$$\lambda_m = \begin{cases} \lambda\left(1 - e^{-\gamma u(m-s+1)}\right), & m \geq s \\ 0 \quad , & m < s. \end{cases} \tag{6.102}$$

where λ and γ are positive parameters and s is a positive integer. It follows that if $m \geq s$, then λ_m grows to the maximum value with increasing m. The same condition also implies that if $\gamma \rightarrow \infty$, we get $\lambda_m = \lambda$, and for $m < s$ we have $\lambda_m = 0$. The expected amount of capital in the next period reads:

$$f(K) = K \sum_{m=s}^{\infty} \lambda_m \widehat{p}_m \tag{6.103}$$

with $\widehat{p}_m$ as the probability that an agent appropriates exactly m resource units under already defined distribution of R (Eq. 6.77). The probability therefore follows Eqs. (6.73), (6.78) and (6.83), which finally yields already known:

$$\widehat{p}_m = \left[\frac{1}{\left(e^{-u/\bar{R}} - 1\right)K}\right]^m \left[1 + \frac{1}{\left(e^{-u/\bar{R}} - 1\right)K}\right]^{-m-1}. \tag{6.104}$$

Considering this equation with Eqs. (6.102) and (6.103), agents' reproduction in the next period defines:

$$f(N) = \frac{\lambda N \theta^{-1}}{\left[1 + N\theta^{-1}\left(e^{-\frac{u}{R}} - 1\right)\right]^{s-1}\left[1 + \zeta N\theta^{-1}\left(e^{-\frac{u}{R}} - 1\right)\right]}, \tag{6.105}$$

where $\zeta = 1/(1 - e^{-\gamma u})$. The difference between this and the Hassel model (Eq. 6.89) consists in replacing N with $\zeta N(>N)$ in the second term in the denominator. Hence, if the amount of allocated resources is taken into account, the model generates lower values than in the case of former Hassel's model. These lower values are the more markable, the smaller is the value of parameter γ.

In order to define upper and lower limits, the highest inequality ($s = 1$) transforms Eq. (6.105) into the Beverton-Holt model:

$$f(N) = \frac{\lambda N\theta^{-1}}{1 + \zeta N\theta^{-1}(e^{-\frac{u}{R}} - 1)}. \tag{6.106}$$

As expected, perfectly equal distribution of resources ($u \to 0$ with fixed $s' = su$) transforms the model into:

$$f(N) = \lambda N\theta^{-1} \exp\left(-\frac{s'N\theta^{-1}}{\overline{R}}\right)\frac{1}{1+\frac{N}{R}}, \tag{6.107}$$

which is the Ricker model multiplied by the growth rate of a Beverton-Holt model. The presence of the Beverton-Holt growth rate then causes that the model generates lower values than in the case of former Ricker model (Eq. 6.91).

The presented model aims to show that the essence of reproduction process, driven by appropriation of additional resources from the outside, is non-neutral to the evolution of resource inequality among competitors. Population consists of independent agents and each agent is considered as a materialized capital. Each agent strives to valorise the amount of capital held in order to reproduce over time. In other words, agents use their capital in order to attain more capital on the market and secure their survival on the market. It is clear from the opening parts of the model that this process is accompanied by rising level of resource inequality. Subsequent parts of the model define lower and upper bound for inequality levels and also show how to operationalize individualized level of resources necessary for reproduction, as well as how to cope with individualized ability of agents endowed with capital to attract additional capital units. Inequality in resource distribution thus depends on the size of the resource unit that an agent can obtain at a time. Outcomes of the model also show that the 'stricter' the competition in economic sense is, it means the more it inclines to ideal contest competition with the exponent in the denominator equal unity, the higher is inequality in resource distribution.

To conclude, the model outlines how reproduction of society depends on appropriation of capital. Of course, there are obvious limits of economic interpretation. One of them may be its randomness which is modelled through various distributions so that model's outcomes remain dependent on the distribution choice. All in all, the final chapter demonstrate that contextualization of the model with market principles produces essential conclusions.

6.4 Chapter Summary

This chapter referred to competition and its possible role in economic distribution. By following this goal, readers were introduced into three models that provide different perspectives on competition. We have started with the Schumpeterian growth model where the prime driver of economic growth are innovations. A rich tradition of economic though starting from Marx deciphered the necessity to innovate as the inevitable process coming from competitive pressures. Innovation activities of each agent naturally lead to increasing production potential on the aggregate level. In order to formulate regular optimization problem, the model uses three types of inputs. Agent's objective is to maximize the flow of expected profits from the innovation process by optimizing the amount of inputs employed in the process. The agent therefore faces trade-offs whether to use inputs in production process or to innovate, whereas successful innovations, which follow Poisson distribution, improve the production process in upcoming future. The Schumpeterian model brings to the light two important outcomes. Firstly, the model concludes that the successful innovator (monopolist) is not motivated to start another innovation process since the value of the next innovation is strictly less than the value of the next innovation to all other actors except the monopolist. The feature of the model is that the monopolist is not permanently exposed to competitive pressures which would weaken monopolist's motivation to innovate. Agents are thus rotating on the position of the monopolist which indirectly moderate long-run evolution of inequality among agents. This is because in different periods there are different monopolists.

Both the average growth rate and the variance of the growth rate increase with higher "arrival" parameter of innovations, with the size of innovations, with the greater endowment of N input, and—in the case of Cobb-Douglas setup—with the level of market power. If we consider arrival parameter and the size of innovations as exogenously given, the competitive capacity of an agent is concentrated in possibilities to innovate. Such possibility is given by the amount of inputs that can be allocated to the innovation process and by agent's market power.

As regards the latter, market power can be defined as the ability to setup prices above the level of marginal costs, which is concerned in the second model of this chapter. The model stresses asymmetric impact of higher prices stemming from higher monopolization on different wealth-groups. The point of the model is that wealthier agents hold disproportionately more corporate assets which means that benefits of higher prices, reflected in returns of corporate assets, are disproportionately distributed as well. All agents as consumers therefore suffer with higher prices, but poorer agents are not compensated by rising returns of corporate holdings as wealthier agents do. After solving the model for eight advanced economies through equilibrium dynamics of wealth, income and consumption shares, we conclude that a significant part of the wealth of the top shares is linked to market power. The model shows that a decrease of market power measured by mark-ups distinctly increases the wealth of the bottom shares, and, conversely, decreases the wealth of those on the top. It is then intuitive that market mechanism transfers economic power from consumers (in proportion to the income they earn) to business owners (in proportion to the wealth or capital they hold). In absolute terms, the most vulnerable are those with high incomes and low business ownership. This goes along with a bunch of research on economic distribution; as an analogy on the global level we can mention famous Milanovic's "elephant graph". In sum, and due to many factors such as decline in employees' bargaining power (unionization), higher profits make in average the wealthy better off at the expense of the poor.

The third model provides a less common perspective on competition. Unlike competitive models in economics, which defines competition predominantly in a 'push' direction, i.e. with an emphasize on supplying the market, models in mathematical biology formulate competition rather in a 'pull' direction. Biological models therefore put an emphasize on the ability to usurp additional (scarce) resources from the outside with the aim to reproduce. In order to incorporate this perspective into our consideration, we have used the model which is convenient in many respects. For instance, it aims to capture inequality in resource appropriation even in the context of individualized subsistence constraints. On the other hand, it does not accommodate economic growth since available resources are fixed, which is an obvious disadvantage compare to most of comparable economic models. In any case, yet the opening part of the model shows that process of appropriation is immanently accompanied by rising inequality measured by variance of the actual amount of resources obtained by an agent. Inequality in resource distribution then depends on the size of the resource unit that an agent can obtain at a time. Also, inequality depends on how strict the competition is. The model demonstrates that the more the conditions of appropriation corresponds to ideal contest competition, the greater is the drive towards divergence.

To conclude, we have presented three models which capture crucial aspects of competitive struggle among agents. Schumpeterian model underlined innovation incentives as the prime driver of economic growth. More competitive markets in this model lead to more intense rotation of the monopolist. Questions of how the growth is distributed then depends on problematizing the role of the monopolistic rent and of the monopolist. Despite the model formulates importance of expenditures on the innovation process, it does not sufficiently differentiate e.g. between established leaders with significant market power and weak followers or capital-unequipped newcomers. The second model confirms this equalizing role of competition from a different perspective, where monopolization and subsequent higher prices have asymmetric impact on wealth of the rich and poor. More intense competition thus not allows high mark-ups which significantly contribute through higher prices to increasing wealth of the richest. The third example therefore presents a 'pull-type competition' model which concludes the opposite—it assesses competitive environment as the diverging factor of agents' reproduction, but under restricting assumption that total available resources are fixed.

References

Aghion P, Howitt P (1992) A model of growth through creative destruction. Econometrica 60 (2):323–351

Anazawa M (2019) Inequality in resource allocation and population dynamics models. R Soc Open Sci 6(7):182178

Baker J, Salop S (2015) Antitrust, competition policy, and inequality. Georgetown Law J 104:1–28
Beverton RJH, Holt SJ (1957) On the dynamics of exploited fish populations. Fisheries Investigations Series II, 19. London
Comanor WS, Smiley RH (1975) Monopoly and the distribution of wealth. Q J Econ 89 (2):177–194
Creedy J, Dixon R (1999) The distributional effects of monopoly. Aust Econ Pap 38(3):223–237
De Loecker J, Eeckhout J, Unger G (2019) The rise of market power and the macroeconomic implications. Quart J Econ (forthcoming)
Ennis S, Kim Y (2016) Market power and wealth distribution. In: A step ahead: competition policy, shared prosperity and inclusive growth. World Bank, Washington, DC
Ennis S, Gonzaga P, Pike C (2019) Inequality: a hidden cost of market power. Oxf Rev Econ Policy 35(3):518–549
Furman J, Orszag P (2015) A firm-level perspective on the role of rents in the rise in inequality. Columbia University, A Just Society Centennial Event in Honor of Joseph Stiglitz
Gans JS, Leigh A, Schmalz MC, Triggs A (2019) Inequality and market concentration, when shareholding is more skewed than consumption. Oxf Rev Econ Policy 35(3):550–563
Hassel MP (1975) Density-dependence in single-species populations. J Anim Ecol 44:283–295
Lotka AJ (1925) Elements of physical biology. Williams & Wilkins, Baltimore
Nicholson AJ (1954) An outline of the dynamics of animal populations. Aust J Zool 2:9–65
Park T (1962) Beetles, competition, and populations. Science 138(3548):1369–1375
Ricker WE (1954) Stock and recruitment. J Fish Res Board Can 11:559–623
Rognlie M (2015) Deciphering the fall and rise in the net capital share. Brook Pap Econ Act 46 (1):1–69
Sweezy P (1968) The theory of capitalist development. Monthly Review Press, New York
Tilman D (1982) Resource competition and community structure. Princeton University Press, Princeton
Tirole J (1988) The theory of industrial organization. MIT Press, MA
Volterra V (1926) Variazioni e fluttuazioni del numero d'individui in specie animali conviventi. Memoria della Reale Accademia Nazionale dei Lincei 2:31–113

Chapter 7
The Dynamic Model of Market Inequality

7.1 Theoretical Context

The aim of the last chapter is to extract and aggregate knowledge from the previous chapters and to formulate a simple model that captures principles of market resource allocation. The model should come with an explicative principle of market inequality in economic distribution for which it abstracts to the utmost from agent's subjectivity, randomness and idiosyncrasies. Therefore, we assume homogeneous agents in order to eliminate individual differences as the determinant of inequality. This assumption secures that inequality detected among agents with the same decision-making process stems from the system characteristics of the production process which is based on the market mechanism. Beside the market-isolating effect, it is necessary to understand that the proposed model concerns abstract principles of the market mechanism which enables to consider not only typical microeconomic actors (firms and households/individuals), but also national states and other geographical or political entities organized by a market system.

To briefly complement already investigated papers, there are also several inspirable papers which refer to economic inequality with homogeneous agents in the context of abstract market principles. A strong position in this question was worked out in econophysics. For instance, Chakraborti's (2002) model is based on exchange between two agents, while the wealth transfer is happening when one of them pays for an object of exchange more/less than it worth. Naturally, we could observe quite a few unanswered questions, for example what the reference price/value is, which is, in addition, highly subjectivized category in modern economics. Among others we can mention series of papers (Boghosian 2014a, b, 2015), later on elaborated by Chorro (2016), whose contribution clearly signalizes that empirical findings on economic distribution are sufficiently well explainable by unstable and diverging models, which is a conclusion that contributes to weakening equilibria obsession in contemporary economics. These results contribute to the foundations of the proposed model as well.

R. Maialeh, *Dynamic Models and Inequality*, Contributions to Economics,
https://doi.org/10.1007/978-3-030-46313-7_7

The issue of inequality requires to be generally viewed as the result of certain creation and appropriation of wealth (resources). Intrinsic features of the production process and concurrently the most influential attributes to researched inequality are 'profit' maximization and a certain level/form of competition. Competitive pressure further prepares soil for innovations through which economic agents enhance their competitiveness. This exhaustibly captures self-preservation and market competition stressed by Horkheimer in the fourth chapter, when saying that 'any slowdown or stagnation brings destruction'. (2012 [1949–67]) Hence, we intuitively understand that every single agent, whose reproduction is subordinated to market conditions, has to adjust her behaviour to them, i.e. maximize the amount of resources for enhancing competitiveness due to competitive pressure.

If any agent does not accept these imperatives in the long run, then the agent loses her competitiveness and the agent is excluded from a given market. Every agent whose reproduction depends on resources from the market thus obeys such rules and agent's behaviour is beyond any preferential ranking—the agent is alleged to prescribed agencies of power.

For reasons mentioned above we assume Schumpeterian growth theory as a starting point for modelling. The reason is that Schumpeterian theory allows to capture an 'infinite' growth via agents' innovation imperatives. Our approach bears a close resemblance to the theory of 'creative destruction' which highly corresponds to the dynamical character of our research. Nonetheless, Schumpeterian theory assumes loans as the source of innovation.[1] However, we adopt a more relevant assumption that accumulation of resources is happening by employing internal savings in the long run. Not to mention broad literature dedicated to 'credit constraints', covered also e.g. by already cited Gomez and Foot (2003), Galor (2009) or Aghion et al. (1999), which also signalize that loans as the source of innovation should be eliminated in our context. The reason is that creditworthiness and imperfections on capital markets[2] in this case might obscure the pure market mechanism.[3] The complete credit market assumption (as the constitutive subset of the capital market) is therefore relaxed due to empirical and theoretical findings (newly for example Getachew 2016 or Hai and Heckman 2017) that prove deepening inequalities caused by capital market imperfections.[4] Without going into depth of these studies, it is enough to perceive that credit is, in general, a function of current resources and their future prospects. We would be therefore forced to consider

[1]Further explanation of Schumpeter's views of capital market as the "headquarter of capitalist economy" is provided by Kurz (2012).

[2]Theoretical insight into persisting inequalities in the context of imperfect capital markets is provided in the first theme of Mookherjee and Ray (2003).

[3]Piketty supports the idea of using own resources by the claim that most of growth relies on domestic, not foreign investments on macroeconomic level (2014).

[4]It is also evident that by assuming perfectly functioning capital market with no credit constraints, where all agents, regardless the amount of their resources, would be able to finance their potentialities, we might observe, upon additional assumptions, converging tendencies, as indicated e.g. in Aghion et al. (1999).

numerous systemic advantages of richer agents, e.g. lower interest rates on loans and better financial services in general, that would intensify diverging tendencies among agents even further. Moreover, an employment of the capital market would lead to serious methodological issues. Capital markets are already a concrete practical application of general market principles, operating in a concrete empirical reality. In contrast to the aim of the book, which focuses on abstract structurally-genetical principles, capital markets work as a subsystem of the general principles. Therefore, an inclusion of such a subsystem does not correspond to the level of abstraction which is desired for composing the model.

For the sake of simplicity, clarity and above-mentioned reasons we use neoclassical emphasis on savings. Hereby we gain a non-stationary frame in which innovations (or new combinations) are the engine of progress meanwhile the innovations derive from agents own unconsumed resources, not from external ones. Then we can claim that everything that has not been consumed is, due to competitive pressures, allocated to strengthen agent's competitiveness. Every investment (actualizing itself in the innovation process) is thus understood as strengthening agent's competitiveness—an activity to which agents are forced by their competitors.

Assuming this, we abstract from intertemporal substitution as exogenously heterogeneous quality of individual agents. In other words, intertemporal transfer of resources often slips into a mere 'psychologized' faculty, concluding e.g. that individuals are born different and those with lower intertemporal substitution necessarily have lower saving rate, while the saving rate is used to be the prime determinant of economic wealth. A real-life decision-making of economic agents is undoubtedly co-determined by such inborn qualities, which, however, say nothing about the role of economic environment on economic distribution. In our abstraction, the intertemporal transfer of resources is therefore exclusively determined by the logic of competitive markets.

Naturally, we can think of numerous extensions of the problem. In our case we can reasonably assume that, if an agent understands reproduction as maintaining the current economic level, the reproduction of a wealthier agent requires more resources than of a poorer agent. Such amount of 'reproductive' resources is thus increasing with economic power, but understandably at a declining pace.

What is also evident is that we do not use game-theoretical terminology since there is no strategy problem. Due to perfectly competitive environment, which underlines the abstract nature of market mechanism, we demystify the naturalized illusion of choice. To be more precise, agents are free to choose in which field, by which means and how they pursue building-up their competitiveness, but certainly they do not have the option to resign on competitiveness as such. The combination of self-preservation and competition for resources attained for further reproduction causes that agents' behaviour is determined by the market mechanism.

7.2 Formulation of the Model

The following model re-formulates income, consumption, savings and investments inspired by Maialeh (2016 and 2017). As regards variables, by R we understand total resources *in various forms* which the agent has before any consumption. Total resources do not refer only to material and monetary resources, but to all resources that can be in any form usable on the market. This is the broadest definition of economic resources which embraces not only wages, capital gains and other assets, but also free time, social capital etc. Further, not all resources can be used to *directly* support the agent's position on the market. Therefore, $\bar{c}$ is assigned to all resources essential for agents' reproduction on a given economic level. It represents the lowest costs that ensure agent's survival on a given market and economic level in the next time-period, which followingly unifies an irreducible multiplicity of subjective positions. In order to follow-up on conventional and already presented economic literature[5], we label this variable as the non-stationary subsistence consumption. Variable of savings is determined by the difference between R and $\bar{c}$. It basically represents how much the agent has at a disposal after meeting his subsistence constraints. This interpretation follows a long tradition of political economy, where the surplus value is determined by the costs on replacement of means of production and necessary consumption, both subtracted from the final product. It means that subsistence consumption $\bar{c}$ in our case contains both replacement of means of production and necessary consumption. Such a value therefore embraces all resources, again in various forms, which an agent is able to use in the competitive struggle; in Schumpeter's language we could talk about resources dedicated to 'new combinations'. In sum, by this we understand all activities and resources which are supposed to strengthen agent's competitiveness after securing his immediate reproduction, which we refer to as investible surplus I.[6] And finally, π represents all scarce appropriable resources on the market—the object of the competitive struggle among agents. These resources π are appropriated above already allocated resources which agent receives in the next period. Based on this we assume that i-th agent faces $R_t^i = R_{t-1}^i \Leftrightarrow \pi_t^i = 0$. This assumption plays a similar role to what we have seen in Rosenzweig and Wolpin (1993) as 'subsistence insurance'.

Except papers dealing with subsistence constraints, there are only few studies which focus on problematizing agents' self-preservation. In concrete, Karni and Schmeidler (1986), as ones of the very few, comes up with their self-preservation model. However, their model is based on a strategic character of preferences in a

[5]Harris similarly defines "necessary consumption" as a "quantity required for consumption in order that a unit of labor may be maintained in production". (1978:55) The term "reproductive consumption" is used in feminist theory. (e.g. Fletcher 2006) Adorno and Horkheimer, inspired by Marx, speak about "cultural minimum". (2002 [1944]:142)

[6]An interesting discussion on investible surplus under competition and subsistence constraints can be found in Edwards (1971) who concludes that competition is harmful for maximizing investible surplus in developing communities.

finite horizon perspective. Slightly more psychologized approach was asserted by Roese and Olson (2007). What is however still useful is Hlaváček's (1999) idea of the perceived threat of extinction r derived through Euclidean distance ρ as the inverse function of the distance to the zone of extinction. Similar ideas are also present in researches where closeness to the subsistence level affects intertemporal substitution. We reformulate the model, hence we get:

$$r(R_t^i) = \left[\rho\left(\bar{c}_t^i; R_t^i\right)\right]^{-1}. \tag{7.1}$$

while the zone of extinction is reached when $R_t^i - \bar{c}_t^i = 0$. The formula says that agent i perceives the threat of extinction the more the smaller is the difference between her total resources and subsistence consumption. Agent i therefore strives for the level of total resources R_t^{i*} at which she minimizes the perceived threat of extinction, i.e.:

$$R_t^{i*} = \arg\min \left[\rho\left(\bar{c}_t^i; R_t^i\right)\right]^{-1}; \text{for } \rho\left(\bar{c}_t^i; R_t^i\right) \in \mathbb{R}^+. \tag{7.2}$$

As is usual in agent-based models, we maximize agent's utility or profit $u_t^i; \Pi_t^i = \max \left[\rho\left(\bar{c}_t^i; R_t^i\right)\right]^{\frac{1}{n}}$; in other words, the agent maximizes the difference between disposable total resources and subsistence consumption. n-th root of the Euclidean distance is a curvature parameter which reflects concavity of utility or production function, depending on whether we model survival of the firm or the individual, which naturally implies whether we refer to utility or profit maximization.[7] The function implicitly contains a form of risk aversion which is usually embedded in economic models through smoothing consumption. In our case, despite concavity of production/utility function plays its role as well, risk aversion is dominantly interpreted via 'disaster-avoiding behaviour', where the agent strives to not fall below a subsistence level. By following e.g. Drèze and Sen (1989) we emphasize that subsistence considerations are present also in the behaviour of those agents who are not immediately at risk of extinction.

In order to refine appropriation of resources, which is in fact a probabilistic process, we need to incorporate a probabilistic frame. The aim to survive, which is immanent to every single agent, is defined as the single mode of agent's action due to inescapable competitive pressure. The probability of survival is hence:

$$P(R_t^i) = \frac{1}{1 + r(R_t^i)} = \frac{\rho}{1 + \rho} \text{ for } \rho = \rho\left(\bar{c}_t^i; R_t^i\right) \tag{7.3}$$

from which we derive that the long distance $\rho\left(\bar{c}_t^i; R_t^i\right)$ gives:

[7]Despite decreasing marginal utility was historically connected rather with logarithmic function (e.g. Daniel Bernoulli), n-th root eases to calculate values of the Euclidean distance (0,1).

$$\lim_{r(R_t^i)\to 0} P(R_t^i) = 1, \tag{7.4}$$

depicting that the probability of survival is approaching to 100% when the perceived threat of extinction approaches 0. Likewise, when total resources of the agent approach the zone of extinction, the probability of survival is limitedly approaching to 0%[8]:

$$\lim_{(R_t^i)\to \bar{c}} P(R_t^i) = 0, \tag{7.5}$$

which demonstrates the fact that if the agent covers mere immediate reproduction without any resources left for enhancing her competitiveness, then competitive environment will ensure that the agent will not be able to appropriate resources on the market in the long-run.

Total resources are the sum of subsistence consumption and investible surplus for strengthening competitiveness of agent i in time t. Then we imply:

$$R_t^i = \bar{c}_t^i + I_t^i. \tag{7.6}$$

Subsistence consumption and investible surplus are defined by the level of total resources $R_t^i = \left(R_{t-1}^i + \pi_t^i\right)$. Average propensity to subsistence consumption is given as a share of subsistence consumption on total resources:

$$ap(\bar{c}) = \frac{\bar{c}}{R} \tag{7.7}$$

and, similarly, average propensity to investible surplus:

$$ap(I) = \frac{I}{R}. \tag{7.8}$$

As regards marginal propensities, marginal propensity to subsistence consumption measures a change in subsistence consumption on changes in total resources; thus:

$$mp(\bar{c}) = \frac{\partial \bar{c}}{\partial R} \tag{7.9}$$

and equivalently marginal propensity to investible surplus:

[8]On the other hand, the "probability of survival" must be understood a bit more loosely since we assumed that agents operate with a "subsistence insurance".

$$mp(I) = \frac{\partial I}{\partial R}. \tag{7.10}$$

For clarity we adopt the standard long-run assumption of equal marginal and average propensities, hence $ap(\bar{c}) = mp(\bar{c}); ap(I) = mp(I)$. Naturally, we follow ordinary relationships between average and marginal propensities, so that propensities change proportionally and inversely:

$$ap(\bar{c}) + ap(I) = 1 = mp(\bar{c}) + mp(I). \tag{7.11}$$

In order to simplify mathematical notation, we posit that $p^{(\bar{c})}$ corresponds to equivalence of long-run marginal and average propensities to subsistence consumption and similarly $p^{(I)}$ corresponds to equivalence of long-run marginal and average propensities to investible surplus. These propensities say what fraction of total resources is dedicated to subsistence consumption and what fraction is left unconsumed for enhancing competitiveness when total resources are changing over time. Further, when we consider a very low level of total resources, let us say $\bar{c}_t^i \to R_t^i$, the agent tends to consume all of them. In this case, propensity to subsistence consumption is approaching to 1. It follows that $p^{(I)}$ is approaching to 0 proportionally as $p^{(\bar{c})}$ is approaching to 1. Subsistence consumption and investible surplus are then given by:

$$\bar{c}_t^i = \bar{c}_{t-1}^i + p^{(\bar{c})}{}_t^i \pi_t^i, \tag{7.12}$$

$$I_t^i = I_{t-1}^i + p^{(I)}{}_t^i \pi_t^i. \tag{7.13}$$

As shown in Eqs. (7.6), (7.12) and (7.13), subsistence consumption $\bar{c}$ and investible surplus dedicated to enhancement of competitiveness I are intertemporally defined by total resources R. It can be also seen that agent's consumption cannot decrease below the level of the previous time period. However strong this assumption is, our focus is put on the ability to appropriate new available resources in the economy (not losing already gained resources) so that such a "floor" for agents' reproduction does not play any important role. This is also backed by empirical findings which intuitively indicate that the present inequality is not driven primarily by systematic losing resources, but rather by systematic inability of poorer agents to appropriate additional resources.

Nevertheless, agent requires a constantly smaller fraction of the additional unit of total resources for her reproduction; the relative amount (relative to total resources) of what the agent necessarily needs to expend is decreasing. It is therefore apparent that subsistence consumption remains to be an increasing function of total resources, however, the dynamics of increments is slower than in case of total resources. This idea is empirically backed e.g. by Carroll et al. (2017).[9] Of course, it reflects the fact that we exclude capital markets, i.e. that agents work only with their own resources. For our case it applies that:

$$\Delta \bar{c}_t^i; \Delta I_t^i < \Delta R_t^i; \Rightarrow 0 \leq \frac{\partial \bar{c}_t^i}{\partial R_t^i}; \frac{\partial I_t^i}{\partial R_t^i} \leq 1. \tag{7.14}$$

Inequality as a dynamic phenomenon therefore requires dynamization of relationships between relevant variables. In other words, we seek a principle that captures individual abilities to gain appropriable resources when total resources of the agent are changing. A narrow case of dynamization was provided e.g. by Gaechter et al. (2017) who studied public good games with dynamic interdependencies. Likewise, Stiglitz (1969), whose article presents implications for the distribution of wealth and income based on alternative assumptions about savings, reproduction, inheritance policies etc., which are investigated in the context of a neoclassical growth model. The author isolates different economic forces in order to evaluate which of those forces tend to make the distribution of wealth in the long run equalitarian and which tend to make wealth unevenly distributed. For this purpose, Stiglitz also models savings as a function of wealth and income but with reverse logic—that greater wealth leads to lower necessity to save. In our case, the dynamization concerns propensities. The dynamic forms require a formulation of the following conditions for one of the propensities; for assumed continuous function $p^{(I)}$: $[0, \infty) \rightarrow [0, 1)$ we have conditions (H):

$$(H)\begin{cases} p^{(I)}(0) = 0 \\ p^{(I)} \text{ is increasing}[0, \infty) \\ \lim\limits_{T \to \infty} p^{(I)}(R) = 1 \\ \exists \varepsilon \in (0, \infty) : p^{(I)} \text{ is convex } (0, \varepsilon); p^{(I)} \text{ is concave } (\varepsilon, \infty) \end{cases}$$

where ε is an inflex point, which is equal to a certain level of total resources where $p^{(I)} = p^{(\bar{c})}$; respectively propensities have values $= 0.5$. An economic interpretation of ε is that for $\{R_t^i | 0 < R_t^i < \varepsilon\}$ agent i prefers (or rather "is forced") to consume a bigger fraction of the additional unit of total resources than to use it in competition, i.e. $p^{(\bar{c})} > p^{(I)}$. Inversely for $\{R_t^i | \varepsilon < R_t^i < \infty\}$ agent i prefers (or rather "is allowed")

[9] The authors find a wide dispersion in the marginal propensities to consume across the wealth distribution. Mostly, less wealthy households have much higher marginal propensity to consume than wealthier households. According to them the ratio between wealth and income is the key determinant of marginal propensity to consume. Theoretical aspects of these determinations were researched in the context of the neoclassical model by Chatterjee (1994). This opposes older statistical estimations of Kuznets (1946) and Goldsmith (1955) regarding long-run constancy of the propensity to consume and redefinitions by Duesenberry (1949) or Friedman (1957). The proposed reformulation however accentuates the necessity to consume which implies that agents are forced to expend relatively less with increasing total resources.

to use in the competitive struggle a bigger fraction of the additional unit of total resources, i.e. $p^{(I)} > p^{(\bar{c})}$. For instance, when assuming a small amount of total resources, let us say $\bar{c}_t^i \to R_t^i$, the agent inclines to consume all total resources. From this we deduce that a still bigger fraction of additional units of total resources is becoming a component of investible surplus. Decreasing propensity to subsistence consumption, respectively increasing propensity to investible surplus when increasing total resources, are derived from the relative amount of resources which agent necessarily needs/is forced to sacrifice—the relative amount is decreasing with increasing total resources. The absolute amount of resources which agent necessarily needs to expend naturally increases and subsistence consumption remains to be an increasing function of total resources.

As a general solution, it can be considered the set of functions $\mathfrak{M}$ which follows H conditions:

$$\mathfrak{M} = \left\{ p^{(I)} \in C\left(\left[0, \infty\right), \left[0, 1\right) \right) \mid (H) \text{ holds} \right\}.$$

However, in order to provide a concrete function solution, we need a concrete functional form that corresponds to $\mathfrak{M}$, i.e. for which propensities are continuous on $[0, \infty)$ with values $[0, 1)$. There are numerous functions that depict outlined relationships. One of these options is to dynamize propensities through inverse trigonometric (cyclometric) or hyperbolic functions. Propensities can be then defined as functions of hyperbolic tangent of total resources (Maialeh 2016 and 2017). A more computationally viable dynamization is conceivable through typical logistic function which easily keeps the evolution of propensities within the allowed interval. Concretely, we have the following sigmoid curves:

$$p^{(\bar{c})}{}_t^i = 1 - \frac{1}{1 + e^{-\varsigma\left(R_t^i - \varepsilon\right)}}, \tag{7.15}$$

$$p^{(I)}{}_t^i = \frac{1}{1 + e^{-\varsigma\left(R_t^i - \varepsilon\right)}}. \tag{7.16}$$

The value of ς is the logistic growth rate which determines "steepness" of the curve.

Here we might identify two contradicting effects. Neoclassical point of view refers to decreasing returns as the result of rising "capital stock" which is translated into slower pace of $p^{(I)}$ increments. On the other side, greater Euclidean distance between total resources and subsistence consumption leads to increasing pace of $p^{(I)}$ increments. Therefore, for $\left\{ R_t^i \middle| 0 < R_t^i < \varepsilon \right\}$ we observe dominating the "Euclidean distance effect", and for $\left\{ R_t^i \middle| \varepsilon < R_t^i < \infty \right\}$ the "neoclassical effect" dominates. Thus, $p^{(\bar{c})}$ is limitedly approaching to 0 when increasing total resources, formally described by:

$$\lim_{R_t^i \to \infty} \left[1 - \frac{1}{1 + e^{-\varsigma(R_t^i - \varepsilon)}} \right] = 0, \tag{7.17}$$

and simultaneously $p^{(I)}$ is limitedly approaching to 1:

$$\lim_{R_t^i \to \infty} \left[\frac{1}{1 + e^{-\varsigma(R_t^i - \varepsilon)}} \right] = 1. \tag{7.18}$$

Agents with a lower amount of total resources then expend relatively a bigger fraction of these resources on subsistence meanwhile agents with a higher amount of total resources can afford to keep a bigger fraction of resources unconsumed in the form of investible surplus. One might argue that by this we overlook one of theoretical determinants of saving rate, concretely interest rate. The elimination however does not cause a distortion of the theory because interest rate is substituted in a sense of appropriated resources flowing from the successful allocation of investible surplus. In other words, deferred consumption is not rewarded by interest rate resulting from savings but by appropriated resources resulting from investments. In sum, agents with a higher amount of total resources can transform unconsumed resources into investments and build up their competitiveness further.

Based on that, it is possible to liken the probability of survival to maximization problem; in our case we can continue with utility maximization. Inasmuch as R is Reimann integrable, we get:

$$\max u_t^i; \Pi_t^i \Leftrightarrow \arg\ \max P(R_t^i) \Leftrightarrow \max \left[\rho\left(\bar{c}_t^i; R_t^i\right) \right]^{\frac{1}{n}} \Leftrightarrow \max \int_0^\infty f(R)\, \mathrm{d}R. \tag{7.19}$$

Here we claim that agent maximizes her utility/profit by maximizing the difference between what the agent has at a disposal and what the agent has to expend in order to reproduce. In our case, it means that the agent maximizes the probability of survival through maximizing total resources. This partial conclusion of the model stays in contrast, for instance, to RCK model in the third chapter, where agents were not motivated to infinitely accumulate wealth due to transversality condition.

For capturing the process of creation and appropriation of wealth/resources—the process generating inequality—we further assume Schumpeterian theory advanced by Aghion and Howitt (1992 and 2009). Subsequently presented growth theory allows to reflect market principles of "profit" maximization and competition. In other words, it eases to see an interlink between economic growth and tendencies of resource allocation. Economic growth g_t (the result of production process) is then calculated as follows:

$$g_t = \frac{A_t - A_{t-1}}{A_{t-1}}, \tag{7.20}$$

where A_t is a technological parameter denoting productivity of inputs in the economy at time t. Technological parameter is bigger at t than at $t - 1$ because A_{t-1} has changed due to innovations and therefore it evinces higher productivity level represented by A_t. Then:

$$A_t = \gamma A_{t-1}; \gamma > 1, \tag{7.21}$$

and thus

$$g_t = \gamma - 1. \tag{7.22}$$

For a successful innovation (as a proxy for competitiveness), i.e. for a subsequent appropriation of resources on the market, the agent must conduct an activity with an economic end; in other words, expend resources in innovation process—in the process of increasing competitiveness. The agent innovates in order to enhance her competitiveness through which she subsequently appropriates scarce resources on the market. It is assumed that the more resources the agent expends the more likely the innovation will be successful (Aghion and Howitt 2009) and, in our case, the more likely the agent appropriates scarce resources at a given time period. Therefore, probability μ_t that the innovation is successful at t is positively related to the amount of resources I_t allocated to the innovation process. Further, the probability μ_t is inversely related to γA_{t-1} which represents a new level of innovation productivity. In other words, the higher the level of productivity we assume the more difficult it is to implement the innovation. The probability is then captured as:

$$\mu_t = \phi\left(\frac{I_t}{\gamma A_{t-1}}\right). \tag{7.23}$$

From above noted we can conclude that probability of successful innovation is increasing with the amount of resources the agent is willing/capable to expend on its realization. At the same time, probability of implementing successful innovation is decreasing the higher the level of productivity the agent strives for. It is also evident that the differentiating factors of inequality are the amount or resources I_t allocated to the innovation and γA_{t-1} representing the new level of innovation productivity. In order to isolate market differences among agents, let us assume equal external conditions for all agents, i.e. identical γA_{t-1}. Then, we can say that the bigger the amount of unconsumed resources the agent has at t, the higher the probability to innovate and to strengthen her competitiveness the agent has at $t + 1$. We can also conclude that resources π exogenously occurs on the market in every period as a result of increasing productivity due to innovation competition.

The following part deals with resource appropriation over time. Firstly, we have to find a balance between two extremes. One of them is that successful appropriation is fully stochastic, and the second one refers to successful appropriation as a fully deterministic process. A sort of compromise between these two is to define appropriation process via computable probability. For our purpose, it is sensible to propose that probability of obtaining additional resources on the market increases with already appropriated resources (Anazawa 2019).

For simplicity, let us construct the model for two agents $\{A, B\}$ who compete for resources on a given market. We assume homogeneous agents and identical γA_{t-1}, i.e. equal market conditions for all agents. Probabilities ${P^{(\pi)}}_t^A; {P^{(\pi)}}_t^B$ to gain appropriable resources on the market are given by the relation of agent's investible surplus which she has at a disposal for the competitive struggle and total investible surpluses of all agents. Further, we define simultaneous moves of agents and zero-sum distribution of appropriable resources, so that the winning agent takes all appropriable resources π available at a given time. By assuming this, we get the following Scheme 7.1:

It is read from the Scheme 7.1 that agents A and B start to compete for appropriable resources π in time t. A's probability of appropriation π_t is given by the amount of resources which A is able to allocate to the competitive struggle $\left({p^{(I)}}_{t-1}^A R_{t-1}^A\right)$ and the total amount of resources allocated to the competitive struggle; in this particular case resources allocated by A and B, i.e. ${p^{(I)}}_{t-1}^A R_{t-1}^A + {p^{(I)}}_{t-1}^B R_{t-1}^B$. Naturally, for agents $\{1, 2 \ldots n\}$ the denominator would be $\sum_{i=1}^n I_t^i$. In $t + 1$, π_t was already distributed and became a part of someone's total resources in $t + 1$. If A appropriated π_t, then A's probability of appropriation π_{t+1} would be higher compare to B's due to A's higher numerator: ${p^{(I)}}_t^A (R_t^A + \pi_t) > {p^{(I)}}_t^B R_t^B$. The 'probability tree' thus shows that the probability to appropriate additional resources is cumulating over time. The probabilistic process can be then simplified as:

$$R_t^i = \begin{cases} R_{t-1}^i + \pi_t, & \text{w/probability } I_t^i / \sum\limits_{i=1}^n I_t^i \\ R_{t-1}^i, & \text{w/probability } 1 - I_t^i / \sum\limits_{i=1}^n I_t^i \end{cases}$$

The resource equation of the winner therefore satisfies: $\pi_t > \Delta I_t > 0$, and is attained by combining Eqs. (7.6), (7.13) and (7.16), which incorporates inequality-accelerating effect of dynamized propensities. Hence, we imply:

$$\frac{1}{1 + e^{-\varsigma(R_t^i - \varepsilon)}} = \frac{I_t^i - I_{t-1}^i}{\pi_t^i}, \tag{7.24}$$

which after inverting and logarithms yields:

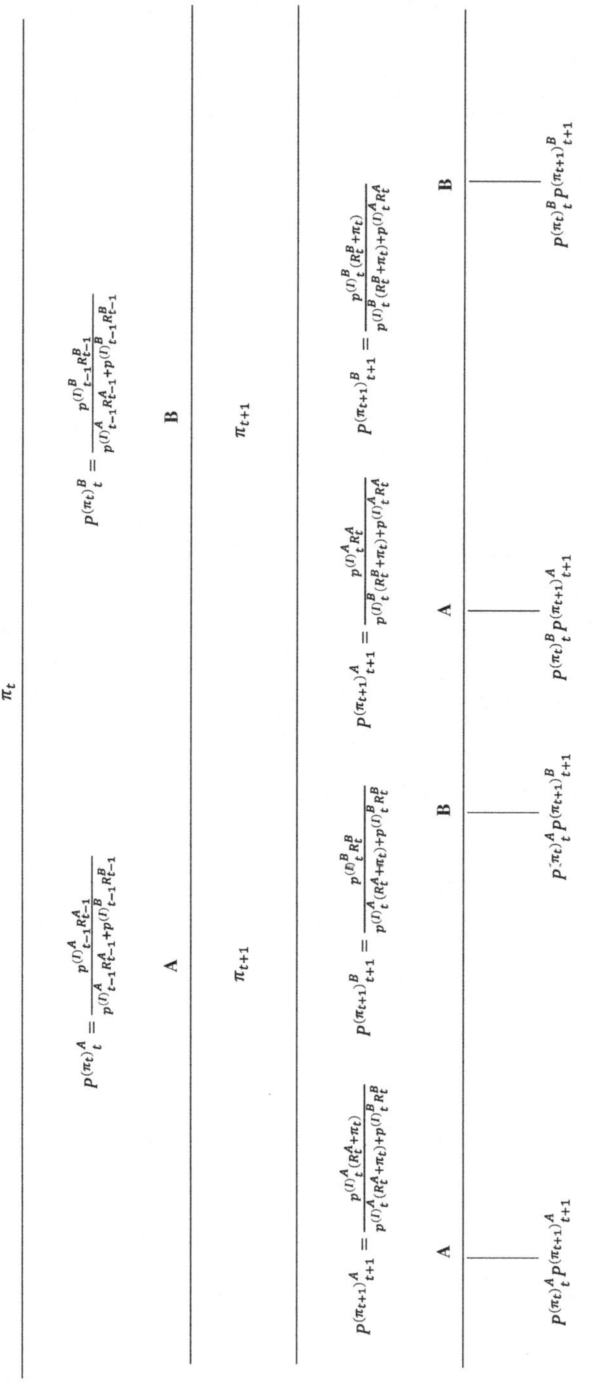

Scheme 7.1 Probabilistic drive towards divergence. Source: Maialeh (2017)

$$-\varsigma(R_t^i - \varepsilon) = \ln\left(\frac{\pi_t^i}{\Delta I_t^i} - 1\right). \tag{7.25}$$

Expressing R_t^i from Eq. (7.25) then defines the final function of total resources of the successful agent:

$$R_t^i = \varepsilon - \frac{\ln\left(\frac{\overset{t}{\pi}}{\Delta I_t^i} - 1\right)}{\varsigma}. \tag{7.26}$$

The resource equation of the non-winner is then simply:

$$R_t^i = R_{t-1}^i. \tag{7.27}$$

7.2.1 Simulation of the Model

In order to inspect the evolution of total resources of two agents organized by market mechanism, we run a discrete simulation of the presented model. The aim is to show that total resource divergence is an immanent part of the market processes. Then, two homogeneous agents face the following simulation set-up based on Maialeh (2020) (Table 7.1):

As can be seen, agents start with a very low level of total resources (as one fiftieth of the propensity inflex point) in order to monitor the evolution of agents' resources from the bottom. The interval for appropriable resources should be also very low (from one-ten-thousandth to one-hundredth) since greater resource units may lead to the rapid increase in inequality (Anazawa 2019; Aghion and Howitt 1992). The simulation then generates the results below (Fig. 7.1):

The main result of the model simulation is that total resources of the two agents are diverging over time. As can be seen, the resource gap between two identical

Table 7.1 Simulation inputs

Number of agents	$n = 2$
Total resources	$R = 1$
Subsistence consumption	$\overline{c} = .99$
Investible surplus	$i = .01$
Logistic growth rate	$\varsigma = .05$
Propensity inflex point	$\varepsilon = 50$
Appropriable resources (uniformly distributed)	$\{\pi \mid .0001 \leq \pi \leq .01\}$
Number of iterations	$= 25\ 000$
Number of simulation repetitions	$= 1000$

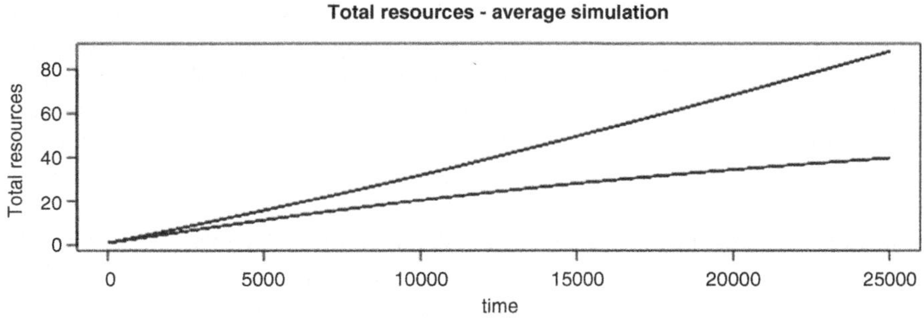

Fig. 7.1 Simulated resource divergence. Source: Maialeh (2020)

agents is increasing since total resources of the more successful agent are increasing convexly, whereas total resources of the less successful agent are increasing concavely. Yet from the model definition we can assume that the main driver of the divergence is the investible surplus. This is not surprising as we know that investible surplus transforms unconsumed resources into strengthening competitiveness, which is then mirrored in a higher probability of appropriation. Subsistence consumption naturally increases with total resources as we assumed that persisting on a higher level of total resources requires to expend more than on lower levels.

The trends observed in simulation results do not depend on parameters choice, but of course, their values influence the dynamics of changes. Firstly, higher logistic growth rate ς causes that agents' total resources are evolving equitably until they approach closely to the inflex point ε, where propensities change abruptly and hence the divergence is rooted in a short interval around the inflex point. In this case, inequality increases all of a sudden, not gradually. A small number of iterations, let us say 500 iterations *ceteris paribus*, would cause that differences between the two agents are negligible and hence the evolution of their total resources would be more equitable. On the other hand, the greater the amount of time periods is considered, the greater (in average) is the difference between agents' total resources. And lastly, a greater higher level of appropriable resources, e.g. $\pi_{const} = 0.1$, would increase divergence significantly. This goes alongside the conclusion of the resource allocation dynamics model (e.g. Anazawa 2019) where inequality was rising with the resource unit appropriable at a time. Not exactly, but similarly in terms of final effects, the variance of the growth rate increases with the size of innovations in the Schumpeterian model (Aghion and Howitt 1992).

7.2.2 *Pareto Efficiency: A 'Nonsensical Optimality' in the Perspective of Market Inequality*

Above mentioned model formulates a concept of inequality based on axiomatized actions of economic agents within fundamental market forces; where the lawful character of agents' contradictory interaction constitutes totality of the market production process. As is clear, the present model opposes typical steady-state equilibrium solutions. By contrast, contemporary economics is obsessed by equilibration—the process which adorably copies gravitation force in physics. But equilibrium does not say anything about how resources will be distributed in the equilibrium state. It could then easily happen that pursuing an equilibrium situation is happening at the expense of undesired inequality. Pareto himself, despite his suspicion of being misinterpreted that redistribution is defective, was originally about to demonstrate that there is no *scientific proof* that redistribution is worth for society. The subsequent part, based on Maialeh (2016), conversely aims to prove that frequent using of Pareto optimality—the established mantra of welfare economics—does not reliably serve as a criterion for market-based inequalities.

Despite the extent of this subchapter does not allow to provide a complete review of Pareto optimal findings in contemporary economics, let us start with a short overview. There are plenty of papers dealing with equilibria in the context of market inequalities whose scientific scope sometimes even exceeds a standard frame of economic theory. The issue was developed, based on Walrasian 'technicist' approach, by many famous economists and mathematicians; few names for that: John von Neumann, John Nash, Nicolas Kaldor in cooperation with John Hicks, John Harsanyi, Kenneth Arrow, Gérard Debreu, Irving Fisher or Milton Friedman. Especially the last one followed a libertarian concept of justice during Robert Nozick's upswing, which contributed to strengthening the position of Pareto efficiency even further. Among others we should also give a credit to Atkinson (1970) and Kolm (1976), whose articles in *JET* significantly contributed to the discussion on the relationship between equality and effectivity. Okun (1975) presented perhaps the most famous contribution based on substitutive understanding of equality and efficiency which inspired numerous followers.

Most of the studies on equality and efficiency (or on general optimality) relates to economic policy. The theoretical frame of economic policy has broadly incorporated Pareto efficiency and economic studies frequently employ respective optimization process, especially on the issue of providing public goods or tax system (e.g. in Cornes and Sandler 2000 or Itaya et al. 1997). The latter article deals with individual utilities while providing public goods in a situation of unequal distribution of income. Authors conclude that the most effective way, in terms of quantity of provided public goods, consists of high inequality, but this account presumes that all public goods are financed by the richest. Dasgupta (2009) reacts on that with his experimental research which assumes Cournot model of two players with identical preferences. Another experimental study was recently elaborated by Gaechter et al. (2014) who dynamically model relationships between economic growth and inequality in the context of public good games. Dynamic modelling that concerns Pareto efficiency was in recent years also advanced by Bommier and Zuber (2012). Olszewski and Rosenthal (2004) then contributes with Pareto optimization through tax system, while their model is based on quasi-linear utility functions, frequently used throughout a broad scope of political economy.[10] Another study was elaborated by Barr (2012) who deals with a broad spectrum of ideological approaches to Pareto efficiency; namely Rawlsian, utilitarian, right-wing-libertarian and Marxist. To have a link to inequality, a combination of Piketty's inequality research with Pareto distribution is the subject matter for Jones (2015).

Optimization of market outputs was highly mathematized from the very beginning, and therefore naturally gravitates to the scope of natural scientists. One of the most famous articles in recent times was elaborated by Venkatasubramanian et al. (2015). The aim of this study is to prove that self-regulated dynamics of free market generates the most effective output in both terms—efficiency and justice. Authors make use of insights in statistical mechanics and thermodynamics and treat them in game-theoretical perspective. Another study (and probably the most famous) that combines natural sciences with political economy is Dragulescu and Yakovenko (2000). Authors demonstrate how thermodynamic theory and Boltzmann-Gibbs distribution (predominantly used in statistical physics) emerges in computer simulations of economic models, particularly of the distribution of money and wealth. These simulations are set for a great number of agents for the purpose to get closer to simulations of molecular dynamics in physics. Authors also admit that despite they work with equilibria, their research due to a limited explanatory power rather serve to detect inefficient states. The crucial disadvantage of these studies is however work with abstract terms. For instance, Venkatasubramanian et al. (2015) treat the term of 'justice' reductively as a mere relationship of contribution and reward, what feeds a justified scorn among other social scientists.

Such deficiencies naturally lead to reverting attention back into social sciences and humanities. One of these authors is Hillman (2000) who models Nietzschean society from the perspective of poverty and inequality. Despite the article focuses on Nash equilibria, it contributes to understanding of asymmetric statuses of agents and their motives to act in favour of optimal societal output. Cohen (1995) in his humanities-oriented research endeavours to reconcile egalitarian approach and weak Pareto optimality. The research was confronted by Shaw (1999) who refuses Cohen's outputs. The author discusses strictly egalitarian standpoint and immense inequality in primary resources which is supposedly incompatible with Pareto efficiency. The icon who deals with the issue in both philosophy and economics is undoubtedly Amartya Sen who confronted Friedman's heritage of utility-oriented Pareto optimality in the early 1990s. In Sen's work (1991) we might also detect an attempt to revive the question of interpersonal comparability of utility which gave birth to the very idea of Pareto optimality.[11]

[10]One of the most cited studies in this regard is Persson and Tabellini (2000).

[11]An interesting article that confronts measurability and hence comparability of performances on the market itself was elaborated by Neckel and Dröge (2002). The article is particularly exceptional in the context of notorious incomparability of interpersonal utilities, asserted particularly by Austrian proponents, e.g. by Rothbard (2011).

To get back to the present model, the following formalization demonstrates above mentioned incompatibility of the general model of market inequality and Pareto efficiency. The model is again simplified only for two agents $\{A, B\}$. Concretely we deal with strong Pareto optimum (*SPO*) which is used in economic models the most and which says that none can be better off at the expense of the other. *SPO* therefore occurs when for any set of feasible situations $\left[\rho^{SPO}(\overline{c}_t^A; R_t^A), \rho^{SPO}(\overline{c}_t^B; R_t^B)\right]$ does not exist any feasible alternative $\left[\widehat{\rho}(\overline{c}_t^A; R_t^A), \widehat{\rho}(\overline{c}_t^B; R_t^B)\right]$ such that:

$$u^A; \Pi^A\left[\hat{\rho}\left(\overline{c}_t^A; R_t^A\right), \hat{\rho}\left(\overline{c}_t^B; R_t^B\right)\right] \geq u^A; \Pi^A\left[\rho^{SPO}\left(\overline{c}_t^A; R_t^A\right), \rho^{SPO}\left(\overline{c}_t^B; R_t^B\right)\right]$$

and

$$u^B; \Pi^B\left[\widehat{\rho}\left(\overline{c}_t^A R_t^A\right)\widehat{\rho}\left(\overline{c}_t^B R_t^B\right)\right] \geq u^B; \Pi^B\left[\rho^{SPO}\left(\overline{c}_t^A R_t^A\right)\rho^{SPO}\left(\overline{c}_t^B R_t^B\right)\right]$$

with at least one of the inequalities strict. In other words, we claim there does not exist a distribution of resources that makes both agents $\{A, B\}$ as well off and making one strictly better off at the expense of the other. An equivalent condition is that for any set of feasible situations $\left[\rho^{SPO}(\overline{c}_t^A; R_t^A), \rho^{SPO}(\overline{c}_t^B; R_t^B)\right]$ must apply:

$$u^A; \Pi^A\left[\hat{\rho}\left(\overline{c}_t^A; R_t^A\right), \hat{\rho}\left(\overline{c}_t^B; R_t^B\right)\right] > u^A; \Pi^A\left[\rho^{SPO}\left(\overline{c}_t^A; R_t^A\right), \rho^{SPO}\left(\overline{c}_t^B; R_t^B\right)\right]$$
$$\Rightarrow u^B; \Pi^B\left[\hat{\rho}\left(\overline{c}_t^A; R_t^A\right), \hat{\rho}\left(\overline{c}_t^B; R_t^B\right)\right] < u^B; \Pi^B\left[\rho^{SPO}\left(\overline{c}_t^A; R_t^A\right), \rho^{SPO}\left(\overline{c}_t^B; R_t^B\right)\right]$$

which says that any set of feasible situations that makes agent A strictly better off must make agent B strictly worse off. Various combination of $\left[\rho(\overline{c}_t^A; R_t^A), \rho(\overline{c}_t^B; R_t^B)\right]$ thus defines the following set of possible combinations of utilities or profits $[(u^A; \pi^A), (u^B; \pi^B)]$:

$$\mathfrak{U} = \left\{\left[\left(u^A; \Pi^A\right), \left(u^B; \Pi^B\right)\right] : u^A; \Pi^A = u^A; \Pi^A\left[\rho\left(\overline{c}_t^A; R_t^A\right), \rho\left(\overline{c}_t^B; R_t^B\right)\right], u^B;\right.$$
$$\left.\Pi^B = u^B; \Pi^B\left[\rho\left(\overline{c}_t^A; R_t^A\right), \rho\left(\overline{c}_t^B; R_t^B\right)\right] \forall \left[\rho\left(\overline{c}_t^A; R_t^A\right), \rho\left(\overline{c}_t^B; R_t^B\right)\right]\right\}$$

which is usually depicted as a graph with $u_i; \Pi_i$ on the x-axis and $u_j; \Pi_j$ on the y-axis. Given the assumption that at least one of the inequalities (see above) is strict, *SPO* occurs on the frontier of the set, except extreme cases of horizontal and vertical points. Pareto optima lie on the edge of the utility (production)—possibility frontier, which is formally expressed as

$$\mathfrak{U}_F = \{[(u^A;\Pi^A),(u^B;\Pi^B)] \in \mathfrak{U} : \exists\Big[\Big(\widehat{u^A;\Pi^A}\Big),\Big(\widehat{u^B;\Pi^B}\Big)\Big] \in \mathfrak{U} : \Big(\widehat{u^A;\Pi^A}\Big) \geq (u^A;\Pi^A) \wedge \Big(\widehat{u^B;\Pi^B}\Big) \geq (u^B;\Pi^B)\}.$$

From the set above we deduce the following: market-based divergence in total resources, enhanced by the accelerating effect of dynamized propensities, deepens differences in individual distances from the zone of extinction between agents $r(R_t^i) = [\rho(\overline{c}_t^i;R_t^i)]^{-1}$ who are motivated by the rational principle of self-preservation $\max [\rho(\overline{c}_t^i;R_t^i)]^{\frac{1}{n}} \Leftrightarrow \max \int_0^\infty f(R)\,\mathrm{d}R$. Then we prove that any equalization of R_t^A and R_t^B, for instance when $\int_{t_0}^t R_t^A\,\mathrm{d}R \gg \int_{t_0}^t R_t^B\,\mathrm{d}R$, would counteract to $\max \int_{t_0}^t R_t^A\,\mathrm{d}R$ and hence to the set of Pareto efficiency $\mathfrak{U}_F$, since

$$\widehat{\rho}(\overline{c}_t^B;R_t^B) > \rho^{SPO}(\overline{c}_t^B;R_t^B) \Leftrightarrow \widehat{\rho}(\overline{c}_t^A;R_t^A) < \rho^{SPO}(\overline{c}_t^A;R_t^A).$$

Based on that we claim that under given circumstances any alternative allocation of resources to agent B may happen only at the expense of agent A, which stands in the very contradiction with Pareto efficiency. That is to say that *any* level of inequality between A and B, which means the difference between R_t^A and R_t^B, and hence between $\rho(\overline{c}_t^A;R_t^A)$ and $\rho(\overline{c}_t^B:R_t^B)$, would be considered as Pareto efficient. The conclusion can be related to the first welfare theorem which states that under certain conditions, which generally corresponds to the definition of the proposed model, markets generate outcomes that are Pareto efficient. The result of the model—a diverging tendency of the market mechanism—therefore disqualifies normative ethos of Pareto efficiency and makes it nonsensical. This conclusion follows-up hitherto non-formalized insights of Sen (1991) and Shaw (1999) and by formal evidences it unmasks the controversy of Pareto efficiency's normativity in the context of market inequality, as well as it unveils a hidden role of Pareto efficiency in permanent legitimation of *status quo* without any justifiable insight.

7.3 Market-Based Inequalities with Cobb-Douglas Agents

The general idea of inequality presented in this book is also applicable to widely known Cobb-Douglas utility (Maialeh 2019). Above already introduced variables, we clarify that $\overline{c}$ is still assigned to all resources essential for agent's reproduction on a given economic level (subsistence consumption). Above that, C is the actual consumption including subsistence consumption, where $\overline{c} \subseteq C$. Therefore, with a higher amount of total resources agent assesses which fraction of the resources to consume and which fraction to keep for strengthening her market position. The term π^{TOTAL} is the total amount of resources available on the market for which all agents compete and π^{SHARE} is interpreted as a share of π^{TOTAL} which agent is able to appropriate on the market at a given time.

The ordinary Cobb-Douglas utility $u(x_1, x_2) = x_1^{\alpha} x_1^{\beta}$, which works with static forms[12], is therefore reformulated (and dynamized in the end) as follows: agent i maximizes her Cobb-Douglas utility in time t composed of actual consumption and investments. The latter is enforced by competitive pressures so that the agent has to strengthen her position on the market, which is, again, happening through investible surplus. The share of actual consumption and investible surplus on final utility is given by propensities to consume and to invest:

$$\max_{C,I} u(C,I) = C_t^{i p^{(C)}{}_t^i} I_t^{i p^{(I)}{}_t^i}$$

$$\text{s.t. } p_{Ct}^{\ i} C_t^i + p_{It}^{\ i} I_t^i = R_t^i. \tag{7.28}$$

where $p_{Ct}^{\ i} = f\left(\rho\left(\bar{c}_t^i; R_t^i\right)\right); p_{It}^{\ i} = 1/f\left(p_{Ct}^{\ i}\right)$ are proxies for prices with ρ as the Euclidean distance between subsistence consumption and total resources.

The idea is that smaller difference in the Euclidean distance refers to higher urgency of consumption which is, in that case, composed mainly by subsistence consumption. In such a situation, the "price" of consumption must be low since opportunity costs of transferring resources to the future through investible surplus are too high, putting subsistence level under a greater pressure. Conversely, a bigger difference in the Euclidean distance signifies that the agent has quite enough total resources. The urgency of consumption is therefore lower and hence consuming more is burdened with a higher price since the agent perceives a lower pressure of subsistence consumption. In order to keep the higher amount of resources the agent is forced to dedicate more resources for competition and the price of transferring resources through investible surplus must be low. The purpose of these prices is to underline that the price of investment is different for poorer and richer agents. We can also see that a "subsistence effect" dominates in the case of poorer agents and a "competition effect" dominates in the case of richer agents.

Here we employ dynamic forms of propensities once again. It is still valid that when a very low level of total resources is considered, let us say $\bar{c}_t^i \to R_t^i$, the agent tends to consume all of them. In this case, propensity to consume $p^{(C)}$ is approaching to 1. It follows that $p^{(I)}$ is proportionally approaching to 0 at the same time. Therefore, for assumed $p^{(I)}$ we have similar conditions *(H)* with the same interpretation as before with an additional assumption: $R > 0 \Rightarrow p^{(I)} > 0$. Therefore:

[12]Except discussions on dynamic modelling with Cobb-Douglas production function in macroeconomics.

$$(H)\begin{cases} p^{(I)} \text{ is increasing}(0,1) \\ \lim\limits_{\tau\to\infty} p^{(I)}(R) = 1 \\ \exists\varepsilon \in (0,\infty) : p^{(I)} \text{ is convex } (0,\varepsilon); p^{(I)} \text{ is concave } (\varepsilon,\infty) \end{cases}$$

As a general solution for dynamized forms of propensities is again the set of functions $\mathfrak{M}$ which follows H conditions:

$$\mathfrak{M} = \left\{p^{(I)} \in C((0,\infty),(0,1)) | (H)\,\text{holds}\right\}.$$

Further, we continue with standard constraint maximization through Lagrangean function (Eq. 7.29) which is interpreted as:

$$\mathfrak{L} = C^{p(C)} I^{p(I)} + \lambda(p_C C + p_I I - R) \tag{7.29}$$

$$\frac{\partial \mathfrak{L}}{\partial C} = p^{(C)} C^{p^{(C)}-1} I^{p^{(I)}} - \lambda p_c = 0 \tag{7.30a}$$

$$\frac{\partial \mathfrak{L}}{\partial I} = p^{(I)} C^{p^{(C)}} I^{p^{(I)}-1} - \lambda p_I = 0 \tag{7.30b}$$

$$\frac{\partial \mathfrak{L}}{\partial \lambda} = p_C C + p_I I - R = 0 \tag{7.30c}$$

with FOC (7.30a), (7.30b) and (7.30c). Assuming $0 < C; 0 < i$,[13] the unique solution for C^* and i^* is:

$$\frac{p^{(C)} C^{p^{(C)}-1} I^{p^{(I)}}}{p_C} = \lambda, \tag{7.31}$$

$$\frac{p^{(I)} C^{p^{(C)}} I^{p^{(I)}-1}}{p_I} = \lambda, \tag{7.32}$$

which naturally gives $p^{(C)} C^{p^{(C)}-1} I^{p^{(I)}} / p_C = p^{(I)} C^{p^{(C)}} I^{p^{(I)}-1} / p_I$. Both terms divided by $C^{p^{(C)}-1} I^{p^{(I)}-1}$ are simplified to $p^{(C)} I / p_C = p^{(I)} C / p_I$, alternatively $p_I I = p^{(I)} p_C C / p^{(C)}$. Then we substitute $p_I I$ back into the third FOC to obtain $p_C C + p^{(I)} p_C C / p^{(C)} - R = 0$. This implies $p_C C = p^{(C)} / (p^{(C)} + p^{(I)}) R$; for C^* we get:

[13]Here we see why must be defined on (0,1).

$$C^{*}=\frac{p^{(C)}}{p^{(C)}+p^{(I)}}\frac{R}{p_{C}}=p^{(C)}\frac{R}{p_{C}} \tag{7.33}$$

and according to $p_I I = p^{(I)} p_C C / p^{(C)}$ it follows that:

$$I^{*}=\frac{p^{(I)}}{p^{(C)}+p^{(I)}}\frac{R}{p_{I}}=p^{(I)}\frac{R}{p_{I}}, \tag{7.34}$$

while the unique solution in $\mathbb{R}_{>0}$ is satisfied as long as $0 < p^{(I)}$, $0 < p^{(C)}$, $0 < p_I$, $0 < p_C$, $0 < R$. To check the constrained maximum, the bordered Hessian is:

$$H=\begin{pmatrix} 0 & -p_C & -p_I \\ -p_C & p^{(C)}(p^{(C)}-1)(C^{*})^{p^{(C)}-2}I^{*p^{(I)}} & p^{(C)}p^{(I)}(C^{*})^{p^{(C)}-1}(I^{*})^{p^{(I)}-1} \\ -p_I & p^{(C)}p^{(I)}(C^{*})^{*p^{(C)}-1}(I^{*})^{p^{(I)}-1} & p^{(I)}(p^{(I)}-1)(C^{*})^{p^{(C)}}(I^{*})^{p^{(I)}-2} \end{pmatrix}$$

where the determinant is

$$\begin{aligned} \det(H) = p_C\Big[& -p_C p^{(I)}(p^{(I)}-1)(C^{*})^{p^{(C)}}(I^{*})^{p^{(I)}-2} \\ & +p_I p^{(C)}p^{(I)}(C^{*})^{p^{(C)}-1}(I^{*})^{p^{(I)}-1}\Big] \\ & -p_I\Big[-p_C(p^{(C)}p^{(I)})(C^{*})^{p^{(C)}-1}(I^{*})^{p^{(I)}-1} \\ & +p_I p^{(C)}(p^{(C)}-1)(C^{*})^{p^{(C)}-2}(I^{*})^{p^{(I)}}\Big] \\ & = C^{p(C)-2}I^{p(I)-2}\Big[-p^{(I)}(p^{(I)}-1)p_C^{2}(C^{*}) \\ & +2p^{(C)}p^{(I)}p_C p_I CI - p^{(C)}(p^{(C)}-1)p_I^{2}(I^{*})^{2}\Big]. \end{aligned}$$

It is clear, given the assumptions: $p^{(C)} + p^{(I)} = 1; 0 < p^{(C)} < 1; 0 < p^{(I)} < 1$, that the determinant is positive. Hence, the stationary point (C^*, I^*) is a maximum.

Additionally, comparative statics is used to explain logically consistent variations of p_C, p_I and R. The following term:

$$\frac{\partial C^{*}}{\partial p_{C}}=-\frac{p^{(C)}}{p^{(C)}+p^{(I)}}\frac{R}{p_{C}^{2}}<0 \tag{7.35}$$

proves that as the difference between subsistence consumption and total resources increases, the quantity of actual consumption tends to decrease. However, actual consumption remains to be an increasing function of total resources—an increase in the difference between reproductive consumption and total resources is possible only when increasing total resources. The fact that increasing total resources relates to increasing actual consumption is proven as follows:

$$\frac{\partial C^*}{\partial R} = -\frac{p^{(C)}}{p^{(C)} + p^{(I)}} \frac{1}{p_C} > 0. \tag{7.36}$$

Further, the model has to be formulated in a special way where $C^*$and I^* are neither substitutes nor complements. In other words, actual consumption is not affected by changes in investible surplus and *vice versa,* but both are determined by changes in total resources. This is simply verified through $\partial C^*/\partial p_I = 0$.

The envelope theorem is also used to look at the effects on the utility of the agent at the optimum. Hence, we calculate the situation $du(C^*(p_C, p_I, R), I^*(p_C, p_I, R))/dp_C$ which is then equal to:

$$\frac{\partial\left(C^{p^{(C)}} I^{p^{(I)}}\right)}{\partial p_C} - \frac{\lambda \partial (p_C C + p_I I - R)}{\partial p_C}. \tag{7.37}$$

The utility function does not depend directly on p_C which implies that the first term is zero. Therefore, we get:

$$du(C^*(p_C, p_I, R), I^*(p_C, p_I, R))/dp_C = -\lambda^* C^*.$$

From the Lagrangean equation we see that $0 < \lambda^*$. In a regular Cobb-Douglas utility case this would imply that increasing Euclidean distance between subsistence consumption and total resources indirectly decreases utility which would be logically inconsistent. Therefore, in the present case, as stated above on the relation of p_C and p_I, an increase in the Euclidean distance inversely and proportionally decreases p_I, which allows to allocate agent's resources in the form of investible surplus. This consequently strengthen her competitiveness when increasing the distance between subsistence consumption and total resources. In other words, the effect of increasing p_C is in terms of maximized utility counterbalanced by the effect of decreasing p_I. Moreover, an increase in p_C is the result of increasing R which has a positive effect on agent's utility. This is derived similarly as above—we get $du(C^*(p_C, p_I, R), I^*(p_C, p_I, R))/dR$ equal to:

$$\frac{\partial\left(C^{p^{(C)}} I^{p^{(I)}}\right)}{\partial R} = \frac{\lambda \partial (p_C C + p_I I - R)}{\partial R} = -\lambda^* \tag{7.38}$$

which confirms that the effect of an increase in total resources is positive on agent's utility. Hence, we say that λ^* captures the effect of changes in total resources on utility at the optimum.

In this Cobb-Douglesian reformulation it can be seen that the agent is, according to presented computations, exclusively motivated to increase her total resources. Therefore, it is crucial to capture the process of resource appropriation which consequently clarifies the issue of economic inequality. For this purpose, it is again assumed Schumpeterian theory advanced by Aghion and Howitt (1992 and

2009). Just to remind, probability μ_t that the innovation is successful at t is positively related to the amount of resources I_t allocated to the innovation process. Further, the probability μ_t is inversely related to γA_{t-1} which represents a new level of innovation productivity. In other words, the higher the level of productivity we go for, the more difficult it is to implement the innovation as our proxy for competitiveness. The probability is then captured as before, i.e.:

$$\mu_t = \phi\left(\frac{I_t}{\gamma A_{t-1}}\right). \tag{7.39}$$

The interpretation of Eq. (7.39) is the same: Assuming constant γA_{t-1}, i.e. equal conditions for all agents, then the bigger the amount of invested resources the agent has at t, the higher the probability to innovate and to strengthen her competitiveness the agent has at $t + 1$, while $\gamma - 1$ represents the growth rate for $\gamma > 1$.

In order to emphasize the role and evolution of the market power, another way of probability-weighted appropriation of additional resources could be also computable through the historical path of the investible surplus:

$$\pi_{it}^{SHARE} = \pi_t^{TOTAL} \frac{\sum_{t_0}^{t-1} I^i}{\sum_{t_0}^{t-1} \sum_{i=1}^{n} I^j} \tag{7.40}$$

where $\sum_{t_0}^{t-1} I$ denotes sum of all invested resources of agent i from t_0 to t for $t_0 \to t$, whilst $\sum_{t_0}^{t-1} \sum_{i=1}^{n} I^j$ represents all invested resources of all agents from t_0 to t for $t_0 \to t$. The term π_t^{TOTAL} denotes the total amount of resources available on the market. Accordingly, π_{it}^{SHARE} is the share of total resources which belongs to i given by the relation of i's and total invested resources.

The divergence among agents is then captured by the intertemporal extension of the basic model; assuming $R_t = R_{t-1} \Leftrightarrow \pi_t^{SHARE} = 0$, we deduce:

$$\max_{C,I} u(C, I) = C_t^{ip^{(C)}{}_t^i} I_t^{ip^{(I)}{}_t^i}$$

$$\text{s.t. } p_{C_t^i} C_t^i + p_{I_t^i} I_t^i = R_{t-1}^i + \pi_{it}^{SHARE}, \tag{7.41}$$

where total resources in t are the sum of total resources in $t - 1$ and appropriated resources gained on the market in t. The latter derives according to Eq. (7.41) from the amount of investments allocated by the agent over a specified time period.

In sum, Cobb-Douglas preferences of agents give the solution (Eq. 7.33) and (Eq. 7.34). Market imperatives, again, force the agent to strengthen competitiveness through competitive pressure. A part of total resources is consumed according to $p^{(C)}$ with regards to p_C. The remaining part of total resources is invested according to $p^{(I)}$ in order to strengthen agent's competitiveness. As it is shown (Eq. 7.41), agent appropriates her share of the total amount of resources available on the market according to the amount of investments allocated to the competitive struggle; in other words, the agent appropriates resources according to her market power. Therefore, each solution for maximizing agent's utility drives the agent to increase her total resources above the subsistence level which is accompanied by increasing inequality among agents.

Our conclusion thus supports the general idea that producing surplus is necessarily connected to hierarchical societies (e.g. Angle 1986). It also goes hand-in-hand with already mentioned econophysics papers. The diverging principle is similar to the one detected by Chakraborti (2002) who presents the model where initial equality among two agents is abolished with the first coin flip. Subsequent transfer of resources necessarily sets up an imbalance between the two which is then reproduced over time. As was the case of market inequality model, the logic of free-market economies is based on a "trickle-up mechanics" which defines the natural inclination of economic resources to flow from the bottom upward.

7.4 Chapter Summary

The last chapter presents a simple model of market inequality that is extended with Cobb-Douglas utility framework. The aim of the model is to formulate general market principles and their connection to economic inequality. For this purpose, it is necessary to abstract from all non-systemic and particular aspects of economic distribution. Therefore, we assume homogeneous agents who face identical market conditions. Agents appropriate scarce resources for their reproduction on the market. For successful appropriation, agents have to continually improve their competitiveness which is done through investing the investible surplus. Agents strive to keep their current economic level for which they have given subsistence consumption. In other words, to keep the current level agents have to meet their subsistence constraints. Naturally, it is also assumed that the higher is the economic level, the more has to be spend in order to keep the current level. Subsistence constraint is thus non-stationary and increases with total resources. A strong assumption of this model is that total resources do not decrease below the level of the previous time period.

The model starts with a maximization function that is based on the self-preserving principle which stands on maximizing the probability of survival (minimizing the probability of extinction). The maximization problem therefore concerns the difference between subsistence level and total resources. Agents then strive to maximize total resources which is conditioned by successful appropriation, while the probability of appropriation is given by the share of agent's investible surplus and total investible surplus of all agents. It means that the more the agent is able to invest compare to others, the higher is the probability of successful appropriation and the better is agent's long-run path of total resources. This is proven by the simulation of the model which clearly demonstrates that even identical agents who face equal market conditions diverge over time. The fact is that from a certain point one of the agents starts to grow convexly while the other one grows concavely, which is caused by intensively increasing investible surplus of the more successful agent. Similar results are reached in the last subchapter, where the proposed model is reformulated in the context of Cobb-Douglas utility. Model's results therefore stand in contradiction to any idea of an "advantage of backwardness" (e.g. Gerschenkron 1962 or Abramovitz 1986).

The crucial aspect of the model is that the main empirical regularities are qualitatively consistent with the model's mechanics. Especially, it covers three key stylized facts about economic inequality: (i) The wealthier the agent is, the greater is her saving rate. (ii) The wealthier the agent is, the greater is the pace of her growth. (iii) A still greater part of the aggregate growth is appropriated by the wealthier agent.

The model is then put into the context of Pareto optimization which still serves as the dominant normative reference point for economic policy. The first section confirms the already known—that competitive markets lead to Pareto efficient states, i.e. there is no possible improvement which would not harm the situation of one of the involved agents. On the other hand, such competitive equilibria do not reflect how (un)equally are resources distributed under these conditions. It is showed that this approach principally ignores any level of inequality which put in doubts any thinkable normative aspect of the theory in terms of market economic distribution.

References

Abramovitz M (1986) Catching up, forging ahead, and falling behind. J Econ Hist 46(2):385–406

Adorno TW, Horkheimer M (2002 [1944]) Dialectic of enlightenment: philosophical fragments. Stanford University Press

Aghion P, Howitt PW (1992) A model of growth through creative destruction. Econometrica 60 (2):323–351

Aghion P, Howitt PW (2009) The economics of growth. MIT Press, USA

Aghion P, Caroli E, García Penalosa C (1999) Inequality and economic growth: the perspective of the new growth theories. J Econ Lit 37(4):1615–1660

Anazawa M (2019) Inequality in resource allocation and population dynamics models. R Soc Open Sci 6(7):182178

Angle J (1986) The surplus theory of social stratification and the size distribution of personal wealth. Soc Forces 65(2):293–326

Atkinson AB (1970) On the measurement of inequality. J Econ Theory 2:244–263

Barr N (2012) Economics of the welfare state. The relevance of efficiency to different theories of society, 5th edn. Oxford University Press, Oxford

Boghosian BM (2014a) Kinetics of wealth and the Pareto law. Phys Rev E 89(4):042804–042825

Boghosian BM (2014b) Fokker-Planck description of wealth dynamics and the origin of Pareto's law. J Mod Phys C 25:1441008–1441015

Boghosian BM, Johnson M, Marcq JA (2015) An H theorem for Boltzmann's equation for the yard-sale model of asset exchange (the Gini coefficient as an H functional). J Stat Phys 161 (6):1339–1350

Bommier A, Zuber S (2012) The Pareto principle of optimal inequality. Int Econ Rev 53 (2):593–607

Carrol C, Slacalek J, Tokuoka K, White MN (2017) The distribution of wealth and the marginal propensity to consume. Quant Econ 8(3):977–1020
Chakraborti A (2002) Distributions of money in model markets of economy. Int J Mod Phys C 13 (10):1315–1321
Chatterjee S (1994) Transitional dynamics and the distribution of wealth in a neoclassical growth model. J Public Econ 54(1):97–119
Chorro C (2016) A simple probabilistic approach of the yard-sale model. Statist Probab Lett 112:35–40
Cohen GA (1995) The Pareto argument for inequality. Soc Philos Policy 12:160–185
Cornes R, Sandler T (2000) Pareto-improving redistribution and pure public goods. Ger Econ Rev 1:169–186
Dasgupta I (2009) Why praise inequality? Public good provision, income distribution and social welfare. IZA Discussion Paper No. 3988
Dragulescu A, Yakovenko VM (2000) Statistical mechanics of money. Eur Phys J B 17(4):723–729
Drèze J, Sen A (1989) Famines and social response. In: Hunger and public action. Clarendon Press, Oxford
Duesenberry JS (1949) Income, saving and the theory of consumer behavior. Harvard University Press, Cambridge
Edwards E (1971) Work effort, investible surplus and the inferiority of competition. South Econ J 38(2):193–205
Fletcher R (2006) Reproductive consumption. Fem Theory 7(1):27–48
Friedman M (1957) Theory of the consumption function. National Bureau of economic research. Princeton University Press, Princeton
Gaechter S, Mengel F, Tsakas E, Vostroknutov A (2014) Growth and inequality in public good games. CeDEx Discussion Paper Series No. 20144-10
Gaechter S, Mengel F, Tsakas E, Vostroknutov A (2017) Growth and Inequality in Public Good Games 150:1–13
Galor O (2009) Inequality and economic development: the modern perspective. Edward Elgar, Cheltenham
Gerschenkron A (1962) Economic backwardness in historical perspective. Harvard University Press, Cambridge, MA
Getachew Y (2016) Credit constraints, growth and inequality dynamics. Econ Model 54 (C):364–376
Goldsmith RA (1955) A study of saving in the United States, vol 1. Princeton University Press, Princeton, NJ
Gomez R, Foot DK (2003) Age structure, income distribution and economic growth. Can Public Policy 29:141–161
Hai R, Heckman J (2017) Inequality in human capital and endogenous credit constraints. Rev Econ Dyn 25:4–36
Hillman AL (2000) Poverty, inequality, and unethical behavior of the strong. IMF working paper no. 00/187
Hlaváček J (1999) Mikroekonomie: Sounáležitosti se společenstvím. Karolinum, Prague
Horkheimer M (2012. [1949–67]) Critique of instrumental reason. Verso, London
Itaya J, de Meza D, Myles GD (1997) In praise of inequality: public good provision and income distribution. Econ Lett 57:289–296
Jones CI (2015) Pareto and Piketty: the macroeconomics of top income and wealth inequality. J Econ Perspect 29(1):29–46
Karni E, Schmiedler D (1986) Self-preservation as behavior under risk. J Econ Behav Organ 7:71–81
Kolm S-C (1976) Unequal inequalities I. J Econ Theory 12:416–442
Kurz HD (2012) Schumpeter's new combinations: revisiting his Theorie de wirtschaftlichen Entwicklung on the occasion of its centenary. J Evol Econ 22(5):871–899
Kuznets S (1946) National income: a summary of findings, NBER

Maialeh R (2016) Fundamental concept of inequality in the perspective of Paretian economics. Polit Econ 64(8):973–987
Maialeh R (2017) Persisting inequality: a case of probabilistic drive towards divergence. Acta Oeconomica 67(2):215–234
Maialeh R (2019) Why market imperatives invigorate economic inequality. Panoeconomicus 66 (2):145–163
Maialeh R (2020) Cumulative advantage in competitive systems. Manuscript in preparation
Mookherjee D, Ray D (2003) Persistent inequality. Rev Econ Stud 70(2):369–393
Neckel S, Dröge K (2002) Die Verdienste und ihr Preis: Leistung in der Marktgesellschaft. Befreiung aus der Mündigkeit: Paradoxien des gegenwärtigen Kapitalismus. In: Franfurter Beitraege zur Soziologie und Sozialphilosophie. Campus Verl, Frankfurt, Main, pp 93–116
Okun A (1975) Equality and efficiency: the big trade-off. The Brookings Institution Press, Washington
Olszewski W, Rosenthal H (2004) Politically determined income inequality and the provision of public goods. J Public Econ Theory 6(5):707–735
Persson T, Tabellini G (2000) Political economics: explaining economic policy. MIT Press, Cambridge, MA
Piketty T (2014) Capital in the twenty-first century. Belknap Press of Harvard University Press, Cambridge
Roese NJ, Olson JM (2007) Better, stronger, faster: self-serving judgment, affect regulation, and the optimal vigilance hypothesis. Perspect Psychol Sci 2:124–141
Rosenzweig MR, Wolpin KI (1993) Credit market constraints, consumption smoothing, and the accumulation of durable production assets in low-income countries: investment in bullocks in India. J Polit Econ 101:223–244
Rothbard MN (2011) Economic controversies. Ludwing von Mises Institute
Sen A (1991) On ethics and economics. Wiley-Blackwell
Shaw P (1999) The Pareto argument and inequality. Philos Q 49(196):353–368
Stiglitz JE (1969) Distribution of income and wealth among individuals. Econometrica 37 (3):382–397
Venkatasubramanian V, Luo Y, Sethuraman J (2015) How much inequality in income is fair? A microeconomic game theoretic perspective. Physica A 435:120–138

Chapter 8
Conclusion

Economic inequality has already become one of the most burning issues throughout social sciences. Numerous effects that influence economic distribution are upon researchers' closer inspection, but the role of market mechanism remains, paradoxically, quite overlooked. It is the more paradoxical when we realize that market as such embodies mechanisms that form the basis for creation and allocation of scarce resources in modern societies. The present book attempted to fill this knowledge gap and outlines how market principles can contribute to explaining current trends in economic inequality predominantly in developed countries.

Despite slightly converging global trends that occurred in the recent decade, economic inequality has been rather on the rise in many respects and according to most of indicators since the 2WW. Furthermore, the nature of the current inequality in developed countries is not of a kind we see e.g. in China, where dramatic increase of inequality is accompanied by increasing living standards of the poor masses. As can be shown on the example of the United States, not only the fruits of growth are distributed by market unevenly, but, in the light of rapid increases at the top end of the distribution, the bottom half of the US citizens have not experienced any change in their real pre-tax incomes since the 1980s.

On the contrary, considering the role of market forces in mainstream economic theory causes (in most cases) convergence that streams from diminishing marginal values. The Ramsey-Cass-Koopmans and Solow-Swan models are the seminal cases materializing these principles on the example of economies' outputs. The thing is that isolation of the market mechanism requires homogeneous economic agents, i.e. we abstract from stochastic, randomly determined particularities, e.g. geographical, psychological, cultural, political, technological etc., as well as from attributes of the concrete economic environment. By contrast, in the framework of the above-mentioned class of models we observe that assuming homogeneous agents necessarily leads to their convergence. The speed of convergence to their steady-state therefore depends on initial levels of wealth so that the agent whose wealth is lower will grow more rapidly. From a different point of view, any inequality is explainable through differences among agents (and hence their

R. Maialeh, *Dynamic Models and Inequality*, Contributions to Economics,
https://doi.org/10.1007/978-3-030-46313-7_8

individualized steady-states) which impedes investigations about how the governing principles of market mechanism influence economic distribution. The distribution among agents is at the end unequal because agents are different from each other. Or put it differently, such framework does not leave any room for inequality between identical agents.

Hence, we dedicated our attention to disregarded aspects of agents operating on the market. Firstly, we concerned subsistence constraints which define the level of resources required for further reproduction. It was shown that considering such constraints restricts agents' ability to save. This ability is nevertheless highly asymmetric—richer agents are in this context allowed to save more not only absolutely, but also relatively, compare to those whose income is close to the subsistence level. The second aspect focuses on competition as the primal principle behind the dynamics of the market mechanism. As was demonstrated, richness of perspectives on competition may lead to ambivalent outcomes. Established consent refers to higher effectivity and lower inequality generated by competitive markets. On the other hand, competitive environment may favour more competitive agents. Be it as it may, agents, whose reproduction depends on resources gained on the market, compete for these scarce resources in order to fulfil their self-preserving imperatives.

Therefore, we introduced a market inequality model that incorporates outlined perspectives on uneven economic distribution, where agents compete for appropriable resources on the market. The probability of appropriation for each agent is based on resources which the agent is able to allocate for enhancing her competitiveness. This investible surplus is given by the difference between agent's total resources and subsistence consumption, similarly as, for instance, the balanced growth path determines consumption as the difference between output and break-even investments in the RCK model. Coupled with empirical findings showing that the main issue for the bottom groups of agents is that they are unable to attain new resources on the market, the probability of appropriation is computed as the share of agent's investible surplus on total investible surplus of all agents. The probability thus serves as a proxy for agent's competitiveness.

Unlike was the case of models presented in the fifth chapter, strictly competitive environment makes the level of competitiveness decisive. For instance, a typical Schumpeterian model assumes that the value of the next innovation, i.e. the value of actualizing investible surplus, is strictly lower for the current monopolist than for others, so that a different agent except for the monopolist will be successful in appropriating resources on the market. However, if we assume hypothetically permanent and unavoidable competitive pressure, the agent having the highest probability of further appropriation is the one with the highest investible surplus (the monopolist in a schumpeterian framework). The value of the next 'innovation' therefore increases with the probability of appropriation, which ensures, in combination with subsistence pressure, that even the monopolist pursues further appropriation.

By following such setting, we might say that possible resource appropriation, the constitutional factor of inequality, is the result of today's resource allocation. Inasmuch as the equations depict interdependency of present and future resources and, thus, they capture the 'history' of the agent, they simultaneously include, according to the set of assumptions and outlined relationships, inherent inclination to deepen inequalities over time. It is clear from 'the model of market inequality' that the amount of unconsumed resources (investible surplus) plays the central role. The reason is that relatively higher investible surplus leads to cumulation of probability of appropriation. But higher investible surplus is attainable only when higher level of total resources exceeds subsistence level; the agent is therefore forced to maximize her total resources in every time period, unless we assume a certain level of total resources from which the agent is free from any relevant competitive pressure. Richer agents therefore have higher probability to be even richer in the future, meanwhile poorer agents have still lower probability of getting better off. In combination with introduced conditions (especially on 'subsistence insurance'), these tendencies cause that the unlucky agent experiences concavely increasing total resources and the lucky one experiences convexly increasing total resources. Constellation of these two dynamics then establishes economic divergence which followingly reflects empirical patterns that poorer agents stagnate or grow slowly while rich agents grow much more rapidly.

Famous researchers have identified various sources of converging (or at least divergence-mitigating) tendencies of markets. As was already mentioned, it is believed that highly competitive markets do not allow to set-up higher mark-ups, basically that all important economic variables are traded on their marginal values, which may cause just temporary differences among agents. To be more concrete, we can mention Simon Kuznets who formulated four factors impeding concentration of savings: (i) government intervention; (ii) demographic changes; (iii) dynamic free market; and (iv) structure of top incomes with lower growth potential. If we focus only on the market-related factors, i.e. on (iii) and (iv), we see that the market dynamics may contrarily favour the richest due to their higher competitiveness. This competitive ability therefore neutralizes the idea that those on the top are dynamically substituted by others. The effect of higher competitiveness also explains, however vaguely, that the growth potential of top incomes is not as limited as marginal theory suggests, but the growth potential conversely rises with the level of economic power.

We can thus observe that even perfectly competitive market with identical agents could have strong monopolizing tendencies. Of course, this depends on specifics of a given market so we can easily imagine that on a highly dynamic market the 'Schumpeterian effect' of switching monopolists could still prevail. All presented models on the other side agree that restricted concentration of savings would mitigate diverging tendencies of the market mechanism.

Also, if we accept that the measure of competitiveness on a given market derives from the scale to which appropriation of resources depends on agents' competitive ability, we conclude that competitive markets allow stronger agents to unlimitedly use their competitiveness against weaker agents. The book therefore shows how slightly different perspective or emphasizing different aspects of already known theories cause significant changes in theoretical view of inequality, for instance that market mechanism can be also seen as an immanent diverging force in economic distribution.

Our conclusions also refer to Pareto efficiency. This equilibrium is frequently used in various branches of economics from game theory to political economy. The final model confirms that *any* level of inequality among agents would be, under the given circumstances of perfect competition, Pareto efficient. This fact however ends-up as a two-fold failure in the context of economic inequality: firstly, as was already posited, richer agents may use more unconsumed resources to enhance their competitiveness and consequently appropriate more resources in the next period. If these richer agents are not restricted in appropriability on the market, perfectly competitive market will ascribe them constantly higher amount of appropriable resources. Further, the only solution for these diverging tendencies is equalization, which, however, does not correspond to Pareto efficiency since it can happen only at the expense of richer agents. Pareto efficiency thus can be proclaimed as logically incompatible with fundamental market forces that implicitly generate economic inequality, because any level of inequality generated on the market is considered as Pareto efficient. Despite normative categories such as effectivity or justice are not the subject matter for this book, the fact that talent and abilities are distributed Gaussian and economic distribution rather follows a kind of power law stimulates the search for different normative criteria applicable on market distribution.

As regards proposed methodology, one might argue that agents do not enjoy any freedom in their decision-making. And we admit that agent-based models in economics mostly demonstrate optimization of alternatives. Nevertheless, limits of these models when focusing on general principles are obvious: to put the following example into our context, optimizing moves of agents can be applied on alternatives that agents have in improving their competitiveness, but certainly not on whether they wish to improve their competitiveness. In other words, such approach, subjected to free-choice doctrine of contemporary economics, focuses on *alternatives* that agents have at a disposal *within* the competitive struggle. The proposed axiomatic approach on the other side helps to grasp *the very imperative to enhance agent's competitiveness*, which exists above the space that is circumscribed for agent's free decision-making. The value added of the model is emphasizing these general laws. This abstract model of market inequality therefore does not aim to copy reality and everyday trade-offs, but the systemic aspects of abstract market mechanism. Isolation of the market in order to distinguish its effect on inequality therefore requires agents to be determined by the market forces, to make them act as mere tools of market imperatives. As a result, the final model of market inequality does not concern particular aspects of economic inequality, but it encompasses a broad spectrum of empirical phenomena which are defining to the current principles of uneven distribution.

In the light of presented results, the book outlines that economic success is not necessarily a meritocratic outcome of agent's talent and effort, as well as economic failure is not necessarily implied by agent's incompetence and effortless. As can be seen, stochasticity (or luck in general) derived from the principles of market mechanism plays a remarkable role and implicitly weakens overestimated and partly unjustified virtues accorded to the rich and stigmatization of the poor. Our conclusions can be further developed through various modifications, for instance the model of market inequality could also serve as a primary reference to inequality predictions and simulations of numerous effects. Among possible extensions we can name e.g. modelling market mechanism as a multi-agent system, putting agents under strategic decision-making without 'subsistence insurance' or formally endogenize economic growth as the result of the interaction among competitiveness enhancing agents. Also, we should not forget that there is a great room for an advancement in philosophically-methodological aspects of the relationship between market and inequality. Generally speaking, despite the generality of provided solutions the model of market inequality sufficiently grasps embedded market logic and stays open to modifications for various supporting empirical inequality researches, from e.g. inter-generational wealth/poverty spillovers to world-systems theories, where it supports dependency theories rather than neoclassical convergence.

With an eye to previous researches, we recognize that market mechanism might have, from a certain perspective and under given assumptions, converging tendencies. However, it has not been sufficiently explored so far how market mechanism driven by competitive imperatives may also generate divergence. This book is a modest contribution to the latter.

The manufacturer's authorised representative in the EU is Springer Nature Customer Service Centre GmbH, Europaplatz 3, 69115 Heidelberg, Germany. If you have any concerns regarding our products, please contact ProductSafety@springernature.com

Printed and bound by CPI Group (UK) Ltd, Croydon, CR0 4YY
30/09/2026
02225709-0006